Simple Mixed Pickles (p.30), with seasonal veggies from my local Farmers' Market.

. We are exhausted.

Artisinal *Shirataki* Maker.

This book is gratefully dedicated to the Oishi family, an extension of our own, and in particular to the memory of Dr. Chikanori Oishi, who opened his heart and home to two young Americans and changed their lives.

MY JAPANESE TABLE

A Lifetime of Cooking with Friends and Family

DEBRA SAMUELS

Foreword by ROY YAMAGUCHI

Photography by HEATH ROBBINS

Styling by CATRINE KELTY

TUTTLE Publishing

Tokyo | Rutland, Vermont | Singapore

Contents

Chapter 5 Meat and Poultry

Chapter 6 Fish and Seafood

Chapter 7 Vegetable and Tofu Dishes

Chapter 8 Bento

Chapter 9 Desserts and Drinks

Having been born and raised in Japan, I often crave the food that I remember from my childhood. Sushi, ramen, and *okonomiyaki* to name a few, immediately transport me back to the sights and sounds of growing up in Japan. As a young child, some of my fondest memories revolved around visiting some of my father's favorite markets looking for octopus, crab, Yellowtail, and one of my favorites: *Himono*, (dried fish).

In *My Japanese Table*, Debra Samuels has captured, and translated many of my early memories of what Japanese food and cooking means to me. From the cooking of my father and mother who would spend hours in the kitchen preparing dinner, it was never fancy but it was always prepared with love.

I try to incorporate Japanese cuisine into my cooking because it reflects my roots and heritage. It is a large part of why I became a chef and who I am.

Although the simplicity of presentation in Japanese cooking expertly cloaks the real complexity of preparation, translating the techniques and ingredients of a centuries old cuisine is not for the faint hearted. Debra has managed to create a compendium that does just that.

The chapter on bento took me back to my childhood, when my mother would pack a bento for my school lunch, it would be as simple as one layer of rice with leftovers from the night before but it always made me happy. When I wasn't enjoying one of my mom's homemade bento, I looked forward to purchasing *eki-bento* when we would travel on the bullet train to far away cities. I loved the variety of *eki-bento* that I had to choose from.

Variety is a large part of what I try to achieve as a chef, incorporating different flavors and textures on a plate is important to me, it keeps peoples interest, it amuses, and satisfies, I think that without really knowing it, I may have derived inspiration from the humble bento.

While desserts have never really been my forte, mochi is my one weakness. Debra's descriptions, and methods of preparation of this Japanese staple make me long for the multi colored, sticky sweets that we would get from department store food courts in Tokyo.

Debra is able to take the intricacies of Japanese cuisine and translate them into a very approachable cookbook that delivers achievable results. *My Japanese Table* takes you on a valuable journey of all the different facets of Japanese cuisine.

From simple street foods to sushi, seafood, and comforting desserts, it is a journey through my memories of Japan.

Roy Yamaguchi, chef and founder of Roy's Restaurants

My red kimono (1972).

Nori Maki, the classic home-style sushi.

ABOVE: My favorite snack, *okonomiyaki*, on display in the Ameyoko shopping district. RIGHT: Simmered Daikon with Citrus Miso (p. 127).

A Lifetime of Cooking Japanese Food with Family and Friends

My taste buds and I came of age together in Japan. In the early 1970s, when I was twenty and just married, my husband, Dick and I arrived in Japan for a semester abroad. Although we had studied Japan and Japanese, we knew nothing of the cuisine. Just like love, there is a first time for everything, and so on our first visit to a Japanese home we were offered a traditional bath and sashimi (in that order)—neither of which we had ever experienced and neither of which we could possibly refuse. Still wet from the bath, we were directed to a low table with a kaleidoscopic platter of gleaming raw fish. Nothing had prepared me for this; I was horrified by the very idea of raw fish—but there was no polite way out. Our smiling hosts watched eagerly as I took my awkward first bite and, sure enough, I could barely swallow the slippery repast. I like to believe that somehow I managed not to embarrass myself or them.

After further language study, our next stop was a home-stay in the port town of Tsukumi, in rural Kyushu.

We lived at the home of a physician, Dr. Chikanori Oishi (Oishi Sensei) and his 15-year-old son Shingo (Shingo's brother, Seichiro, and sister, Eriko were away at university). As is common among Japanese doctors, the doctor's home was also a small hospital, with beds for patients. Ordinarily, the doctor's wife would run the home, but Shingo's mother had died the year before, so a small staff of nurses and a housekeeper looked after the patients, the doctor, his son, and now us. Each day we awoke to the smell of miso soup, steamed rice, and roasted fish. I hung around the kitchen and helped the staff prepare the lunches. The aromas in that home remain imprinted on my senses today and are strongest when I prepare the basic Classic Miso Soup you will find on page 81.

After graduation, my husband began his graduate studies, and his field research brought us back to Japan in the late 1970s with our then 5-month-old son, Brad. For 2 ½ years we lived in a tall gray concrete apartment complex in a working class Tokyo neighborhood.

Odagiri Sensei and my classmates (1984).

Crabmeat and Seaweed Salad (p. 76)—
my favorite side dish.

Me at Yushima Shrine—eating my way through
the food stalls!

Our apartment was spare—two small tatami mat rooms with a kitchen/dining area. We slept on a futon, Japanese style—Brad in between us—which I folded up and stored away every morning. Our small washing machine was outdoors on our tiny cement terrace, and my kitchen was a six-foot counter with a 2-burner stove top and a toaster oven. The fridge was "dorm room" size, so like all my neighbors, I shopped daily. Dick, who is 6'4" (193 cm) felt cramped, but I was thrilled. He began a lifetime of banging his head against low doorways and ceilings, while at 5 feet tall, everything was in arm's reach for me. In downtown Tokyo my taste buds were educated by my kind neighbors and, after a while, more formally when I enrolled in classes to learn Japanese homestyle (*katei*) cooking.

The famous Tsukiji fish market was just across the Sumida River, which ran next to our apartment building. Our neighbors there adopted us. No one spoke English and my Japanese was still tentative. I would not have survived but for the "kindness of these strangers." I have never forgotten how they embraced our family, and I have spent the rest of my life trying to reciprocate by helping others who find themselves in similar situations. As I settled into the rhythms of Japanese life, I began looking forward to the sound of the tofu vendor's horn on his bicycle, to the rhythmic call of the roasted sweet potato hawker in his rickety truck, and to the daily banter with the local shopkeepers. My love affair with

Japanese food was well underway. Daily shopping made me appreciate serving the freshest food possible. Each new ingredient provided an opportunity for mini cooking lessons with my neighbors. They showed me how to put together a chicken hot pot (*mizutaki*) and lent me the clay pot (*donabe*) to do it. I learned how to rinse short grain rice until the freezing cold water ran clear or my reddened hands seized up.

Half way through our stay we moved from downtown Tokyo to the suburbs. Brad went to Japanese nursery school, I went to work, and Dick finished his dissertation. We returned to the States with a three-year-old and a baby on the way.

In the mid-1980s we returned to Japan when Dick began research for a new book. Now we had two boys in tow—Brad was 6 and Alex was 3. I marketed daily at the small shops in Hamadayama, a Tokyo suburb. My bicycle had a grocery basket in the front and a seat for Alex in the back. With him perched on his little throne, we would cruise up and down the high street, buying ingredients for dinner. Alex quickly became fluent in Japanese and soon knew that the locals found him different and cute (*kawaii*). He was quick enough to know that if he said "*oishii sō*" (that looks so yummy!) while staring directly at a mountain of just-fried chicken, the granny behind the counter would offer him a crispy piece. Then he would bow and say "*domo*" (thanks), and out would

ABOVE: Making Mochi with my "brother" Shingo in Tsukumi (1972). RIGHT: Chef Masashi Ishida's Gorgeous Spread at JJ's.

Tai Yaki—Waffle Stuffed with Sweet *Adzuki* Bean Jam.

Hand crafted roasted rice crackers on Jizo Dori in Sugamo.

come another one! The kid had his routine perfected, and by the time we were on the way home he was full.

Brad was a first grader at the local elementary school, so I learned to prepare Japanese-style boxed lunch (bento) for him. These box lunches were culinary masterpieces—at least when in the ways the other moms prepared them. Brad made it clear that American-style peanut butter and jelly sandwiches in a brown paper bag just wouldn't do! Far from thinking these moms were mad to be spending an hour preparing cute lunches for their kids, I embraced the idea. I bought myself a Japanese book called *100 Obento Ideas* and a little blue plastic bento box in the shape of a car for Brad. For the rest of the school year I made my way through that book, letting him pick his lunches by looking at the pictures. Maybe I was mad too, but he always finished his lunches.

This was also when I started taking Japanese cooking classes at the home of Michiko Odagiri, an elegant and well-known cooking teacher who, like Julia Child, taught cooking on Japan's public television network, NHK. Her class was aimed at Japanese women, and I was the only foreigner in attendance. I could understand her oral instructions, but her recipes were written in Japanese, which I had not fully mastered. Fortunately, my fellow students read the recipes to me after each class, and I translated and transcribed them into my notebook. These recipes formed the base of my practical training, and

many appear in some form in this cookbook with the kind permission of Odagiri Sensei's daughter Shigeko.

Here is where I learned to make Dashi (Fish Stock) (p. 35), my first sushi roll, and the delicate *sanbaizu* vinegar dressing. The first class I spent on knife skills cutting paper-thin slices of ginger. Another was spent separating the whites and yolks from hard-boiled eggs and then pressing them through a wire mesh tool that acted as a ricer, to create a decorative flower garnish. The attention to detail was paramount. How would I ever keep this up?

About that same time, I bought *The Simple Art of Japanese Cooking* by Shizuo Tsuji, first published in 1983 by Kodansha International. It was, and in my opinion still is, the go to reference on standard Japanese cuisine. It just was revised and re-issued in 2008.

We left Japan after another year. By now I had a solid technical base in Japanese cuisine. I began teaching and doing workshops upon my return to Boston.

We returned again in the 90's for another of Dick's book projects and this time I spent a year learning the food of everyday meals: Chicken and Egg Rice Bowl (*Oyako Donburi*), our favorite Stuffed Savory Pancake (*Okonomiyaki*), Chunky Miso Chowder (*Tonjiru*). Brad and Alex were now middle and high school students.

By the time Dick and I celebrated our 30th wedding anniversary, we had lived in Japan on and off for nearly a

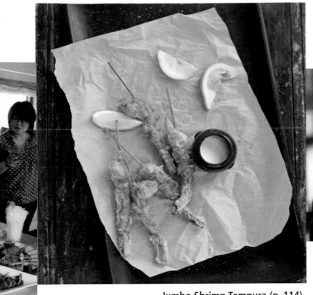

Feeding baby Brad (1977).

Our 30th wedding anniversary at Iwanoyu Onsen in Nagano. Kampai! (June 2002).

Jumbo Shrimp Tempura (p. 114).

decade. We marked the occasion at a hot spring *onsen* in the mountains of Nagano known for its healing waters, its elegant pottery, and its amazing food. Each meal was designed to mirror nature in miniature—each morsel was a delight and each dish was exquisite. One memorable dish was a small roasted trout, set upon a dish resembling a river and looking as though it had paused midstream. We reflected on the arc of our life in Japan together. Our sons had been in nursery, elementary, and high school in Japan, and we had lived all over the Tokyo metropolitan area, as well as in Kyoto and Kyushu. Japan had long since become our second home. With each decade that passed I had a new persona in Japan. In the early 1970s, the neighborhood kids called me *oneesan* (elder sister); a decade later I had become "*Buraado-kun to Arekisu-kun no okaasan* (Brad and Alex's mom); by the 1990s I was *Debi obasan* (Auntie Debbie). These days my friends in Japan all ask if I am an *obaachan* (grandmother) yet.

All that reminiscing brought us back to the ways in which Japanese foods and aesthetics are not solely the domain of elegant and isolated retreats. It is often said that in Japan "one eats with one's eyes," and that every customer is an "honored guest" (*okyakusama*). Quality and presentation of the food are important, even in prepared foods in supermarkets and urban convenience stores. Slices of tuna atop a bed of shredded white daikon radish with a perfect pinch of grated ginger—placed just-off center—are thoughtfully designed for take out at even the most unassuming market.

Nor is Japanese food just a matter of daily consumption; it is also about gift giving. Most department store basements (*depachika*) have two levels, one entirely devoted to food for gift giving. Railway stations across the country offer themed, regional specialties in the form of "station box lunches" (*eki-ben*). Some are consumed on the trip and others are brought along as gifts for fortunate friends and relatives. But their passions embrace more than just their native cuisine.

Japan has been adapting foreign cuisines to local tastes and sensibilities for centuries. Many dishes that originated abroad are now part of the repertoire of both home cooks and restaurants alike: Curry rice, originally from South Asia; ramen, gyoza, *shumai*, noodles and dumplings from China; *yakiniku* barbecue beef and spicy pollock roe *mentaiko* from Korea; deep fried *tonkatsu* cutlets and tempura from Portugal; and pasta from Italy are all now thoroughly standard Japanese meals in homes across the archipelago.

Conversely, the rest of the world has discovered and embraced Japanese food. Sushi and ramen are staples in supermarkets in North America and Western Europe; tofu no longer terrifies Western consumers; and words like edamame, teriyaki, and wasabi no longer need translation or italics.

ABOVE: Fresh Tuna Rice Bowl with Cucumber, Avocado and Spicy Mayonnaise (p. 86) LEFT: Chef Masashi Ishida comes to Lexington and makes Dashi (Fish Stock).

Junko Joho teaching Elsa Tian.

A Farmer displays her produce.

I saw the embrace of Japanese cuisine in my own family. As soon as they could express their preferences, my sons asked for octopus (*tako*) and seaweed (nori) instead of steak and mashed potatoes. They may have had a head start, but they certainly are not alone. Today, American kids do not need to wait an entire lifetime to educate their palates. Instead of a pizza on a Friday night, ten-year-old kids ask for California rolls, a thoroughly American invention that has made its way back over the Pacific. Many opt to snack on edamame in instead of potato chips. I have been teaching my nephew, Brandon, how to make sushi rolls since he was eight, and every time I visit we make something new. He is now nearly twenty and has never been to Japan, but he recently begged me to teach him how to make "inside-out" rolls. Although not considered pure sushi by some, these American concoctions are as popular in Japan as "American" bagels are in Israel.

There are many sources for the recipes in this book. In addition to cooking and eating in my friends' homes, I have been inspired by imaginative meals at Japanese pubs called *izakaya*. Here chefs offer small plates, like Spanish tapas, that match creatively styled fish, meat, and vegetables with beer, grape wines, rice-based sake, and (mostly) potato-based *shochu*. Other recipes come from festivals *(matsuri)* at Japan's shrines and temples. Whether celebrating the harvest, the coming of the rains, school entrance examinations, or the appearance of spring blossoms, these festivals are celebrated with street food from itinerant vendors' stalls featuring the savory and sweet snacks that form the core of millions of Japanese childhood memories.

And, given my sons' experiences, how could I not include a chapter on box lunch bento? But bento is not just for kids. They have already caught on in the United States, and there are many instructional websites in English. You can purchase bento boxes on-line or seek out alternatives, as I will show you. These attractive, appropriately portioned, and nutritionally balanced boxed meals will be a boon to you and your family's health.

In writing this book I have called upon a lifetime of experiences and upon a great many Japanese friends who have influenced my work (and play) in the kitchen. I hope it will appeal to experienced readers who already have an interest and knowledge about Japanese cuisine, as well as to beginners poised to discover all it has to offer. Many of the recipes are from classes I teach on Japanese home style cooking designed for students to achieve success on their own. My philosophy is that we should leave the fancy stuff to the pros (sushi chefs train for years for a reason). But you can still enjoy sushi and sashimi, served home style. Join me in the kitchen to discover some of my favorite Japanese recipes and it won't take you a lifetime to learn them.

Mixing spices in Kyoto.

This is a bento lunch in my favorite handmade box.

Dick and I visting with the Itoh and Oishi families.

Red daikon radishes.

Teaching

Despite my degree in elementary education, I have been teaching everywhere but in a conventional classroom. My first job, as 4-H agricultural agent, took me right to the farm and exposed me to the fundamentals of canning, baking, and pickling.

But teaching about food started as an informal exchange with a group of four Japanese women whose husbands, like mine, were studying at the Massachusetts Institute of Technology (MIT) in the mid-1970s. Masayo, from rural Shikoku, was the mom of a middle schooler; Emi was a Tokyo social worker; Harumi, from Yokohama, was interested in the Japanese arts of tea and kimono, and Yoshiko was a Tokyo office worker. We each started with the basics of our cuisines: I taught them how to bake bread and can jams, and they taught me how to make Japanese rice and rolled sushi. And so it was that when Dick and I returned to Tokyo to live for three years, I could navigate a market, recognize food labels, and guess what to do with the product.

My transition to formal teaching was gradual. It started with an English lesson in a supermarket for a Japanese mom with two kids back in Boston in the early 1980s. Supermarket English lessons evolved into tutorials on American food ingredients and eventually into American cooking lessons for groups of Japanese women. Along the way I was asked to teach classes on Japanese food and culture to American college students interested in Japan.

One thing always leads to another in life, and so it was with teaching and me. Between five subsequent yearlong stays in Japan that enabled my continuing education in Japanese cuisine (including formal classes in Japanese cooking), I started a catering business that I called "Eats Meets West" (pun intended) because there was now so much of Asia in my repertoire. Meanwhile, there was increasing demand for cooking classes on both Western and Japanese cuisine. In the early 1990s I began working in the Japan Program at the Boston Children's Museum and offered teacher workshops about Japanese food and culture, often focusing on kids' bento lunch boxes; I have subsequently done similar programs in Boston, New York, Washington D.C., and Tokyo. While at the museum, I developed the "Kids Are Cooking" program, which focused on introducing children to a world of cuisines, cooking fundamentals, and nutrition. Writing about food and culture for *The Boston Globe* was a natural next step in my rather unconventional journey.

Debra G. Samuels

Debra Samuels

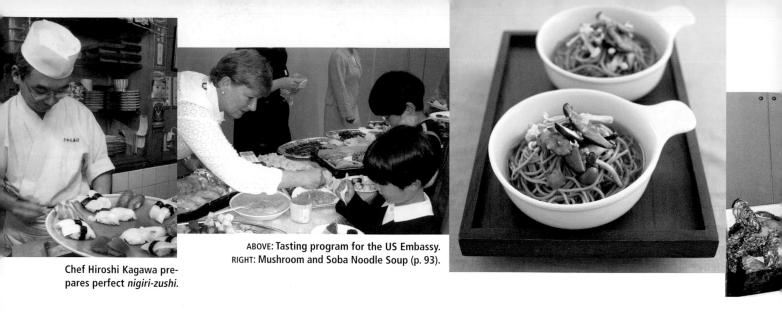

ABOVE: **Tasting program for the US Embassy.**
RIGHT: **Mushroom and Soba Noodle Soup (p. 93).**

Chef Hiroshi Kagawa pre-pares perfect *nigiri-zushi*.

Thoughts About Japanese Cuisine

I do not have a Japanese mother or mother-in-law and I did not grow up with Japanese food, flavors, or cooking techniques. The only soy sauce I encountered had caramel food coloring and lots of salt. In fact, my dear mother, Rona Greenberg, did not react very well when I told her in 1977 that we would be going to Japan with her first grandchild. "But what will he eat?" she wailed. "Tofu," I tossed out. This only made her cry harder. Who in suburban New York knew from tofu at that time—or much about Japanese food beyond the theater of knife twirling chefs in Japanese steak houses? Sure, the counter-culture set was dabbling in macrobiotic food with some Japanese roots, but we were still several years away from Japan's emergence as a global economic power and from the Japanese culinary boom that followed. Thankfully, in the subsequent four decades I have had dozens and dozens of surrogate mothers, sisters, aunties, and certified teachers who took me under their collective wings. (Rona still won't eat tofu, but she loves *yakitori*.)

My experience has distilled into a singular, powerful impression of how Japanese cooks—professionals and home cooks alike—respect the process, the product, and the details of a meal. They commit themselves to the high-est quality of each and establish an aesthetic that appeals to every sense. Setting a perfect leaf just off center on a plate of sliced persimmon is for your eyes; pressing a hard-boiled egg through the tight wire mesh of a ricer (*ura-goshi*) produces a velvety texture for your tongue; twisting

a *yuzu* peel for a burst of citrusy bouquet is for your nose. What may seem like small enhancements actually are the essence of the Japanese table. Each is second nature to the Japanese cook, and now, after decades, to me as well. Hopefully they will appeal to you too.

Like cooks everywhere, Japanese cooks have always been curious and innovative. Although tofu was intro-duced to Japan through China as early as 600 AD, it was the Buddhist monks and the aristocracy who mainly consumed it. It became part of the commoners' diet in the 16th century. This was about the time when Portuguese merchants and clergy introduced deep fried pork (*tonkat-su*), deep fried fish and vegetables (*tempura*), and sweet pound cake (*kasutera*). French pastries became *Japonaise* after the Japanese themselves ventured out in the 19th and 20th centuries. And now, as the world eagerly embraces their cuisine, they are still absorbing new ingredients and adapting to a rapidly globalizing world food market. Take *wafu* (Japanese style) pasta for example. One version mar-ries shredded seaweed with spaghetti and spicy pollack roe (*mentaiko*). This is actually a "two-fer"—the pasta is from Italy and the spicy roe is from Korea. The novelty of put-ting it all together is purely Japanese.

So, what are the elements that make food Japanese? In Italy, one encounters *alio* (garlic), *olio* (olive oil), and *prez-zemolo* (parsley) in most dishes. Korean cuisine features *pa* (scallions), *manul* (garlic), and *chamgirum* (sesame oil).

A side of *maguro* at the Tsukiji fish market.

ABOVE: This is a display of my favorite array of fillings for a hand roll sushi party. LEFT: Shoko unpacks a case of oysters.

Kimie Sato preparing dinner for us.

Japanese cuisine also has its own distinctive flavor profile found in its seasonings (*chomiryo*). *Sa, shi, su, se, so* (さ し す せ そ) is a line of sounds in the Japanese *hiragana* syllabary that captures many of the essential elements and the order of the seasonings of a Japanese dish. **Sa**to is sugar; **Shi**o is salt; **Su** is vinegar; **Se**iyo is an old fashioned word for soy sauce; and **Mi**so is fermented bean paste. But there are five more seasonings: mirin (sweet rice wine), sake (rice wine), kelp (*kombu*), dried shiitake mushrooms; and dried *katsuo* (bonito used to make fish stock), and you have a palette of Japanese flavors. Sugars and alcohol (mirin and sake) are added in the beginning to flavor and cook down the alcohol content, and strong seasonings like soy sauce and miso come later to maintain maximum flavor.

These days the word *umami*, commonly referred to as the savory fifth taste, is on everyone's tongue. *Umami* was identified by a Japanese scientist a century ago and occurs naturally in kelp (*kombu*), mushrooms, and fermented foods like soy sauce, miso, and Dashi (Fish Stock). The chemical base of *umami*, glutamates, is synthesized in MSG through a fermentation process. Some people have sensitivity to MSG, but in moderate amounts this flavor enhancer has not proven to be harmful.

Japanese cuisine has five important elements: seasonality, presentation, quality, portion size, and balance. Flavors peak and different local foods are available at different times of the year, so the season often dictates restaurant and recipe choices. The first bamboo shoots of the spring are eagerly anticipated for adding to rice (*takenoko gohan*). Eel (*unagi*) is fresh and abundant in the summer, when its rejuvenating powers are especially appreciated. This is also the season for

cold noodles in refreshing light vinaigrettes. In the autumn, the long, silver-bodied Pacific saury (*sanma*) are grilled simply with salt (*shioyaki*) and meals are finished with giant, thick-skinned, purple-blue grapes. Daikon radishes are sweetest in the winter, when hot pots with bubbling stocks are favorite communal dishes. The season not only influences the choice of food, but also the tableware. Earthy fall and winter pottery often give way to decorative porcelain and glass in the spring and summer.

This relationship of vessel and food is captured by the Japanese expression that one eats with one's eyes (*me de taberu*). This aesthetic is not reserved just for gift food, like handsomely wrapped Japanese sweets (*wagashi*) or high-end formal meals, with their multiple, gorgeously arranged dishes. It is also incorporated into the most routine fare: takeout from a convenience store so thoughtfully constructed that you'll forget it was mass produced; bento box lunches that entice you to eat every last bite; even the garnish of contrasting colors on the home dinner plate. The Japanese culinary aesthetic is spare. Odd numbers of dishes are often arranged in asymmetric patterns. A thin green chive blade will set off the flesh of a single plump and perfect scallop. A square of grilled tofu is topped by thinly spread miso with a sprinkling of poppy seeds. Not all Japanese meals are elegant and minimalist, but most are appetizing. Brimming bowls of hot ramen and spicy curry rice—two of the most modest and popular meals—and feathery mounds of bonito flakes atop a Stuffed Savory Pancake (*Okonomiyaki*) are always presented in an appealing way.

Food is expensive in Japan, and Japanese consumers do not shy away from spending a large potion of their budget

Stuffed Rice Balls (p. 88).

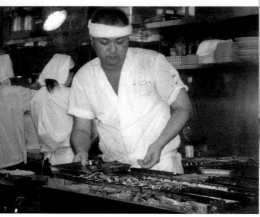

Yakitori being prepared for takeout.

Our cache of everyday chopsticks.

Eating Tako Yaki at Yushima Shrine Festival.

for high quality ingredients. Everyone has heard of the pampered cows that produce the famous, highly marbled Kobe beef (*wagyū*), and of the meticulously tended vines that produce intensely sweet (and expensive) melons. This insistence on high quality, labor-intensive production extends to prepared foods as well. All major department stores have food emporia, usually in their basement, where shoppers can see their food prepared, cooked, and packaged. The tofu makers on the premises use clear running water and the pleated dumpling crafters scoop freshly prepared fillings into thin, hand cut wrappers. A great deal of labor goes into Japan's love for high quality food, and they have little tolerance for sloppiness. One way to maintain access to high quality food within a household budget is to reduce the volume, a tactic that fits naturally with the emphasis on smaller portion sizes.

Portion sizes for most meals served in Japan are small to moderate by western standards. It is rare that one plate will hold an entire Japanese-style meal. Portions are dictated by the size of the plates on which they are individually served, and most meals feature multiple small plates, none of which is intended to overwhelm the others. Side dishes (*okazu*) each make a distinctive contribution to the meal and these vegetables, soups, and pickles are not mixed together. The main protein, such as a piece of grilled fish, is typically less than 4 ounces (100 g). Formal presentation of a meal is usually done on a lacquer tray. Even this relatively austere practice incorporates each of the central elements of a Japanese meal, including balance.

Japanese meals are balanced in many ways, from cosmology to cooking techniques. The oldest balancing act comes through Chinese beliefs about interaction among five components: wood, fire, earth, metal and water; their corresponding colors: green, red, yellow, white, and black—each of which corresponds to organs in the body; and their corresponding tastes: bitter, salty, sour, sweet and savory. Whether consciously or not, most Japanese cooks use these concepts to guide their menus and enhance well being. A formal meal also balances cooking methods, and will include items that are stir-fried (*yaitamono*), simmered (*nimono*), deep-fried (*agemono*), grilled (*yakimono*), and steamed (*mushimono*). The Japanese diet is also balanced by a rich variety of fermented foods that are eaten daily in some form. Miso, soy sauce, fermented soy beans (*natto*), and pickles (*tsukemono*) all have distinct health benefits, work as appetite enhancers, aid in digestion, are nutrient rich, and help balance the body's chemistry.

Above all, the Japanese meal is balanced around rice. One of the many Japanese words for a meal is *gohan*, which also refers to cooked rice; indicating just how central rice is to the Japanese diet. Japanese rice is the short grain and medium grain japonica variety. Often called "sticky rice" outside Japan, it is different from the glutinous rice (*mochigome*) that the Japanese and other Asians refer to as sticky rice. Japanese rice farming has been heavily subsidized by the government and is one of the few foods that Japanese farmers produce in self-sustaining volume.

And, of course, Japan is an island nation that depends upon the ocean for much of its protein. Seafood is consumed in many forms: raw, dried, cooked, ground, and whole. Low in fat, high in omega fatty acids and calcium, fish is eaten in greater volume in Japan than beef, pork, and chicken combined. The sea is also a source of one of Japan's

Vegetarian bento in a black box with a chrysanthemum motif.

Brad and Alex's childhood friends forever Ko and Yume
Takeuchi eating Korean BBQ.

Delicate Seafood Consommé (p. 79).

most popular and nutritious vegetables: seaweed, which comes in staggering number of varieties. Used to make stocks, in salads, and to wrap around rice, seaweed is high in vitamins B and C and is a natural source of glutamates.

Japanese cuisine is far broader than rice and the ocean's bounty. Noodles have their own food culture and are often a meal of their own. Buckwheat noodles (*soba*) are nutritious, chewy, and simple to prepare. Their thicker, white wheat-based cousin, *udon*, is popular in soups and hot pots. Ramen retains its Chinese influence and has reached cult-like status, while the thin angel hair threads of *sōmen* are served cold and minimally adorned. Noodle stocks can range from a Fish Stock-soy based broth, to the rich ramen soup made from a mixture of pork and beef bones, often with a chicken carcass thrown in for good measure.

Beef, pork and chicken are also used in main dishes, though in lesser quantities than in Western meals. Beef is often simmered in a sweet soy stock (*sukiyaki*), while pork is stir-fried with ginger (*shogayaki*) or enjoyed as deep-fried cutlets (*tonkatsu*). Chicken pieces are grilled on skewers (*yakitori*), deep fried (*kara age*), and simmered to make a topping for a rice bowl (*oyako donburi*). Tofu and tofu products are a prominent source of non-animal protein in soups, hot pots, salads, and dressings.

Every region and, it seems, every village, town, and city is justifiably proud of its specialty dishes (*meibutsu*). Fukuoka and Nagasaki are famous for their Chinese influenced noodles (*chanpon*), while Hokkaido, to the north, is known for its salmon hot pots. My friends from the Kansai region (Osaka and Kyoto) insist that their *sukiyaki* is special—they add the seasonings one-by-one instead of making a sauce

and adding it all at once, as Tokyoites do. A stay in the mountains of Nagano yields trout (*ayu*) as well as dishes rich in wild vegetables and herbs (*sansai*), such as bracken (*warabi*) and fiddlehead ferns (*zenmai*). And the wild boar served in other mountain regions as a hot pot meal (*botan nabe*), is exquisitely arranged on a platter in the shape of a peony. Can you see that preparing and serving Japanese cuisine is a thoughtful endeavor? To me this is the essence of this cuisine. The details, the flavor combinations, the concentration on eating foods for well-being, and, above all, the consideration of presentation together make it special.

Putting together your own Japanese table will be easier than you might think. Most of the tableware photographed for this book is part of my own collection, and when I serve a full Japanese meal or teach a class, I always incorporate western dishware as well. In addition to embracing the idea that everything does not have to match, you also should downsize. The western dinner plate becomes a serving platter or tray, the salads plate for the main dish, and saucers and dessert plates are perfect for side dishes. I accent the table with Japanese bowls and condiment dishes, and I follow Japanese etiquette by placing chopsticks parallel to the front of the diner's plate or bowl, with the tips pointing to the left, set on a chopstick rest. These functional rests also add decorative elegance to the table. Although napkins are not part of a Japanese place setting, I set rolled white organdy napkins with blue embroidered flowers from my Nana's wedding trousseau just above the chopsticks. It's these touches that make this my Japanese table, and now, using this book, I hope you will enjoy creating your own.

A Simple Guide to Japanese Ingredients

Basic Japanese ingredients are now available at supermarkets everywhere. The international section usually has short grain rice (for sushi), roasted seaweed (*yaki nori*), soy sauce, rice vinegar, and sesame oil. You will find fresh tofu, dumpling (*gyoza*) wrappers, fresh shiitake, and possibly even miso in the produce section. Edamame will be in the frozen food section. Organic markets have some of the lesser-known ingredients, such as seaweed, pickled plums (*umeboshi*), and miso. But, at least for the time being, you still may need to visit an Asian market or an on-line vendor for some of the dry or shelf stable ingredients like sweet rice flour (*mochiko*) or spring rain noodles (*harusame*) (p. 21). I know what it is like to buy one exotic spice for a recipe and never use it again, so I have given you multiple recipes for each ingredient. I have an extensive collection of Japanese ingredients in my pantry, but if you start with these 13 basic items—11 for the shelf and 2 for the fridge—you will be on your way to building your own collection.

Bonito Flakes

For Your Pantry
Soy sauce (I use low sodium)
Mirin
Sake
Bonito flakes (*katsuobushi*)
Kelp (*kombu*)
Wakame
Roasted seaweed (*yaki nori*)
Roasted sesame seeds
Short or medium grain rice
Sesame oil
Rice wine vinegar

For the Refrigerator
Miso
Tofu

Adzuki Beans (*Adzuki*) This petite red bean is high in fiber and very nutritious. In many Asian cuisines it is used mostly for making desserts. In Japan, where red and white are celebratory colors, it is also mixed with glutinous rice to make the dish, *sekihan*, which is eaten on special occasions. The canned beans come prepared whole and sweetened for topping fruit and ice cream and for baking in pastries. The sweetened paste (*anko*) comes in two textures—smooth (*koshi an*) and chunky (*tsubu an*). They are found in plastic pouches in the refrigerator section at Asian markets.

Bonito Flakes (*Katsuobushi*) Bonito flakes are the building block for most Japanese soups, sauces, and seasonings. They are made from dried, smoked, and fermented bonito, a large dark-fleshed relative of the tuna. The dried body of the fish is planed into papery curls that look like wood shavings. The large flakes, along with kelp (*kombu*), are used to make the classic Dashi (Fish Stock) (p. 35). This stock is full of natural glutamatic acid and is associated with the term *umami*, what we now associate with the savory "fifth taste." The flakes also come finely shredded and are used as a topping for savory pancakes, salads, dressings, and for a filling in Stuffed Rice Balls (p. 88).

Bonito Granules (*Hon Dashi*) These dried granules are made from *katsuo*. Some may include salt, MSG, and sugar. Japanese cooks like the convenience of Bonito Granules, which they can dissolve in boiling water to make an instant stock. Use 1½ teaspoons in 2½ cups (625 ml) of water, although it will depend on the type of Bonito Granules used. There are other convenience products on the market called "dashi packs" that have processed bonito flakes in a square paper pouch (like a large tea bag), that drop directly into boiling water.

Chinese (Napa) Cabbage

Green Onions (Scallions)

Fresh Ginger Root

Daikon Radish

Fresh Shiitake Mushrooms

Daikon Sprouts (*Kaiware*)

Garlic Chives (*Nira*) These paper-thin, flat green chives are also known as Chinese chives and have a distinctly garlic flavor. They are used in the filling for dumplings. They are not always easy to find, so I substitute regular chives or the tops of green onions (scallions) when Garlic Chives are not available.

Ginger (*Shoga*) Ginger is an aromatic rhizome that grows horizontally underground in knobby clumps. It has a clean spicy flavor. The skin is peeled and the flesh is used fresh, not dried. Ginger is used in stir-fries, it is pickled for condiments, grated for seasoning, and its juice is extracted for sauces and dressings. The skin of the ginger is light tan and should be smooth, not wrinkled. Young ginger is long, thin, and very tender.

Gari Shoga This is the ginger that is served in little mounds alongside sushi and sashimi. Paper-thin slices are marinated in a bath of sweet-and-sour vinegar. Found in the refrigerator sections, it is usually light pink due to the addition of food coloring. It is made from young ginger, which is less fibrous. In sushi restaurants you may find the natural light tannish-yellow slices.

Beni Shoga These neon red shreds of salty and sharp pickled ginger are scattered atop, or mixed in with Scattered Sushi Rice Salad (p. 50) or as a condiment eaten with Japanese style curry rice (*kare raisu*).

Green Onions (Scallions) Green onions (scallions) most closely resemble the Japanese long onion *naganegi*. It is mild with a long white onion stem and green top. Both are used in soups, salads and as a garnish. Although not perfect, the tops can be used as a substitute for chives.

Chinese (Napa) Cabbage (*Hakusai*) This long leafy cabbage is used in stir-fries, for stuffing, to make pickles, and in hot pots. It is not usually eaten raw in Japanese cuisine and quickly cooks into a soft pliable leaf. The white stem area is edible and crunchy and has a fresh celery-like flavor.

Daikon Radish Daikon radish is a long thick white cylindrical root. The radish can be sliced and salted to make pickles. When grated or shredded for salads and sauces and consumed raw, it has a spicy bite, but turns mild when cooked.

Daikon Radish Sprouts (*Kaiware Daikon*) These spicy sprouts have bright green clover-like petals atop 2-inch (5 cm) long white stems. Their length makes them perfect for sushi hand rolls (p. 46). You can also use them in salads.

When not available substitute watercress or spicy radish sprouts.

Edamame The fact that this entry is not in italics is testament to how much a part of the American culinary landscape edamame have become. These green beans grow on stalks in fuzzy pods and are served as a nutritious snack, boiled and salted in their pods, or folded into cooked rice. Outside Japan, they are mostly shelled and used in salads or used to make sauces for fancy sushi rolls and as a dip.

Garlic (*Ninniku*) Garlic is not a classically Japanese seasoning, but is used in Japan because Korean, Chinese, and Italian cuisines have become staples in the Japanese home. Garlic, a member of the onion family, is a strong aromatic used in stir-fries, to season ground meat for dumplings, and as a condiment.

Dried Red Pepper

Wasabi Paste

Wasabi Powder

Red Pepper Powder

Japanese Citron (*Yuzu*) This Japanese citron is prized as much for its aromatic zest as for its juice. The fruit is full of pits, and produces very little juice, so it can be quite expensive. It is rare to find this fresh citrus outside Japan, although it is sometimes available at Asian markets. The juice comes in small bottles and is highly concentrated. It is used to flavor dressings and the zest is used for soups and teas.

White Miso

Red Miso

Hot Spices Although Japanese food is not thought of as a particularly spicy cuisine, plenty of heat is often added to cooked dishes, through such condiments as wasabi in sushi or red pepper flakes (*togarashi*) sprinkled on a bowl of noodles.

Dried Red Pepper (*Togarashi*) These dried red peppers are used whole in pickling or ground and sprinkled on cooked foods. red pepper powder (*Ichimi togarashi*) can be part of a spicy blend called *shichimi* that includes seven other peppers and spices.

Dry Yellow Mustard (*Karashi*) Dry yellow mustard seeds are ground and mixed with flour. Dry Yellow Mustard must be mixed with water. It is also available as a paste. This very spicy mustard resembles English style mustard, but is a darker yellow. It is used for dipping fried foods, such as pork cutlets and oyster or shrimp fry, with roast pork, or steamed fish balls (*oden*).

Wasabi This is a fresh water root cultivated in rural Japan. Freshly grated for eating with sushi and sashimi, it was once used to mask the smell of fish and is reputed to have powerful antibacterial and anti-parasitic function when eaten with raw fish. Fresh wasabi is expensive and very hard to obtain outside Japan. Most of us are familiar with it as a paste that comes in a tube or as a powder to mix with water. Both the paste and the powder come mixed with other ingredients, such as horseradish. Combined with soy sauce, wasabi is also a dressing for vegetables.

Miso Miso is fermented soybean paste. Soybeans are steamed with grain, yeast, and salt and then are fermented, forming a variety of pastes of varying strengths. The most common and mild miso pastes are the white ones (*shiro*) that are used with bonito stock to make miso soup. The darker and saltier red miso (*aka*) is also used for soup. A mixture of white and red pastes (*awasemiso*) is also very popular. Miso can be used to marinate fish and vegetables, and is a base for sauces such as Sweet Miso Sauce (p. 32). It usually comes in clear plastic containers and pouches. Be sure to check the label, as some include the stock (Dashi) for convenience.

Trumpet Mushrooms
(*Eringhe*)

Oyster
Mushrooms

Enokitake (*Enoki*)

Fresh Shiitake

Honshimeji (*Buna Shimeji*)

Spring Rain Noodles
(*Harusame*)

Buckwheat
Noodles
(*Soba*)

Dried *Udon*

Mushrooms There are a large variety of wonderful mushrooms available for Japanese dishes:

Enokitake These thin white mushrooms have a small smooth cap and a narrow, long 3-inch (7.5 cm) stem. They grow in a bundle and are often used in soups and hot pots and in combination with other mushrooms. They taste clean and delicate, and their texture includes a bit of a crunch. They have recently become popular and can be found in cellophane packages in many western supermarkets. They keep for about 1 week in the refrigerator.

Shimeji These stumpy mushrooms grow in clumps and can have white or light brown triangular-shaped caps on a 1 or 2-inch (2.5-5 cm) stem. They have a meaty texture and must be cooked. Break up the clump into smaller sections for cooking.

Shiitake Sometimes called black mushrooms, or Chinese mushrooms, shiitake are available both fresh and dried. These mushrooms are grown in Korea, China, and Japan. Fresh shiitake are now widely available in western supermarkets and must be cooked before being consumed. They are used in hot pots, stir-fries, and soups and can be quite meaty. The cap is light brown and has a smooth soft texture. The stem tends to be woody and is not usually eaten, but saved to add to a stock for flavor. Dried shiitake mushrooms must be reconstituted and are more intensely flavorful than the fresh ones. Use the tasty soaking liquid to cook the mushrooms as well as for stocks and sauces. Dried shiitake can have thick brown caps with white cracks or can be thinner and darker with a slightly yellowish underside. The soaking time varies according to the thickness of the mushroom. They stay indefinitely on the shelf in an airtight container. Once reconstituted, you can use dried shiitake in any dish calling for shiitake. However, fresh shiitake is not suitable for all recipes.

Noodles come in a variety of flavors and shapes:

Udon These creamy, white, thick wheat noodles are used in soups, hot pots, and stir-fries. They come both fresh and par cooked in nests of single serving sizes, usually in the refrigerator sections of Asian markets. They also come dried in long cylindrical cellophane packages. Recently, I have seen some of the par cooked variety in the Asian section of supermarkets in shelf stable packages.

Buckwheat Noodles (*Soba*) These nutritious noodles are made from a combination of buckwheat and wheat flours, and come in individual serving sizes packed in cylindrical bundles. They have a chewy texture and an earthy nutty flavor. In Japan, during the summer, they are often eaten cold, served simply with a dipping sauce and green onions (scallions). However, they are also cooked and served in a hot broth.

Spring Rain Noodles (*Harusame*) The name "spring rain noodles" is fitting for these translucent vermicelli made from either potato or yam starch. Sold dry they are re-constituted in boiled water and then used in cold noodle salads and hot pots and do not fall apart when simmered in soups or sauces. They come in cellophane packages and are sometimes referred to as saifun noodles.

Short Grain Brown Rice   Short Grain White Rice

Soy Sauce   Sesame Oil   Sake   Mirin   Rice Vinegar

Brown Rice (*Genmai*) Brown rice is un-polished short grain rice with the layer of bran left intact. It is more nutritious than white rice, but not that popular in Japan yet. It needs to be cooked longer, but uses the same amount of water. Although it is almost never used for making sushi in Japan it is gaining in popularity due to an increase in organic health food restaurants and stores.

Rice (*Kome*) Short and medium grain rice, japonica, is stickier than the long grain variety. This is the rice eaten daily and used in making sushi. Do not confuse it with the sticky rice (glutinous or sweet rice) that is used to make *mochi* and Japanese sweets.

Mirin This is a sweet rice wine used for cooking. *Aji-mirin*, which has sugar and salt added, is the variety most commonly found in markets. *Hon mirin*, with no additives, and higher alcohol content, is sold only in liquor stores in Japan and is very hard to locate elsewhere. Some of my Japanese friends say they mix a little sugar and sake together, but it isn't the same thing.

Rice Vinegar (*Su*) Rice vinegar is milder and is less acidic than the sharper western vinegars made from fermenting fruit. It is used for making salads (*sunomono*) and dressing for sushi. Do not mistake pure rice vinegar for bottles of seasoned rice vinegar (*sushi-zu*), which contains sugar and salt. I prefer to make my own seasoned rice vinegar.

Soy Sauce (*Shoyu*) Soy sauce is a brown liquid made from crushed, fermented soybeans, wheat, and salt. It is ubiquitous in Japanese cuisine and is associated with the term *umami,* the savory "fifth taste." It also acts as a preservative. There are a variety of soy sauces on the market, but Japanese soy sauce is generally less salty than its Chinese counterparts. It may seem counter-intuitive, but light soy sauce (*usukuchi shoyu*) is saltier than regular soy sauce. Cooks who do not wish their food to darken often use the lighter soy sauce. Regular soy sauce is used directly for dipping. I use low sodium soy sauce in most of my recipes and at the table as well. It has about 30% less sodium.

Sake This clear and potent rice wine, made by brewing short grain rice in porcelain or wooden casks, is used for cooking or drinking. Much like wine grown abroad, breweries are highly localized and each region of Japan produces its own signature sakes. It can be served hot or cold.

Sesame Oil This aromatic oil is made by pressing hulled roasted sesame seeds, and is used in dressings, sauces, and to stir-fry vegetables. It is often added to flavor neutral oil in making tempura.

Seaweed and
Sesame

Red Shiso
and Plum

Homemade Dried Fish
and Sesame Seeds

Hijiki

Wakame

Dry Mixed Seasoning for Rice (*Furikake*) Furikake
is a savory dried mixture for sprinkling on top of, or
mixing into, hot rice. The varieties are endless and
can include combinations of dried ingredients such
as seaweed, herbs, sesame seeds, fish, egg, sour plum,
salt, sugar and sometimes MSG. Commercial brands
are plentiful and delicious, but you can also make your
own combination (p. 31)

Salt (*Shio*) Sea salt is most commonly used in
Japan. The sea salt is moist and sold in plastic
pouches. It is used for making pickles and seasoning sauces. I use either a fine grain sea salt (as moist
as I can find) or kosher salt.

Seaweed This sea vegetable is an integral part of Japanese meals and
can be purchased and eaten in both dried and fresh forms. Nutri-
ent-dense seaweed is used in salads, soups, as a stock, and, most
famously, to wrap sushi.

Hijiki One of the most nutritious seaweeds, *hijiki* is rich in protein, minerals, and high in fiber, it comes dried in short thread-like
strands. It has a chewy texture and is used in simmered and fresh
salads with seasoned tofu, carrots, and soybeans. *Hijiki* is great when
stir-fried in sesame oil. I find the flavor has a hint of licorice to it.

Nori (**Laver**) This seaweed is dried, but doesn't need to be
reconstituted. Roasted Seaweed (*yaki nori*)comes in sheets, squares,
or rectangles and is used to wrap plain or sushi rice. It is made from
chopped pieces that are dried and pressed into sheets. It is also cut
into strips and used as a garnish and as part of a savory rice sprinkle
mix used on or mixed in with plain rice.

Kelp (*Kombu*) It almost always comes as a dried flat rectangle,
in a variety of lengths and widths. It is used directly for seasoning
stocks, in the water for rice, and sometimes to add depth to dressings. It is rich in the natural glutamates that appear as a light white
dusty coating on the surface of the seaweed. Kelp becomes thick and
slimy after soaking and is removed before eating. But don't throw it
out. It can be chopped and simmered in soy sauce and seasonings
and used to make the condiment *tsukudani* for rice.

Wakame This is the seaweed most often used in soups and
vinegared salads. You are most likely to find it in dried form outside
Japan, probably cellophane packages of foot-long (30 cm) threads
or 1-inch (2.5 cm) pieces. It is high in Vitamins B and C. *Wakame*
is mild and has a velvety texture. It only needs a short soak before
expanding to almost triple its size.

White Sesame Seed

Black Sesame Seed

Sesame Seeds Both white (*shiro goma*) and black (*kuro goma*) sesame seeds are versatile accents in many Japanese dishes. Often they are toasted and crushed in a special grooved ceramic bowl called a *suribachi* to bring out their nutty flavor. These seeds are mixed in with salads, used as a garnish, as a condiment, in sauces and in desserts. Japanese brands of sesame seeds are packaged in plastic pouches or plastic jars. Look for the word *iri goma*, which means the seeds have already been toasted. I usually re-toast them in a dry skillet for an even deeper flavor. White sesame seeds are roasted, crushed and pressed to make sesame oil.

Fresh Shiso Leaves

Shiso This member of the mint family is my all-time favorite Japanese herb. Like other members of the mint family, it grows like a weed. This perennial has been growing happily in my garden for 10 years. Known in English as Beefsteak plant or Perilla, it has a distinctive flavor—some combination of mint and basil with a hint of coriander leaves (cilantro). It is a beautiful serrated-edge leaf that is used with sushi. Chop it up and add it to salads, or deep-fry it for tempura. Its seeds and blossoms, when salted and preserved, can be added to warm rice. There are two varieties: the more common green (*aojiso*), and the red (*akajiso*), used mostly for adding color rather than flavor.

Sweet Rice Flour Granules   Sweet Rice Flour

Sugar (*Sato*) People are surprised that so much sugar is used in Japanese cuisine. Most Japanese sugar is made from sugar cane. It is white and moist and resembles the texture of brown sugar. This is what is used in cooking. It is totally different from the granulated sugar used in the West. I use granulated sugar in most of the recipes in this book unless otherwise indicated. Many Japanese use a brown sugar (san on tou) instead of the white, which has a slight caramel flavor. I substitute light brown sugar, which is slightly stronger but works well.

Sweet Rice Flour (*Mochiko*) Sweet rice (glutinous) flour is made from milled and ground sweet short grain rice. This flour is used in making desserts and is also suitable as a thickening agent. For recipes in this book I use Koda Farms brand, which comes in 1-pound (500 g) boxes and is available in most Asian grocers or online. Other sweet rice flours are not suitable for substitution.
Sweet Rice Flour Granules (*Shiratamako*) are a sweet rice (glutinous) flour that has been dried into smaller than pea-size granules. It is used in making Japanese sweets and can also be a thickener. The granules are mixed with water and heated to form sticky dough. *Shiratamako* comes in tubular cellophane packages and is available at Japanese grocers as well as Asian grocers, or online.

Sencha   Matcha   Hojicha

Tofu Tofu is made from the "milk" of cooked soybeans that are mashed, sieved, and mixed with a coagulant and poured into molds while it drains and sets. A nutritious block of non-animal protein and amino acids, it has been the mainstay in vegetarian and Asian diets for centuries, and it long ago crossed over to the mainstream in Western cuisines. Tofu comes in a myriad of textures both dried and fresh, and is eaten both raw and cooked, in soups, stews, salads. It absorbs the flavors of whatever is cooked with it. Two of the most common forms of tofu in supermarkets are soft and firm, but there are many varieties within that range. Soft or silken tofu (*kinu*) is used in soups, dressings and on its own. Firm tofu (*momen*) is commonly used in soups, stews, and salads.

Tonkatsu Sauce This vinegary sweet, thick, rich brown sauce is a Worcestershire-like sauce that combines tomato paste, fruit, and a variety of seasonings. It is used as a dressing and dip for fried dishes, like Fried Pork Cutlets (*Tonkatsu*) (p. 104) and Fried Oysters (*Kaki Furai*) (p. 113). The most popular commercial brand is Bull-Dog Sauce and it comes in a plastic rectangular bottle. Similar sauces are used for topping Stuffed Savory Pancakes (*Okonomiyaki*) (p. 60) and are mixed into Fried Noodles with Cabbage and Pork (*Yaki Soba*) (p. 94), but they vary in sweetness and viscosity.

Umeboshi Sour, reddish purple, with wrinkly skin the dried pickled Japanese apricot, sometimes referred to as a plum, is a standard condiment on every Japanese table.

White Bait (*Chirimen/Chirimen-jako*) These miniscule dried or semi-dried baby anchovies are mixed into salads or rice directly. They are also used as part of a Homemade Savory Sprinkles (*Furikake*) (p. 31). They come separately in shelf stable cellophane packets or in the freezer section of Asian markets. Toast them, like sesame seeds, for an added protein crunch.

Green Tea (*Sencha/Ocha*) This is the most common Japanese beverage. Imported from China centuries ago, Japan's tea bushes grow in perfectly mounded and manicured rows. The young leaves are picked, steamed, and then dried. The amount of tea, the temperature, the grade, and brewing time are important factors in serving a good cup of green tea. Unlike black tea, (*kocha*) which requires boiling water poured onto the tea leaves, the temperature for making green tea is lower—about 160-170°F (70-80°C) depending on whether it is spring picked *sencha* or summer harvested *bancha* or *genmaicha*.

Powdered Green Tea (*Matcha*) This is the ground, powdered green tea famously used in Japanese tea ceremonies. It is made from leaves that have been grown in the shade and has a deep moss green color and bitter flavor. It has high caffeine content and is packed with antioxidants such as Vitamins C and E. Unlike other teas, where leaves are steeped in water and should not be swallowed, with *matcha* one ingests the dissolved leaf, thus increasing its health benefits. *Matcha* is no longer just for tea ceremonies or drinking. You can now order *matcha* latte and shakes and find it in Japanese and western confections. *Matcha* is sold in small tins or foil pouches and is more expensive than *sencha*.

Hojicha This is also referred to as *bancha*, a rustic blend of roasted older tea leaves and twigs. It has a dark brownish color and a deep smoky flavor. It is a very satisfying drink at anytime of the day because it has less caffeine than *sencha*. Unlike *sencha*, you pour boiling water directly on the leaves.

Useful Equipment

Bamboo Rolling Mat (*Makisu*) This mat is used for making sushi rolls. There are two types of mats. The one with cylindrical sticks bound together by string woven through the mat vertically. This is the most common and used with roasted seaweed, rice, and fillings to make a variety of rolls. It is covered in plastic wrap to make inside out rolls where the rice is on the outside and the seaweed is rolled inside the rice. The other mat is flat on one side and round on the other. This mat is used for both maki rolls and for shaping the Seasoned Rolled Omelet (*Tamago Yaki*) (p.34).

Chopstick Rests (*Hashi Oki*) Chopstick rests hold the tips of the chopsticks that diners place in their mouth when not in use. The rests can be made of porcelain, clay, wood, treated Japanese paper or even a natural stone (washed of course).

The rests come in all different shapes and colors and generally complement the season and food. They can be fun, fanciful, or elegant (At a pub I saw one made with a screw and two bolts). Mine do double duty as knife or dessert fork rests.

Cooking Chopsticks (*Saibashi*) Cooking chopsticks come in lengths from 12 inches to 18 inches (30 cm-45 cm) and can be made of bamboo or metal. They keep fingers away from hot sauce and oil while turning or plucking food from pots. There are also cooking chopsticks with particularly narrow tips that are useful in garnishing a dish and special serving chopsticks with flat surfaces.

Drop Lids

Drop Lids (*Otoshibuta*) These wooden lids are made to fit inside pots and rest directly on top of cooking food. The lid keeps the sauce from evaporating and concentrates it directly into the food. You can use parchment paper circles to achieve similar results.

Chopstick Rests

1. Stirring Spoon
2. Ladle
3. Bamboo Skewers
4. Wire Mesh Strainer
5. Cooking Chopsticks
6. Wood Skewer
7. Decorative Slotted Spoon

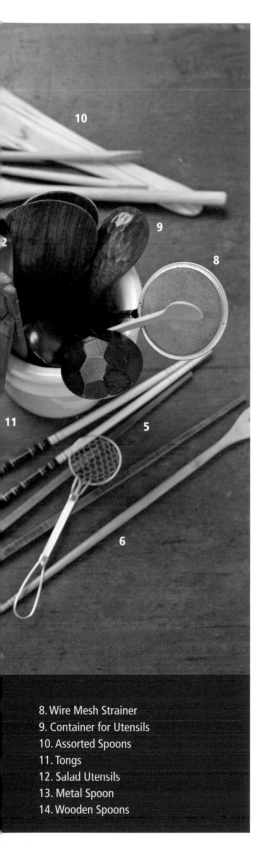

Grater Box   OXO Julienne Peeler

and other food. The two part graters that set a plastic grater atop a box are very useful as the grated food falls directly into the box. Substitute microplane graters and box graters to obtain desired texture.

Rice Cooker (*Suihanki*) The electric rice cooker is probably the most common item in Japanese kitchens and increasingly in western kitchens as well. They range from simple to sophisticated with sensors that have timers for soaking and automatic switch on. Many include a multitude of settings for cooking brown rice, porridge and sushi rice. All of them keep the rice warm. Rice cookers come with special 1 cup rice (1 *ichi go*) measures that are about ¾ cup (160 g). These cookers also cook terrific *takikomi gohan* (rice cooked with a variety of ingredients).

Graters and Peeler (*Oroshiki*) Graters are used frequently in the preparation of Japanese food and for accompaniments for dishes. Graters do different jobs and can be made of metal, porcelain, and plastic. All have very sharp raised teeth that efficiently grate ginger, daikon radish, wasabi, onions,

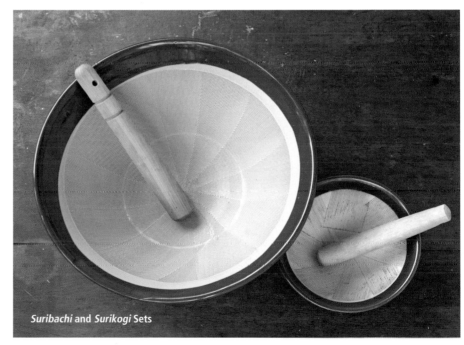

Suribachi and *Surikogi* Sets

8. Wire Mesh Strainer
9. Container for Utensils
10. Assorted Spoons
11. Tongs
12. Salad Utensils
13. Metal Spoon
14. Wooden Spoons

Japanese Mortar and Pestle (*Surib-achi* and *Surikogi*) Clay bowls with an unglazed grooved surface interior and a wooden stick are primarily used for grinding toasted sesame seeds and making pastes. When the toasted seeds are

ground in a circular motion a nutty appetizing aroma is released from the seeds. The crushed seeds are used in sauces and as a tasty garnish. The bowls are also made in plastic, but the grinding stick remains wood.

Basic Recipes

It is a good idea to make these basic ingredients and keep them in your refrigerator and pantry to make things easier when you cook your way through this book. Many of these sauces have commercial brand equivalents, but many have additives that you don't get when you make your own. I like the idea of having a big jar of Teriyaki Sauce in my refrigerator, because I don't hesitate to make recipes that call for it. Making things from scratch also gives you a good base knowledge of your materials, some of which will be new to you. *Gambatte*! You can do it!

Soy Ginger Vinaigrette

The tang of lemon juice and the zing of ginger juice give this dressing a snappy flavor. I use it on mixed salads to give them an Asian flair. Sprinkle on a combination of toasted sesame seeds and a sprinkle of sea salt or kosher salt just before serving. (The Ginger People manufactures a very good fresh bottled ginger juice that you can substitute for grating ginger and squeezing your own.)

Makes 1 cup (250 ml)

½ cup (125 ml) soy sauce, preferably low sodium
¼ cup (65 ml) canola oil
1 tablespoon sesame oil
2 tablespoons ginger juice
1 tablespoon fresh lemon juice
3 tablespoons rice wine vinegar
1 garlic clove, crushed
2 teaspoons sugar
½ teaspoon salt
¼ teaspoon pepper

Combine all the ingredients in a glass jar, cover and shake. This will keep in the refrigerator for about 3 weeks.

NOTE HOW TO MAKE GINGER JUICE
It is easy to make your own ginger juice. Take a knob of ginger and, using a Japanese porcelain grater or microplane or using the smallest holes on a box grater, grate the ginger into a mound. Pick up the grated ginger with your fingers and squeeze to release the juice into a small bowl.

Spicy Mayonnaise

This quick dressing is commonly used for dabbing inside sushi rolls, mixing with fresh and canned tuna, and for use as a dipping sauce.

Makes ½ cup (125 ml)

½ cup (125 ml) mayonnaise
2-3 teaspoons Sriracha sauce or spicy chili oil (or more, to taste)
2 teaspoons sesame oil
2 teaspoons soy sauce, preferably low sodium

Combine the ingredients in a mixing bowl and whisk together. Store in airtight container in the refrigerator.

Wasabi Soy Sauce Dressing

This is a tasty, spicy dressing that is great over simply cooked vegetables like asparagus, fiddlehead ferns, or broccoli. This recipe calls for powdered wasabi, but you can use wasabi paste instead. Dilute in a little bit of water and add to the soy sauce.

Makes ¼ cup (65 ml)

1-2 teaspoons wasabi powder
2 teaspoons water
¼ cup (65 ml) soy sauce, preferably low sodium

Add the wasabi powder and water to a small bowl and mix well. Add the soy sauce and mix again. Store the mixture in an airtight container in the refrigerator.

Tofu Dressing Shiro-ae

This seasoned, mashed tofu dressing adds protein to a simple bowl of steamed or boiled vegetables, such as spinach, green beans, or carrots. Tofu is highly perishable, so use it within 1 or 2 days. Silken or soft to medium soft tofu is best, but you can use a firm tofu.

Makes 2 cups (500 ml)

1 block of soft or silken tofu
1 tablespoon toasted sesame seeds or ¼ cup (25 g) toasted walnuts
1 tablespoon sugar
½ teaspoon salt

1 Place the tofu on a plate and microwave for 30 seconds. Drain the water from the plate.
2 Place the sesame seeds or walnuts in the bowl of a food processor. Pulse several times.
3 Add the tofu, sugar, and salt. Process until smooth.

Akiko's Sesame Seed Dressing

Akiko Nakajima, a neighbor, took me under her wing and introduced me to the daily life of a suburban Japanese family. The term multi-task might have been invented for her. Her rat-a-tat speech and physical speed were hard to keep up with. She showed me all sorts of time saving short cuts in the kitchen. A jar of Akiko's Sesame Seed Dressing has been in my fridge for 32 years—ever since she taught me how to make it. I use it on steamed vegetables, as a salad dressing, or on steamed fish. The coarsely ground roasted sesame seeds provide a nutty taste and texture. I learned to make it by grinding the seeds in a *suribachi*, a pottery bowl with grooves. But these days I often make quick work of it in the food processor. Nakajima-san would be proud!

Makes 1 cup (250 ml)

½ cup (125 g) white sesame seeds, toasted
2 cloves garlic, minced (optional)
½ teaspoon salt
½ cup (125 ml) canola oil
¼ cup (65 ml) soy sauce
1 tablespoon sugar

1 Place the toasted sesame seeds in the bowl of a food processor. Pulse 3 times until the aroma is released.
2 Add the remaining ingredients and process for 30 seconds or until the desired consistency is achieved. Store in an airtight jar in the refrigerator. This will keep for several weeks.

Odagiri Sensei's Sanbaizu Vinegar Dressing

This *sanbaizu* recipe is from my cooking teacher, Odagiri Sensei. *Sanbaizu* is a classic dressing used often in the vinegary *sunomono*, which is a part of almost every meal in Japan. "San" means "three," so *Sanbaizu* means "vinegar plus 3 other ingredients." Soy sauce, Dashi (Fish Stock), and mirin are the three ingredients in this dressing. A few tablespoons of this dressing transforms a plate of sliced cucumbers, crabmeat, or steamed chicken into a delicious salad.

Odagiri Sensei always added a few more ingredients to make it special. A piece of kelp (*kombu*) is added to release natural glutamates into the dressing and one pickled plum (*umeboshi*) contributes a sour tone. These elements are called "hidden flavors" or *kakushiaji*. (In order to test our taste buds, Odagiri Sensei used to ask us "Can you tell what is in this dressing?" A trained palate would recognize the combination of flavors in this sauce.)

Makes ⅓ cup (80 ml)

3 tablespoons rice vinegar
1 tablespoon soy sauce, preferably low sodium
1 tablespoon Dashi (Fish Stock) (p. 35)
1 tablespoon fresh lemon juice
1 tablespoon mirin
1 pickled plum, (*umeboshi*) (optional)
One 2 in (5 cm) piece of kelp (*kombu*)

Mix the vinegar, soy sauce, Dashi (Fish Stock), lemon juice, mirin and pickled plum if using, in a small bowl. Add the kelp to the bowl and let sit for 20 minutes. Remove and discard the kelp and pickled plum.

Crunchy Cucumber Pickles

My friend, Atsuko Fish, made these quick, simple, and crunchy cucumber pickles (*shiozuke*). Their refreshing taste is a great accompaniment to a Japanese meal.

6 mini cucumbers or one English cucumber
1½ tablespoons sea salt or kosher salt
Dash of sake
Dash of soy sauce, preferably low sodium

1 Wash and dry the cucumbers. If you are using an English cucumber, slice it in half lengthwise and then scoop out and discard the seeds with the tip of a spoon.
2 Rub each cucumber with about 1 teaspoon of the salt and set it in a bowl.
3 Leave the cucumbers in the bowl for about 30 minutes. Remove from the bowl and squeeze any liquid from the cucumbers.
4 Set the cucumbers on a cutting board. Cut in half lengthwise again and then slice into ½-inch (1.25 cm) pieces. Mix with a sprinkle of sake and soy sauce before serving.

Simple Mixed Pickles Tsukemono

Every Japanese meal is accompanied or completed by crunchy pickles (*tsukemono*) to either enhance the appetite or aid in digestion. Daikon radishes, eggplant, cucumbers, turnips, and Chinese (Napa) cabbage are popular choices. I used to see, in my friends' kitchens, deep plastic boxes with tops outfitted with what looked like a giant screw with a disc attached. Large heads of Chinese (Napa) cabbage sliced in quarters and salted were placed under the disc. After four turns the disc pressed down upon the cabbage to squeeze the liquid from the vegetable. This is a simple salted pickle (*shiozuke*) and is the easiest to make. Other styles of pickling can be done with vinegar (*suzuke*), burying vegetables in rice bran, (*nukazuke*) and rubbing vegetables with miso (*misozuke*). the famous sour salted pickled plum (*umeboshi*) is consumed almost daily.

Although many people used to make their own pickles, and some still do, the high quality of mass-produced *tsukemono* has reduced that number. However some do contain food coloring and additives. Making your own *shiozuke* is a snap. For this recipe instead of making one type of vegetable I use a mélange of vegetables. The vegetables are cut into similar sizes and salted to remove excess water. For extra color, I like to use the rotund red radishes or slender French red radishes. Cut the vegetables into similar lengths not only for the aesthetic, but it makes it easier to pick them up with chopsticks.

Makes approximate 4 cups (1 liter)

½ head (12 oz-1 lb/375-500 g) Chinese (Napa) cabbage cut into 2 in (5 cm) pieces
1 large carrot, peeled and cut into 1 x ¼ in logs (2.5 cm x 6 mm)
2 mini cucumbers or half English cucumber, skin on, and cut into 1 x ¼ in logs (2.5 cm x 6 mm)
6 radishes, cut into 8 wedges
1-1½ tablespoons kosher or sea salt

1 Have on hand a very large bowl.
2 Place the Chinese cabbage in a colander and rinse under cold water. Drain and place in the large bowl.
3 Add the carrots, cucumbers, and radishes to the bowl.
4 Sprinkle on the salt and toss together to thoroughly coat the vegetables.
5 Set a piece of plastic wrap on top of the vegetables and place another bowl that fits just inside the larger bowl on top of the vegetables. Take two 1 pound (500 g) cans of food from your pantry and set them into the bowl to use as weights.
6 Set the mixture aside for about 2 hours. Remove the weights. Take a handful of vegetables and in the sink squeeze the excess water from the vegetables. Place the vegetables in a clean dry bowl. Repeat with the remaining vegetables.
7 Store the vegetables in an airtight container for one day before using. They will last for about 2 weeks in the refrigerator. Serve in small bowls.

> **NOTE** To vary the taste of the pickles just before serving drizzle on
> 1) Lemon juice and mirin
> 2) Sesame oil and toasted sesame seeds

Preparing Japanese Rice

Japanese rice (japonica) is a short or medium grain rice and an accompaniment to most meals. I first learned how to make rice properly from my neighbor, Kai-san. With her baby, Keiko, strapped to her back and with Brad strapped to mine, she showed me how to properly rinse, drain, and soak the rice. She taught me to measure the water and rice by placing my hand flat atop the rice. There was enough water when it was just over the knuckles on the back of my hand. Today's directions on packages of Japanese rice in the United States tell us not to rinse the rice. all my Japanese friends still rinse their rice before cooking.

Soak the rice for at least 20 minutes until the grains plump up and turn white. Depending on the age of the rice, this can take anywhere from 25-45 minutes. After soaking, I drain my rice for 20 minutes before starting the cooking process. When using a rice cooker this step is often eliminated. The newer, and very expensive, "smart" rice cookers have sensors and will time the soaking and cooking with a push of a button. When using the simpler (and more widely available) rice cookers, you have to presoak the rice. In 30 minutes, including steaming time, you will have perfect rice. You can make one pot rice casseroles in the rice cooker by adding vegetables, chicken or salmon. If you don't have a rice cooker, here is a stovetop recipe that yields excellent results. The rice should be toothsome and sticky, but not mushy. When making rice for sushi, use a little less liquid, as you will be adding a dressing to the hot rice.

If you are in a hurry you can eliminate the soaking, but the rice will be harder. Instead, make more rice than you need and freeze it in plastic wrap while it is still hot. I was taught this by my friend (and coauthor of *The Korean Table*), Taekyung Chung. Heat them in the microwave for 2 minutes and you have hot steamed rice. Japanese rice cookers come with a measuring cup, a special measure just for rice (1 *go*) with a volume of ¾ cup (160 g) (an American cup is 200 grams). The recipes in this book use the standard American measure. For example: 3 cups (600 g) raw rice equals just over 4 Japanese rice cups. If you have a Japanese rice cooker and measuring cup, follow the manufacturer's instructions.

Makes 4 cups (approximately 800 g)

2 cups (400 g) short-grain white rice
Water for soaking the rice
2 cups (500 ml) water

1 Put the rice into a large mixing bowl and set in the sink. Run cold water into the bowl, and with your hand, swish the rice around, and then carefully drain the water into the sink. Repeat this about 3 times until the water runs clear. Fill the bowl of rice with water to cover—about 3 cups. Set aside for 20 minutes; the rice will become white and plump. Pour the rice through a sieve and set it aside again for 10 minutes.

2 Combine the rice and the 2 cups of water in a medium saucepan. Cover with a lid. Cook the rice over medium heat for 10 minutes. Turn the heat down to low and simmer for 10 minutes or until the rice is tender (total cooking time is 20 minutes).

3 Turn the heat off and let the rice sit for 20 minutes more.

Homemade Rice Seasoning Sprinkles

Furikake

We always dress up our plain rice bowl with a sprinkling of this condiment. These savory sprinkles are made from crispy flakes of bonito flakes, seaweed, sesame seeds, dried egg, and teeny white bait. They come in jars or plastic pouches in the condiment section in Asian markets. You can make your own. It is good to have a package of tiny, whole, boiled, and dried fish, *chirimen-jako* or *shirasu* on hand. They freeze well and add calcium to a bowl of rice.

Makes 1 cup (40 g)

1 cup (40 g) white bait (dried *shirasu*/**Japanese anchovy or dried, fried white bait simmered in soy sauce, sake and mirin (***chirimen-jako***)**
½ cup (125 g) white sesame seeds

Put the dried fish and sesame seeds in a medium skillet over medium heat. With a wooden spoon, gently mix the fish and seeds around the skillet as they brown. This will take about 8 minutes. The fish will turn light brown and become crispy. Store in an airtight container on a shelf. This will last for about 2 months.

Teriyaki Sauce

Teriyaki sauce is the Swiss Army knife of Japanese sauces. It combines many of the elements that, when combined, makes this sauce and anything on which it is used as identifiably Japanese. Once the sauce cooks, it thickens slightly to a glossy mixture. Brush this sauce on chicken, beef, fish, vegetables, and tofu for a lustrous glaze. I often use Teriyaki Sauce as a marinade before grilling meat (although pork is one of the few meats it doesn't enhance).

Makes 2½ cups (625 ml)
Prep Time: 5 minutes
Cooking Time: 40 minutes

2 cups (500 ml) mirin
2 cups (500 ml) sake
6 tablespoons light brown sugar
1 cup (250 ml) soy sauce
6 slices ginger, smashed

1 Combine the mirin and sake in a medium saucepan over medium heat and bring it to a boil. Continue boiling for 2 minutes. This will cook off the alcohol.
2 Add the sugar and cook until dissolved.
3 Add the soy sauce and ginger and bring to a boil for 1 minute. Turn the heat to medium and continue to cook for about 15 minutes, stirring occasionally. The sauce will begin to thicken. Reduce the heat to medium low and simmer for about 25 minutes until the sauce thickens to a light syrupy texture.
4 Store in an airtight container in the refrigerator. This will keep for several months.

Tempura Dipping Sauce

Tensu

This is the classic dipping sauce for tempura. It is sweet and salty, perfect for tempura on its own, and for drizzling over tempura-topped rice bowls.

It is mixed with grated daikon for a spicy punch. The daikon also aids in breaking up the oil from the deep-frying and helps with digestion.

Makes ¾ cups (190 ml)

½ cup (125 ml) Dashi (Fish Stock) (p. 35)
3 tablespoons soy sauce
3 tablespoons mirin
Salt to taste

Add the Dashi (Fish Stock), soy sauce, and mirin to a medium pot over medium heat and bring to a boil, add salt to taste. Remove from the heat and cool before storing in an airtight jar in the refrigerator. This will keep for 2 weeks.

Sweet Miso Sauce   Dengaku

This sweet miso sauce, called *dengaku*, is used for grilled and boiled foods. I learned to make this sauce from Odagiri Sensei and it soon became a favorite. It combines the salty taste of miso with the sweetness of sugar and mirin. The sauce is cooked to meld the flavors and then is spread on top of eggplant, tofu, and scallops, which are then grilled. I pass the vegetables under the broiler for a caramelized finish. You can use a combination of red and white miso, or just white for a milder flavor.

Makes ½ cup (125 ml)

3 tablespoons white miso
2 tablespoons sugar
2 teaspoons mirin
1 tablespoon sake
2 tablespoons Dashi (Fish Stock) (p. 35) or water

In a small saucepan add the miso, sugar, mirin, sake, and Dashi (Fish Stock). Heat over low heat until the mixture comes

to a boil. Turn off the heat and let it sit. When it has cooled, store in an airtight container and let sit for 20 minutes.

Quick Tonkatsu Sauce

This thick, sweet cousin of Worcestershire Sauce is used with fried dishes, like Fried Pork Cutlets (*Tonkatsu*) (p. 104), and is mixed with fried noodles like Fried Noodles with Cabbage and Pork (p. 94). The popular commercial brand, Bull-Dog Vegetable and Fruit Sauce, comes in a plastic rectangular bottle with a white cap, and there's always a bottle in my fridge. Once only available in Asian grocers, it has now crossed over to many well-stocked supermarkets. Should you not be able to find it, make this simplified version using Worcestershire sauce, tomato paste, and grated apple. The standard Worcestershire sauce available in American markets is more peppery than its Japanese counterpart.

Makes ⅔ cup (160 ml)
Prep Time: 5 minutes
Cooking Time: 5 minutes

½ cup (125 ml) Worcestershire sauce
2 tablespoons tomato paste
1 tablespoon sugar
2 tablespoons grated apple (skin on)
¼ cup (65 ml) water

Combine the Worcestershire sauce, tomato paste, sugar, and apple in a small saucepan. Bring the sauce to a boil over medium heat and cook for 1 minute. Reduce the heat to low and simmer another 3 minutes. Turn off the heat and add the water.

Debra's Shiso Pesto

I have a *shiso* bush that looks like it was fed steroids, but all it gets is great sun and water. With the end of September bearing down, there are still hundreds of beautiful, tasty leaves on it. You can't freeze them, because they turn black, and there are just so many you can press on your friends. Then I remembered what the Italians do with hyperactive basil plants at the end of the season. They make pesto! Why not *shiso* pesto? I combine *shiso*, pine nuts, canola oil, and soy sauce, and a little lemon juice and blend it in my food processor. The scent of fresh cut *shiso* is terrific and the thought of having that taste throughout the year is almost more than I can bear. I use this pesto on *soba* noodles, grilled chicken, and tofu.

Makes about 1 cup (250 g)

20-30 *shiso* leaves (1 oz)
¼ cup (65 ml) canola oil or olive oil
1 teaspoon sea salt or kosher salt
½ cup (65 g) pine nuts, lightly toasted
2 teaspoons soy sauce, preferably low sodium
1 teaspoon fresh lemon juice

Place the *shiso*, oil, salt, pine nuts, soy sauce, and lemon juice in a food processor or blender. Pulse about 5 times until the *shiso* is finely ground. Store the mixture in a glass container. This will keep in the refrigerator for more than 3 months.

Kyoko's All-Purpose Dashi Soy Sauce Concentrate

One day, when my old friend, Kyoko Wada, was sitting in my kitchen, I asked her to taste a packaged dashi soy sauce that had been recommended by another Japanese friend. She dipped the tip of her pinky in the spoon I proffered and in an emphatic tone said, "You can make this!" Her recipe for this multi-purpose soy sauce concentrate includes bonito flakes, shiitake, and kelp. Use one part sauce, and mix it with three parts water as a base for noodle soups, tofu dishes, simmered vegetables, and salad dressings. And, yes, it is better than the pre-made sauce. Never one to waste a scrap, Kyoko makes a delicious condiment from the steeped leavings of the sauce, which is great when mixed into hot rice or soup.

Makes 1¾ cups (400 ml)

1 cup (250 ml) soy sauce, (preferrably low sodium)
½ cup (125 ml) mirin
½ cup (125 ml) sake
One 4 in (10 cm) kelp (*kombu*)
2 dried shiitake
1 handful of bonito flakes (*katsuobushi*)

1 Combine the soy sauce, mirin, sake, kelp, and shiitake in a medium size saucepan over medium heat. Bring to a boil and immediately turn off the heat.
2 Add the bonito flakes and let the mixture steep for 10 minutes.
3 Place a sieve over a bowl and pour the sauce into the sieve. Let the mixture cool. Pour into a jar and keep in the refrigerator for up to 2 months.

Kombu Shiitake Mix

1 Separate the kelp, bonito flakes, and shiitake.
2 Roughly chop the kelp into small dice-sized pieces. Place them in a saucepan.
3 Remove the stem from the mushroom and discard. Chop the mushroom into small dice-sized pieces and add to the seaweed.
4 Roughly chop the bonito flakes and add to the kelp mixture.
5 Add 1 tablespoon of sugar and ¼ cup (65 ml) water to the pan.
6 Bring the mixture to a boil over medium heat and then reduce the heat. Stirring occasionally, simmer until all the liquid has been absorbed. Store in an airtight container in the refrigerator. This will keep for several weeks.

Black Sesame Seed Salt
Goma Shio

This simple combination of toasted black sesame seeds and kosher or sea salt livens up a rice ball, a bowl of rice, or a salad. Sprinkle on steamed vegetables for contrast and flavor.

Makes ¼ cup (30 g)

¼ cup (30 g) black sesame seeds
2 teaspoons kosher or sea salt

1 Spread the black sesame seeds evenly in a single layer in a medium skillet over medium heat.
2 Gently heat the seeds, shaking back and forth until you hear them begin to pop and their aroma is released. This takes about 5 minutes.
3 Let the seeds cool down and then transfer them to a small bowl. Mix with the salt and store in a glass spice jar. They will last for several months at room temperature.

Seasoned Rolled Omelet Tamago Yaki

This is, literally, an egg roll. Eggs, Dashi (Fish Stock), sugar and salt are beaten and then cooked in a special rectangular pan to make a multi-layered, thick omelet log. This rolled omelet is sliced and served cold in lunch boxes, as well as used inside and on top of sushi. Build up the log one layer at time by adding small amounts of the egg mixture to the pan and rolling the growing omelet back and forth in the pan each time you add a layer of batter. It does take a bit of practice, and having the right equipment helps. You can easily find rectangular skillets in a well-stocked Asian grocery. However, I have made the log, with success, in a round skillet by trimming the edges to make a log shape. For a quick version, my friend, Junko Ogawa, demonstrated how to cook this in a regular round-shaped non-stick skillet and then cut it into wedges. She makes this for her daughters' bento lunch box.

Makes one 2.5 x 5-inch (3.5 x 7.5 cm) thick roll

4 large eggs
½ cup (125 ml) Dashi (Fish Stock) (p. 35) or water
1 tablespoon sugar
½ teaspoon salt
1 tablespoon oil

1 Beat the eggs, Dashi (Fish Stock), sugar and salt in a large mixing bowl.
2 Pour the oil into a rectangular, non-stick Japanese omelet pan or a small 6-8 inch (7.5-9 cm) skillet and heat over medium low for 30 seconds. Wipe the oil out with a paper towel and set it in a dish next to the stovetop.
3 Take about ¼ cup (65 ml) of egg mixture and pour it into the hot pan and tilt it around the pan to cover the surface. Let it set for about 30 seconds.
4 With a rubber spatula or pair of chopsticks, pick up the edge furthest from you and roll it forward forming a little log. Now push it back to the opposite side of the pan.
5 Rub the oil-soaked paper towel over the bottom of the pan. Pour in another ¼ cup (65 ml) of the mixture into the pan. Lift up the roll and tilt the pan so the egg slides under the roll. Let it set for a few seconds and then roll the omelet forward with your spatula or chopsticks. Your roll has gained another layer.
6 Push your roll back and repeat with the remaining batter. Continue with this until you have completely used up the eggs. This will take about 6 rounds.
7 This step is optional but helpful in giving shape to your roll. Turn the omelet onto a bamboo rolling mat (or piece of parchment paper), if you have one, and wrap the roll snugly into the mat. Set aside for 20 minutes. Remove the mat. The roll is ready to cut or to place in plastic wrap in the refrigerator until ready to use. Cut into 6-8 slices.

> **NOTE TO CUT FOR SUSHI ROLLS**
> Make long logs for sushi rolls by cutting the roll in half length-wise. Then cut each half into about four ¼-inch (6 mm) strips for a total of 8 strips.

Seasoned Egg Shreds

Use these shreds on Scattered Sushi Rice Salad (p. 50) or instead of the egg strips used on sushi rolls. Place a heaping line of the shreds alongside the ingredients on a *maki-zushi* roll.

½ recipe for Seasoned Rolled Omelet

1 Fry one quarter of the egg mixture in a small hot skillet that has been lightly greased. Spread into a thin crepe and cook just until bubbles appear. Turn over and then transfer to a plate and continue until all the egg is used. Stack the crepes and cut into shreds.
2 Repeat with the remaining egg mixture and stack one pancake on top of another. Cut the stack of egg pancakes into shreds. Set aside.

Seasoned Egg Wedges

Makes one 6-inch (15 cm) round, cut into 6-8 wedges

1 recipe for Seasoned Rolled Omelet
2 teaspoons canola oil

1 Add oil to a non-stick 6-inch (15 cm) skillet with a lid, over medium heat for 1 minute. With a paper towel, wipe out the oil.
2 Pour in the egg mixture and bring it to a bubble.
3 With a flexible, heat resistant rubber spatula, pull the edge of the omelet from the pan and tip the loose egg mixture over the edge of the omelet and back underneath the omelet. Continue to do this until most of the mixture is set.
4 Cover the pan with the lid and cook for 1 minute or until the egg is set.
5 With a wide spatula carefully lift and flip the omelet over and continue to cook for another 1-2 minutes. Slide the omelet onto a plate and let stand for several minutes before cutting. Or refrigerate and cut when it's cold.
6 Cut the round into 6-8 wedges and set into individual paper or silicon cups for a bento lunch or picnic.

Sweet Simmered Mushrooms

This dish, more than almost any other, embodies the essence of Japanese flavors for me. Japanese use this tasty soaking liquid to cook the mushrooms as well as in other dishes. The classic combination of soy sauce, sugar, mirin, and sake are combined with the liquid and cooked with the mushrooms until all the liquid has been absorbed.

Depending on the thickness of the mushrooms, soaking time can be between 20 minutes and 1 hour. When I first learned how to make these from my cooking teacher, Odagiri Sensei, I cooked the mushrooms whole in the seasoning liquid and then sliced them. My friend, Kyoko Wada, showed me a shortcut that is particularly useful when making sushi rolls, hand rolls, and the Scattered Sushi Rice Salad (p. 50) that uses these mushrooms. Kyoko slices the mushrooms first and then cooks them. Every crevice picks up the seasonings. They are earthy, salty, meaty, and sweet—an intense and evocatively Japanese combination.

Yield: 4 oz (125 g)
Prep Time: 25 minutes
Cooking Time: Approx. 15 minutes

8 dried shiitake mushrooms
1½ cups (375 ml) water,
**   reserve liquid**
1 tablespoon sugar
1 tablespoon sake
1 tablespoon mirin
2 tablespoons soy sauce

1 Place the dried mushrooms and water in a medium size bowl. Soak the mushrooms for 20 minutes or until the mushrooms are soft.
2 Remove the mushrooms from the liquid and rinse under cold water. Reserve the soaking liquid. Cut off the stems and slice the mushrooms into ¼-inch (6 mm) slices. The size generally depends on the recipe. Sometimes the mushrooms are left whole.
3 Carefully drain the soaking liquid.

4 Combine the mushrooms, and sugar in a small saucepan. Over medium heat, melt the sugar. Add 1 cup (250 ml) of the soaking liquid, sake, and mirin and simmer for 5 minutes.
5 Add the soy sauce, increase the heat and cook, frequently stirring until the sauce is completely absorbed into the mushrooms. This will take about 10 minutes. The mushrooms are now ready to use in recipes. They can be cooked whole as well.

NOTE I always reconstitute more mushrooms than I need for a recipe. I take the whole reconstituted, uncooked mushrooms and place 6-8 inside a plastic bag, press out the air, seal, label with the date and freeze. They are great to have on hand when you don't have time to wait for mushrooms to soak.

Dashi Dried Katsuo Flakes and Kelp

Dashi (Fish Stock) is the cornerstone of Japanese soups, sauces, and many dishes. There are no bones to roast, no hours of simmering making it an easy and flavorful stock to make from scratch. All you need is dried bonito flakes (*katsuo bushi*). *Ichiban* dashi ("first stock") results from the steeping of the first batch of ingredients and is good for clear soups. *Niban* dashi ("second stock") is made from the left over kelp and bonito flakes that still retain some of their flavor and is good for miso and noodle soups. I generally use first stock for most recipes. Double the recipe for *ichiban* dashi and freeze some of it in 1-cup (250 ml) bags for soups or in mini muffin tins (about 2 tablespoons) or in ice cube trays (1 tablespoon).

The fresh Dashi (Fish Stock) will last for several days in the refrigerator. Although I have encouraged you to make this stock from scratch, most people either use convenient premeasured packets or buy the perfectly serviceable *hon dashi* (dashi powder) and either dilute it for soups or add it directly to dressings and sauce. These powders often include sugar and MSG.

Makes 1 quart (1 liter)
Prep Time: 20 minutes
Cooking Time: 8 minutes (including time for fish flakes to settle in the water)

4 cups (1000 ml) of water
Two 5 in (12 cm) strips kelp (*kombu*)
1 heaping cup (30 g) loosely packed bonito
**   flakes (*hanakatsuo*)**

1 Add the water and kelp to a medium size pan. Let the flakes settle to the bottom of the stock, which will take about 3-5 minutes. Then bring the water and kelp to a boil over medium heat.
2 Toss the flakes into the boiling water and turn off the heat. Let the flakes settle to the bottom of the stock, which will take 3-5 minutes.
3 Set a tightly woven mesh strainer over a mixing bowl. Line the sieve with a cheesecloth or a linen dish towel. Pour the stock through the strainer. Reserve the fish flakes and kelp for making *niban* Dashi, or a tasty *tsukudani*.

Chapter One

Sushi

Today, sushi is everywhere. Like bagels, pasta, and espresso before it, sushi has been embraced around the world. I bought sushi takeout at the supermarket down the block from our son's apartment in Berlin, in a market in Nova Scotia, and at a kosher restaurant in Brooklyn, New York (all for research purposes of course)! But when I saw a shelf filled with sushi rolling mats (*maki-su*), short grained sushi rice, wasabi, and ginger at a neighborhood grocery in Tel Aviv, Israel, I realized that folks not only buy sushi, they make it as well.

Sushi is not raw fish. That's sashimi. Sushi is the combination of vinegared rice and what you put on, around and inside of it—including vegetables, eggs and even a piece of rare beef—determines the type of sushi. For the most part, handling raw fish should be left to professionals. Proper storage temperatures, knife and cutting board hygiene are critical for a safe eating experience. Always purchase fish for sushi at a trusted source. Much of the raw fish in our markets is caught and frozen right on the fishing vessels. This "super freezing" process is done quickly and at the appropriate temperatures, and "sushi or sashimi grade" refers to fish that has been handled in this manner. Freezing kills parasites, so in this case "previously frozen" is a good thing.

What we now call "sushi" started out as a way to preserve fresh fish. At one time, raw fish was set between layers of rice for preservation and would begin to ferment, and the rice was discarded before the fish was consumed. Like many happy accidents, this turned the rice into something special and a new cuisine was born. One dish that did evolve directly from that layering of rice and fish is pressed sushi (*oshi-zushi*), which is then cut into rectangles. Try my version with Smoked Salmon Pressed Sushi using Spicy Mayonnaise, and *shiso* leaves (p. 53). It's great for when you have a sushi-loving crowd to feed.

This chapter will introduce you to homestyle sushi. Part of almost every home cook's culinary skill set is to be able to make a thick roll of sushi rice stuffed with vegetables and seafood (*futo-maki*), wrapped in roasted seaweed. Try your hand at the Classic Sushi Roll (p. 40). I leave *nigiri-zushi*, the little rice pillows with a smear of wasabi and raw fish set on top, to trained professionals.

Good sushi means learning the proper way to make and season sushi rice (p. 38). Short and medium grain rice both are suitable and are a matter of personal preference. I tend to use short grain rice, as I like the feel of the smaller grain in my mouth. The rice is dressed in a sweet and sour mixture of rice vinegar, sugar, and salt (*sushi-zu*). The sweetness of the rice varies by region in Japan, with the Osaka-style being sweeter than its Tokyo competitor. Since much of my time has been spent in Tokyo, you may want to slide that sugar scale upward.

Sushi made with brown rice (*genmai*) may be heretical to many, but it has been embraced outside of Japan, even by some Japanese. I have come around to seeing it as a welcome innovation (p. 39). Make a roll (*maki*) or use it in hand rolls for A Sushi Hand Roll Party (p. 46) for a home-style sushi feast.

How to Make Sushi Rice

Knowing how to make good rice is the key to good sushi. Short and medium grain japonica rice is the only variety used to make sushi rice. Long grain rice is not suitable. In the West, we are used to adding rice to boiling salted water, but short grain rice has a cold water start. Please note in this recipe that I am using an American measuring cup. If you are using a Japanese measuring cup it will be about 4 of those cups. Conventionally, the rice is rinsed, drained, and soaked before cooking. This helps to plump it and make it tenderer. When the rice is done and still hot, it is seasoned with a sweet-and-sour dressing made of rice vinegar, sugar, and salt. Simultaneously, the rice is cooled down with a fan or even a magazine or newspaper.

Talc used to be added to rice, but for the most part new milling techniques have reduced the amount of rinsing you need to do for your rice. Now you will find instructions on most bags of Japanese rice telling you to cook the rice without rinsing or soaking. I have experimented with several techniques, and believe that you will get a superior taste and texture when you rinse, drain, and set the rice to dry in a mesh colander before cooking. **However**, if you are using a rice cooker when making sushi rice you can skip the soaking step. Sometimes the rice gets a little too soft for sushi—you want sushi rice to be a bit toothsome.

You cannot refrigerate plain sushi rice because it hardens. So plan to cook the rice and make the sushi on the same day. You can even make the rice several hours ahead of time. Place in a plastic container, set a piece of plastic wrap directly on the rice, and then close tightly with a lid. This also gives the rice a chance to absorb the flavor of the Sushi-zu Seasoning.

Hiroko Shimbo, Japanese food expert and cookbook author of *The Sushi Experience*, suggests setting the plastic tub of sushi rice into a warm water bath to warm it back up before using.

Makes about 7 cups (about 1.2 kg)
Prep Time: 50 minutes (includes soaking and drying time)   Cooking Time: 30 minutes (includes 10 minutes of resting time)

3 cups (600 g) short grain rice
3 cups (750 ml) water
1 tablespoon sake
1 small strip of kelp (*kombu*), 2 x 3 in (5 x 7.5 cm)

Sushi-zu Seasoning
7 tablespoons rice vinegar
3 tablespoons sugar
2 teaspoons salt
1 tablespoon mirin

1 Pour the rice into a bowl or pot and place under running water. Rinse the rice until the water becomes clear.
2 If you are going to use a rice cooker, do not soak the rice. Place a wire mesh colander in the sink and drain the rice into a colander and set aside for 30 minutes. If you are using a pot, soak the rice for 20 minutes. Then drain into a mesh colander and set aside to dry for 30 minutes.
3 If using a rice cooker, add the 3 cups of water, sake, and kelp if using, and cook according to manufacturer's instructions. If using a pot, add the water, sake, and kelp, if using.
4 When the rice is done, transfer the rice to a large bowl and fold and lift the rice. Do not mash and mix it.
5 For stove top cooking combine the rice and the 3 cups of water in a medium saucepan. Cover with a lid. Cook the rice over medium heat for 10 minutes. Turn the heat down to low and simmer for 10 minutes or until the rice is tender (total cooking time is 20 minutes). Turn the heat off and let the rice sit for 10 minutes more.
6 While the rice is steaming combine the seasonings for the rice in a small saucepan. Heat until the sugar and salt dissolve. Set aside to cool down before pouring over the hot rice.
7 Sprinkle the seasoning mixture, a few tablespoons at a time, onto the rice as you toss the rice, coating all the grains until shiny. Taste the rice after each addition of seasoning. You may not need it all. Fan the rice to cool it down. When you are done, sprinkle on the mirin and give it a final toss.
8 Place in a shallow serving bowl and cover with plastic wrap until it's ready to be served.

Brown Sushi Rice

Brown Sushi Rice is popular in the United States but foreign to the Japanese. When I asked my friends in Japan if they had ever eaten brown rice sushi, they all emphatically answered "no!" They explained that the more delicate white rice is more appealing in combination with various fillings and toppings; brown rice is too chewy and doesn't have the same stickiness needed to hold the rice together. Like California Rolls, brown rice sushi is an American twist on the Japanese national dish. I have been asked many times to teach how to make sushi with brown rice, but thinking it wasn't "authentic," I resisted. Not anymore.

Boston, rebel restaurateur, Kazu Awano, serves only brown rice sushi at his restaurant, Snappy Sushi. He admits that this is still unthinkable to most Japanese, even his mother! He uses a high quality brown rice that he then mills a bit further to take off a small amount of the outer coating which makes the rice easier to cook but still keeps the bran intact.

He prepares it the same way that he would prepare white rice sushi. His sushi is creative and delicious if not delicate, and there is rarely an empty seat in his restaurant. In the United States, brown rice sushi is sold nation-wide. Unfortunately there is no one-size-fits-all recipe for making brown rice sushi. Different brands produce different results. You will have to experiment with the brand of rice available in your local market. I followed Awano-san's directions, which was basically to treat brown rice the same way I would white rice and it came out great. I use Kagayaki Brown Haiga Rice widely available in Asian supermarkets or online (www.asiangrocer.com) as this produces the best results. This brand of brown rice has been processed to take off just a bit of the outer layer, just like they do at Snappy Sushi. This recipe works like a charm in the rice cooker. Once the rice is cooked, season it while it is hot because this is when it best absorbs the dressing.

Makes 3 cups (425 g)
Prep Time: 50 minutes (includes soaking and drying)
Cooking Time: 30 minutes (includes 10 minutes of resting time)

1 cup (200 g) short grain brown rice
1¼ cups (300 ml) water
Water for soaking
1 tablespoon sake

Sushi Dressing
3 tablespoons rice vinegar
1 tablespoon sugar
¼ teaspoon sea salt or kosher salt

NOTE Another widely available brand (in many supermarkets) Nishiki Medium Grain Brown Rice, will work if you soak it for one hour, drain, and then add to your rice cooker with 1½ cups (375 ml) water. When the rice is done, leave it for 20-30 minutes to steam. Season while the rice is warm. The results are a bit chewy but passable.

1 Add the rice to a bowl and rinse and drain once. Add water to cover the rice and soak for about 30 minutes. Drain.

2 Drain the rice into a mesh colander and let sit for 20 minutes. If you are using the stove top method, add the rice, water and sake to a medium size pot with a lid and cook according to instructions on page 38.

3 If you are using a rice cooker, add the rice, water and sake to the bowl of the rice cooker and cook as you would for white rice, do not use the brown rice setting (if your rice cooker has one).

4 If you are using a pot, combine the rice, sake and 1¼ cups of water in a medium saucepan. Cover with a lid. Cook the rice over medium heat for 10 minutes. Turn the heat down to low and simmer for 10 minutes or until the rice is tender (total cooking time is 20 minutes). Turn the heat off.

5 Once the rice is done, open the lid, fluff up the rice with a paddle, close the lid and let the rice sit for another 10 minutes (or longer if necessary), before seasoning.

6 Meanwhile, mix the Sushi Dressing ingredients in a microwave proof dish or a small saucepan. Heat for about 1 minute or until the sugar and salt are thoroughly dissolved.

7 If you have a wooden salad bowl, this is the perfect receptacle for seasoning and mixing the rice. If not, glass or pottery is fine as long as it is non-reactive.

8 With a wet wooden spoon or rice paddle transfer the rice to the bowl. Gently fold and mix the rice.

9 Sprinkle 2 tablespoons of the Sushi Dressing over the rice and continue to gently fold the seasoning into the rice. With a fan or magazine, fan the rice periodically to cool it down. This helps to give the rice a nice shine.

10 Sprinkle another tablespoon of Sushi Dressing over the rice and continue folding and fanning. Taste the rice for seasoning. Sprinkle on one more tablespoon of Sushi Dressing if necessary. Be careful not to add too much liquid or it will become moist and mushy.

11 Cover the rice with plastic wrap until ready to use. Or store in a plastic ware container. If the rice is made in the morning for use later in the day, set the container in a bowl of warm water just before using. This will make the rice easier to handle.

Classic Sushi Rolls Maki-zushi

This is the very first sushi roll I ever made. I learned the technique in the home cooking studio of Michiko Odagiri. Once I mastered it, it felt like the training wheels had just come off my first bicycle. Literally a "thick roll," *futo-maki* is stuffed with fillings like sweet simmered vegetables, egg omelet and seafood. Odagiri Sensei explained that choosing 5 different colors for the filling was important for both nutritional balance and visual appeal. Several of the techniques needed for this hand roll will be useful in other Japanese dishes. The Sweet Simmered Mushrooms (p. 35) and the Seasoned Rolled Omelet (*Tamago Yaki*) (p. 34) are two important ones. Cut all the filling ingredients to about the same length and to a similar width for easy eating. You can make these ahead of time, but do not cut them until you are ready to serve. The nori absorbs some moisture from the rice and becomes softer, but that is fine.

Makes 5 rolls   Prep Time: 1½ hours
Cooking Time: 1 hour

7 cups (about 1.25 kg) cooked sushi rice (p. 38)
1 large carrot, peeled and cut into ¼ in (6 mm) strips
1 tablespoon sugar
1 cup (250 ml) water
Egg Omelet Roll, cut into 10 strips or Omelet Shreds (p. 34)

Cucumbers

2 mini cucumbers, or ½ English cucumber, deseeded and cut into ¼-inch (6 mm) strips
Sweet Simmered Mushrooms (p. 35)

Rolled Omelet

1 Seasoned Rolled Omelet or Seasoned Omelet Shreds (p. 34)

Fish

8 sticks imitation crab legs or 8 oz (250 g) fresh crabmeat, cut in half lengthwise
5 sheets of roasted seaweed (*yaki nori*)
1 teaspoon vinegar plus 1 teaspoon water, mixed in a small bowl
1 tablespoon toasted sesame seeds (optional)
Bamboo rolling mat

NOTE For easier cutting, lay a piece of plastic wrap loosely over the length of the roll and cut, as instructed above, through the plastic wrap. You will still need to wipe your blade, but it is not as sticky. This is particularly helpful for inside out rolls.

1 Before starting you should have all the ingredients organized in piles on a tray and within easy reach. The sushi rice should be covered with a piece of plastic wrap when not in use. Place a bowl half filled with water near you.

2 Place the carrots in a medium size skillet over medium heat. Add the sugar and water and bring to a boil. Cook the carrots until all the water is absorbed and carrots are tender, set aside. Place the bamboo-rolling mat (*makisu*) on a table or counter top. Place one sheet of roasted seaweed onto the mat, short edge and rough side up, lined up on the edge closest to you.

3 Dampen your hands and take about 1¼ cups (225 g) of sushi rice and form a loose log. Place it in the center of the seaweed. With your fingertips, gently spread the rice downward, upward, and outward on the seaweed. Make sure the rice gets spread to both edges. Do not mash the rice. Leave ½ inch (125 mm) of open space on the top edge of the seaweed.

4 Starting from the bottom third, and taking one fifth of the ingredients, make a line of each ingredient, going end-to-end. Set the ingredients next to each other (you can stack some of the ingredients on top of each other as well).

5 Dip your finger into the vinegar mixture and dab onto the exposed area of seaweed, this will be the "glue" that holds the seaweed in place.

6 Holding the ingredients in place with your fingertips and starting from the end closest to you, in one movement, lift the mat and seaweed up and over the vegetables. Still holding the mat, apply moderate pressure with your hands across the length of the mat.

7 Now lift just the mat from the roll and with the palms of your hands, continue rolling it forward, keeping the mat free from being wrapped, until the entire roll is encased in the seaweed.

8 Roll the bamboo-mat around the finished roll and apply light pressure along the roll to shape and compress the ingredients. Unroll the mat and cover the roll loosely with plastic wrap. Continue with the remaining ingredients. You may make these rolls several hours before serving.

9 To cut the rolls you will need a sharp knife (not serrated) and a damp cloth or paper towel at hand. Each time you make a cut you will wipe the blade with the damp towel. Set the roll, seam side down on a cutting board. Starting in the middle, with a see-saw motion, then cut the roll in half. Then take one half and cut that into half, wiping between cuts. You now have 2 pieces. Wipe your blade and cut in half again. You will have 4 pieces. Repeat with the other half for a total of 8 slices. Repeat with remaining rolls. Make sure you cover the cut rolls with plastic wrap until ready to serve.

10 Serve with soy sauce and slices of pickled ginger if you like. Pickled ginger is generally used when raw fish is included but it has become a favorite condiment for Americans.

Making the Sushi Rolls

1. Spread the rice evenly onto the rough side of the seaweed. Leave ¼ inch (6 mm) exposed at the top.

2. Line up the ingredients, end to end on the rice. Set each ingredient next to each other.

3. Holding the ingredients in place, in one movement lift the bamboo mat up and over the vegetables.

4. After enclosing the roll in the seaweed and applying light pressure to compress the mixture, unroll and place on a cutting surface.

5. With a damp paper towel or cotton cloth wet the blade of the knife. Cut the roll in half.

Step-by-step Inside-Out Rolls

1. Sprinkle toasted sesame seeds over the surface of the rice.

2. After flipping the rice onto the plastic wrapped surface, spread a thin line of Spicy Mayonnaise mixture down the center of the seaweed.

3. Set the crabmeat on the mayonnaise.

4. Hold the plastic wrapped mat and ingredients in place and in one movement fold the seaweed over the crabmeat.

5. Unroll the mat and set the roll on a cutting surface.

Crab and Avocado Inside-Out Rolls

You don't have to be a magician to get the rice on the outside of inside out rolls (*ura-maki*). Cover your bamboo rolling mat (*makisu*) with plastic wrap, set a half piece of roasted seaweed (*yaki nori*) down, spread on sushi rice, sprinkle on sesame seeds or fish roe for a coating, and 1, 2, 3—flip! Turn the rice and seaweed blanket over so that the rice is now facing the wrap and the seaweed is facing you. Fill and roll—presto you've got a Crab and Avocado Inside Out Roll.

Although this roll is now popular in Japan, it was born in America when many Japanese sushi chefs crossed the Pacific in the 1970s. Their creativity blossomed once they were freed from the hierarchy and rigid rules of traditional sushi making and were presented with an array of new raw materials.

This is basically restaurant sushi. When I ask Japanese friends if they would make this roll at home, they often say "it is very difficult"—which is Japanese for "no way." They're right if you are aiming at perfection, but if you are aiming to have some fun and feel like learning a new technique, this is a good place to start. For a demonstration I was giving, I forgot the bamboo mats and had to use the only thing at hand—a piece of wax paper. It worked perfectly—just like magic!

Makes 6 rolls
Prep Time: 1 hour
Cooking Time: 1 hour

½ recipe (3 cups/600 g) of cooked
  sushi rice (p. 38)
3 sheets roasted seaweed (*yaki nori*)
½ lb (250 g) fresh crabmeat
1 avocado, sliced into 12 wedges
1 tablespoon lemon juice
2 oz (50 g) flying fish roe (*tobiko*)
1-2 tablespoons Black Sesame Seed
  Salt (p. 33)
½ cup (125 ml) Spicy Mayonnaise
  (p. 28)
Soy sauce, preferably low sodium,
  for dipping
Wasabi, for dipping

> **NOTE** Use the fish roe on top of the rice instead of sesame seeds. Spicy Tuna Salad (p. 88) is also a good filling for this dish instead of the crabmeat.

1 Have on hand a tray or baking sheet covered with wax paper. Tear a piece of plastic wrap twice the size of the bamboo mat. Enclose the mat into the plastic wrap.
2 Fold the roasted seaweed in half horizontally. Gently tear or cut along the fold. Set one half sheet of the seaweed on the mat at the edge closest to you. Spread ½ cup rice over the entire surface of the seaweed. Sprinkle the sesame seeds over the rice.
3 Pick up the seaweed and rice and flip it over. Now the rice side is down and the seaweed is on top facing up. Spread about 2 teaspoons of the spicy dressing in a line down the middle of the seaweed. Take ⅙ of the crabmeat and spread it on top of the dressing.
4 Lay two pieces of avocado, end-to-end on top of or just next to the crabmeat. Spoon the fish roe on to the avocado or crab.
5 Pick up the mat and with your fingers holding the seaweed, with one movement fold the seaweed over the crabmeat. Holding the mat over the roll, gently, and evenly compress the mat with your hands to shape the roll.
6 Now lift just the mat from the roll and with the palms of your hands continue rolling forward, keeping the mat free from being wrapped, until the entire roll is complete.

7 Roll the bamboo-mat around the finished roll and apply light pressure around the roll to shape and compress the ingredients. Unroll the mat and cover it loosely with plastic wrap.
8 Set the roll on a baking sheet covered with wax paper. Repeat with the remaining ingredients.
9 Set the roll, seam side down on a cutting board. Set a piece of plastic wrap on top of the roll so that it covers the surface. Do not wrap it around the rice, just over the rice.
10 Starting in the middle with a see-saw motion, cut the roll in half. Wipe the blade with the moist paper towel. Then take one half and cut that into half, wiping between cuts. You now have 2 slices. Wipe your blade and cut in half again for a total of 4 pieces. Repeat with the other half for a total of 8 slices. Repeat with the remaining rolls. Make sure you cover the cut rolls with plastic wrap until you are ready to serve. Serve with soy sauce (preferably low sodium), ginger, and wasabi.

Tuna and Cucumber Rolls Tekka-maki

This is another thin roll (*hoso-maki*). The roasted seaweed is cut in half, then lined with fresh tuna strips and crunchy cucumbers.

Makes 6 rolls
Prep Time: 1 hour
Cooking Time: 50 minutes

3 sheets roasted seaweed (*yaki nori*), cut in half lengthwise
3 cups (600 g) ½ recipe of cooked sushi rice (p. 38)
1 tablespoon wasabi
¼ lb (125 g) fresh tuna
2 mini cucumbers, skin on, cut into 12 strips ¼ inch (6 mm) in diameter
Soy sauce, preferably low sodium, for dipping

1 Have on hand a tray or baking sheet covered with wax paper.

2 Fold the roasted seaweed in half horizontally. Gently tear or cut along the fold. Set one-half sheet of the seaweed on the mat at the edge closest to you. Spread ½ cup (100 g) of the rice over the seaweed leaving an ⅛ inch (3 mm) border on the top and bottom of the seaweed.

3 Put the wasabi in a little dish and dip your finger in the dish and make a line down the middle of the seaweed.

4 Take 2 pieces of tuna and lay them end-to-end on top of the wasabi.

5 Lay two pieces cucumber just next to the tuna.

6 Pick up the mat and with your fingers holding the seaweed, with one movement fold the seaweed over the filling. Holding the mat over the ingredients gently and evenly compress the mat with your hands to shape the roll.

7 Now lift just the mat from the roll and with the palms of your hands continue rolling forward, keeping the mat free from being wrapped, until the entire roll is complete.

8 Roll the bamboo-mat around the finished roll and apply light pressure around the roll to shape and compress the ingredients.

9 Set the roll on a baking sheet covered with wax paper. Repeat with the remaining ingredients.

10 Set the roll seam side down on a cutting board. Set a piece of plastic wrap on top of the roll so that it covers the surface. Do not wrap it around the rice, just over the rice.

11 Starting in the middle, with a see-saw motion, cut the roll in half. Wipe the blade with the moist paper towel. Then take one half and cut that into half, wiping between cuts. You now have 2 slices. Wipe your blade and cut in half again for a total of 4 pieces. Repeat with the other half for a total of 8 slices. Repeat with the remaining rolls. Make sure you cover the cut rolls with plastic wrap until ready to serve. Serve with soy sauce (preferably low sodium), ginger, and wasabi.

Hayashi Sensei's Mini Sushi Balls

Temari-zushi

Japanese cookbook author and teacher, Keiko Hayashi, came to my home to teach a class to members of the Japan Society of Boston. She demonstrated how to make these simple creations using sushi rice. Each ball highlights a single ingredient molded and wrapped in one step.

Everyone was thrilled to learn an accessible method for making this attractive morsel. A piece of plastic wrap is the only tool you'll need. Set thin cucumber slices or a shrimp on a square of the wrap, top with some rice, bring the edges up and twist into a ball. Remove the wrap or keep the wrap and tie the little packet closed with a short colorful ribbon for fun or a piece of raffia string for an elegant presentation. This is great for bento boxes. Hayashi Sensei makes a dainty 1-inch ball (2.5 cm) that is a perfect appetizer size. Sprinkle on some fresh chives for a little color and bite.

Makes sixteen 1 in (2.5 cm) or 8 2 in (5 cm) balls
Prep Time: 30 minutes
Cooking Time: 40 minutes

2 cups (400 g) cooked sushi rice (p. 38)

Suggested Toppings
1 mini cucumber, cut into ¼ in (6 mm) slices
¼ teaspoon sea salt or kosher salt
Sweet Simmered Mushrooms (p. 35), keep them whole
2 oz (50 g) smoked salmon, cut to fit the size of the rice ball you are using
Shrimp, cooked and split in half along the back
¼ lemon wedge
2 pea pods, blanched

1 Place the cucumbers in a bowl and sprinkle them lightly with salt. Let stand for 5 minutes. Squeeze out excess water. Set aside.
2 Set the Sweet Simmered Mushrooms on a small plate.
3 Place the shrimp in a bowl. Squeeze a quarter of lemon juice on the shrimp and toss.
4 Slice the smoked salmon into 2-inch (5 cm) pieces. Set aside.
5 Remove the string along the spine of the pea pods and separate the pods into two identical halves.

To Assemble the Sushi Balls

1 Take a piece of plastic wrap and lay it on the table.
2 Place a single topping in the center of the wrap, face down. Take ⅛ cup (25 g) of the sushi rice and place on top of the ingredient.
3 Bring the plastic wrap up around the rice and topping and gently mold into a ball. If you want to keep the ball in plastic wrap, secure with a ribbon. Make these balls in the morning for an afternoon picnic. They will not need refrigeration as the vinegared rice acts as a preservative.

A Sushi Hand Roll Party

This is the way to entertain! And this is the way Japanese families eat home made sushi. There are no rules; anything you can think of to pop onto your rice goes! Hideko Itoh, my Japanese niece, tells me that in her family cheese is always part of the selection. Cheese in sushi? Yes! (This is mild American cheddar style cheese and it goes great with salmon.) Preparation is key; once you have seasoned the rice, cut squares of crisp roasted seaweed, and arranged a platter of vegetables and fish your job is almost done.

The beauty of a meal like this is that everyone can take their time and choose their favorite filling. Lay it on a bed of rice, wrap it in roasted seaweed and take a bite. Crunch! Make sure ingredients are similar in size; this makes for easier eating. Steam the carrot sticks and asparagus spears. You can use fresh tuna, Spicy Tuna Tartar (p. 49), smoked salmon, shreds of poached chicken, and cooked shrimp. My personal favorite is super fresh scallops with a squeeze of lemon and a *shiso* leaf. *Oishii* (delicious)!

And wasabi isn't the only thing that can give your roll a bite. Place a bowl of Spicy Mayonnaise (p. 28) on the table and use daikon radish sprouts, watercress, or arugula. Any soft leaf lettuce, like butter (sometimes called Boston) lettuce also make a great wrapper instead of the seaweed. Use as many or as few ingredients for your platter as you like. You may even want to try some cheese. You have nothing to do but dip, dab, and enjoy!

Serves 8
Prep Time: 1 hour
Cooking Time: 1 hour

7 cups (1 kg) cooked sushi rice (p. 38) divided into 4 serving bowls (keep covered with damp paper towel and plastic wrap until you are ready to serve)

Suggested Fillings

8 oz (250 g) smoked salmon, cut into 2 in (5 cm) pieces
12 cooked large shrimp, cut in half along the back
8 oz (250 g) crabmeat
8 oz (250 g) raw sushi grade tuna (*maguro*), cut into ½ in x 2 in (1.25 x 5 cm) strips

4 large scallops, sliced into 4 slices each for a total of 16
4 oz (100 g) salmon roe (*ikura*)
4 oz (100 g) flying fish roe (*tobiko*)
2 cups (500 ml) water
2 carrots, peeled and cut into ¼ by 2 in (6 mm by 5 cm) logs
1 tablespoon sugar
1 teaspoon salt
12 asparagus spears, trimmed
Sweet Simmered Mushrooms (p. 35)
2 mini cucumbers, deseeded and cut into ¼ by 2 in (6 mm by 5 cm) logs or ½ English cucumber, deseeded and cut in half again and each half into 8 strips
2 oz (75 g) daikon radish sprouts (*kaiware*) (or watercress or arugula), rinsed and trimmed
20 *shiso* leaves
2 avocados, (ripe but firm) cut into 12 slices per avocado
1 tablespoon fresh lemon juice
10 sheets of roasted seaweed (*yaki nori*), cut into quarters with scissors
Wasabi
Soy sauce, preferrably low sodium

Suggested Condiment

½ cup (125 ml) Spicy Mayonnaise (p. 28)

1 Group salmon, shrimp, crab, tuna, and scallops on a platter leaving spaces in between for the vegetables.
2 Place the salmon roe and or flying fish roe in little bowls or cups. Set on the platter.
3 In a shallow skillet, bring 1 cup of water to a boil. Add the cut carrots and sprinkle with sugar. Bring to a boil, reduce heat to medium and simmer for 8 minutes until most of the water is absorbed. Arrange on the platter. Rinse the skillet.
4 In the same skillet, bring the remaining water to a boil. Add the salt. Add the trimmed asparagus and turn the heat down. Simmer for 3 minutes. Remove from the pot and plunge the asparagus into cold water, drain and pat dry with paper towels. Place on the platter.
5 Arrange the mushrooms, cucumber strips, radish sprouts, *shiso* leaves, and avocado on the platter.
6 Just before serving, cut roasted seaweed squares with scissors and place on 4 plates.
7 Provide each diner with a bowl for the rice, and the soy sauce poured into small plates.
8 Take a generous tablespoon of the rice and place onto the rough side of the seaweed square.
9 Each diner spreads the rice with a dab of wasabi and the ingredients of their choice. Roll into a cone and dip into soy sauce. Do not overstuff your roll or it will be hard to shape and eat.

Lobster Rolls with Wasabi Mayonnaise

Lobster, (along with cod, baked beans, and the Red Sox) is one of Boston's calling cards to the world. New England's legendary lobster rolls have four ingredients: lobster, mayonnaise, celery and a buttered, toasted hot dog bun. Just as sushi restaurants in California adopted avocadoes and came up with "California rolls," Boston sushi makers offer fancy lobster rolls that switch out the buttered bun for rice and seaweed. I guess you could say the New England lobster is going back to its roots—or weeds, as it were. Here is a simple (and "wicked awesome") hand roll: Cook a 1¼ lb (625 g) lobster to get ¼ lb (125 g) of delicious, sweet, briny meat. This does not sound like a lot, but the meat is so rich, you don't need much. Make sure you keep the shape intact and the distinctive red and white markings visible. After all, you want your guests to know they are eating "lobstah"—that's how we say it here in New England.

Makes 8
Prep Time: 30 minutes
Cooking Time: 40 minutes

1¼-1½ lb (625-750 g) cooked lobster
½ cup (125 ml) mayonnaise
1-2 teaspoons wasabi paste
1 teaspoon soy sauce, preferably low sodium
1 celery stalk, cut into matchstick strips
4 sheets roasted seaweed (*yaki nori*)
2 cups (400 g) cooked sushi rice (p. 38)
Soy sauce, preferably low sodium, for dipping

1 Remove the lobster meat from its shell. Cut the claws in half vertically. Cut the tail in half and then each half into quarters. Remove the knuckle meat. Set the lobster meat aside.
2 Combine the mayonnaise, wasabi, and soy sauce in a small bowl. Set aside.
3 Set the celery sticks on a plate.
4 Cut the seaweed in half horizontally. Set on a plate.
5 Place the sushi rice in a bowl on the table.

To Assemble the Lobster Rolls

1 Take one half-sheet of seaweed in your hand or set it on a plate.
2 Place about 2 tablespoons (30 g) of rice on the left hand section of the seaweed on the diagonal and flatten just a bit.
3 Spread the wasabi mayo on the rice. Add the celery sticks and then a piece of lobster.
4 Take the lower left corner of the seaweed and bring it over the lobster, holding the seaweed down with your thumb.
5 Take the seaweed on the right and twist it around the ingredients into a cone shape and dip in soy sauce.

Spicy Tuna Tartar

When I visit my nephew, Brandon, we always enjoy a sushi-making extravaganza with his friends. When he was 8-years-old, I taught him how to make sushi rolls. At 15 he requested inside out rolls with shrimp tempura. Recently he asked for my Spicy Tuna Tartar recipe, a tuna tartar mixed with a piquant sauce. We went shopping together and he reached for a fresh tuna steak in the supermarket when I reminded him, only sushi-grade tuna will do. We went to the local sushi restaurant and bought the raw tuna from them. If your guests are anything like Brandon and his friends, these will disappear as soon as you plate them.

When trimming tuna for hand rolls or sashimi I cut away the odd triangular pieces and pulse the extra bits in a food processor to make this mixture. You can also use this filling in other types of rolls. It is best suited to thin rolls (*hoso-maki*) that use half sheets of roasted seaweed. Follow the rolling technique for Tuna and Cucumber Rolls (p. 44), or Crab and Avocado Inside Out Rolls (p. 43). For hand rolls, place the tuna mixture in a mound and let the diners help themselves. Here I make a cone with large *shiso* leaves, but you can use roasted seaweed or even soft leaf lettuces, like Boston or red leaf.

Makes 1 cup (about 300 g)
Prep Time: 15 minutes

½ lb (250 g) fresh tuna
2 teaspoons Sriracha sauce or chili oil (or more to taste)
¼ cup (65 ml) mayonnaise
1-2 teaspoons sesame oil
2 teaspoons soy sauce, preferably low sodium

1 Add the tuna to the bowl of a food processor and pulse until completely ground.
2 Transfer to a mixing bowl. Add 1 teaspoon of the Sriracha sauce. Set aside for 5 minutes.
3 In a small bowl, combine the mayonnaise, remaining Sriracha sauce, sesame oil and soy sauce. Add to the ground tuna and mix well. Adjust the seasonings. Refrigerate until you are ready to use.

Tuna Tartar Shiso Wraps

Tuna Tartar Shiso Wraps

I have *shiso* growing in my garden and about half way through the summer, the leaves become really large (over 3 inches or 7.5 cm) and are perfect for wrapping. If you don't have this delightful problem, you can use 2 *shiso* leaves per wrap or less tuna and rice so that it wraps without spilling over.

Makes about 12

1 portion Spicy Tuna Tartar (see recipe on this page)
1 cup (200 g) cooked sushi rice (p. 38)
12-16 *shiso* leaves (as large as possible)

1 Rinse the *shiso* leaves and set to dry for 10 minutes on a baking sheet covered with a paper towel.
2 Have the Spicy Tuna Tartar and sushi rice in bowls on your work surface.
3 Take a *shiso* leaf, vein side up and spoon on about 1 tablespoon of rice into the center of the leaf.
4 Add a spoonful of the tuna and fold the sides of the leaf over the mixture. Dip, leaf side down, in soy sauce.

Scattered Sushi Rice Salad

Chirashi-zushi

I think of Scattered Sushi Rice Salad as a large, deconstructed sushi roll. My editor at the *Boston Globe*, Sheryl Julian, calls it a rice salad. Elaborate versions of this are served in sushi restaurants with arrangements of cooked and raw fish and vegetables set on top of sushi rice. But it is also part of the repertoire of every Japanese home cook. It is a festive dish often served on Girls' Day (March 3) and other holidays. When I have a large gathering, I make Scattered Sushi Rice Salad the edible centerpiece on my buffet table. It is also a perfect picnic food, as the vinegary rice acts as a preservative. The Japanese use a shallow wooden tub made of cypress (*sushi-oke*) to mix the rice. I also use this rustic vessel as a serving dish. Use a wooden salad bowl if you have one available (a glass or pottery bowl will also do).

Serves 8
Prep Time: 1½ hours
Cooking Time: 1 hour

7 cups (1 kg) cooked sushi rice (p. 38)
1 cup (250 ml) water
2 carrots, peeled and cut into matchstick strips
1 tablespoon sugar
⅛ teaspoon salt
½ lb (250 g) of cooked shrimp, sliced along the back
1 cup (125 g) frozen green peas, thawed or ½ lb (250 g) green beans steamed and cut into 1 in (2.5 cm) pieces
1 recipe Sweet Simmered Mushrooms (p. 35)
2 oz (65 g) pea pods, strings removed and blanched
½ recipe Seasoned Egg Shreds (p. 34)
Shredded red pickled ginger (*kizami* shoga) for garnish (optional)

1 Prepare the sushi rice and place in a large mixing or serving bowl.
2 Bring 1 cup (250 ml) of water to a boil in a medium saucepan over medium heat. Add the carrots and sprinkle with sugar and salt. Simmer for 8 minutes until most of the water is absorbed. Transfer to a plate and set aside.
3 Place all of the ingredients in separate plates or bowls and set on the counter.
4 Take three quarters of all the ingredients except for the Seasoned Egg Shreds and ginger, if using, and scatter over the rice. Gently fold into the rice and distribute evenly.
5 Arrange the remaining ingredients attractively on top of the rice.

CUTTING TIP To cut carrots into thin uniform strips: peel the carrot and trim off the stem. Make a cut on the diagonal. Continue to cut slices, of desired width, on the diagonal. This will give you the largest cutting surface. Stack about 3 slices of carrot and cut into matchstick strips.

Preparing Scattered Sushi

1. Gently lift and fold the warm rice in the bowl.

2. Add the sushi seasoning a little bit at a time to the rice, while fanning to cool the rice down

3. After adding the various toppings, fold them into the seasoned rice.

Smoked Salmon Pressed Sushi Oshi-zushi

Smoked Salmon Pressed Sushi or *Oshi-zushi*, is a dish made with layers of sushi rice and fish, then cut into bite-size pieces—it's a great way to make sushi for a crowd. In Japan, a special box made from cedar is used in constructing this dish. A slightly smaller square lid is set on top and weighted to compress the mixture. I happen to own a beautiful box, but you don't have to have one to make this dish. When I teach a cooking class or write an article it is important for me to find acceptable alternatives for these hard to find items—enter your ordinary square or rectangular baking pan! I cover the pan with plastic wrap before putting in the ingredients for a no-fuss removal of the pressed layers. A heavy cookbook can serve as a weight.

Traditionally, marinated mackerel slices are the fish of choice, but sushi-grade mackerel is not easy to find and has a strong distinctive flavor that's not universally appreciated. I'll use smoked salmon, Spicy Mayonnaise, and *shiso* leaves for a terrific trio. If *shiso* isn't available then use basil or an assertive green, like arugula or watercress instead. Once the mixture is pressed and cut up, serve them as appetizers, tuck a few into an bento or bring it along on a picnic. Vary the filling by using cooked shrimp, slices of avocado, soft leaf lettuces, like Boston or red leaf. Serve with soy sauce. To dip the pieces, turn them salmon side down; if you dip the rice end first, the pieces will fall apart.

Makes about 30 bite-size pieces
Prep Time: 1½ hours
Cooking Time: 50 minutes (for the Rice)

Rice
4-5 cups (800-1000 g) cooked sushi rice (p. 38)

Toppings
¾ cup (375 ml) mayonnaise
2 teaspoons liquid hot sauce (Sriracha sauce)
1 teaspoon dark sesame oil
2 teaspoons soy sauce
35 *shiso* leaves or 2 cups arugula leaves
12 oz (375 g) smoked salmon
1 oz (30 g) salmon roe, for garnish
2 green onions (scallions), finely chopped for garnish (optional)
Soy sauce (for dipping)

1 Set a 9 by 13-inch (22.5 x 32.5 cm) pan or an 8-inch (20 cm) square pan on the counter. Line the bottom with 2 pieces of plastic wrap, letting 8 inches (20 cm) hang over all sides. With moist hands, place half the sushi rice in the bottom of the pan. Press lightly to make a smooth layer.
2 Stir together the mayonnaise, hot sauce, sesame oil, and soy sauce in a bowl.

Spread half the mayonnaise mixture on the rice.
3 Reserve 5 *shiso* leaves for garnish. Lay half of the remaining *shiso* leaves (or arugula) on the rice. Top the *shiso* with half the salmon slices. The salmon should completely cover the leaves.
4 Repeat the process with the remaining rice, mayonnaise mixture, *shiso*, and salmon. Fold the extra plastic wrap over the top layer. Place a large book on top and gently apply pressure. Set aside for at

least 15 minutes or for up to 1 hour.
5 Open the plastic wrap and use it to lift out the sushi. Sprinkle on the chopped green onions, if using. Decorate the top with additional *shiso* leaves and salmon roe. Set it on a cutting board. With a wet paper towel, moisten the edge of a sharp knife. Cut the sushi into rectangular pieces about 1 x 2 inches (2.5 x 5 cm) each. Sprinkle with green onions. Serve with soy sauce.

Chapter Two
Snacks and Appetizers

Like zen, haiku, or anime, Japan's cozy neighborhood pubs (*izakaya*), are another gift to the world from Japan. Each one serves its own creations on small plates, like tapas but Japanese style, with an entire menu of appetizers. One of our favorite dishes in our Tokyo neighborhood is a small bowl of pasta tossed with spicy fish roe in a soy cream sauce, topped with a small mountain of shredded seaweed. They also served a salad of daikon radish ribbons garnished with fried *udon* noodles in martini glasses. In contrast to these western-influenced appetizers, you'll also find a bamboo basket filled with custard-like tofu served with a wooden spoon, which couldn't be more traditional.

Other examples of light eating fare are the snacks found at the food stalls (*yatai*) during Japan's many festivals (*matsuri*) that take place on and around the grounds of Shinto shrines. The hot, humid summers are high season for festivals, a time when Japan turns into one big outdoor party and almost everyone is wearing the cool (and I mean that both ways) cotton kimono (*yukata*), and men and little boys don comfy loose pajamas (*jimbei*).

The *yatai* stands are lined up chock-a-block. Vendors wear *hachimaki*—a twisted cloth tied around the forehead or colorful bandanas as they labor over hot griddles blanketed with the Savory Stuffed Pancakes (p. 60), or Fried Noodles with Cabbage and Pork (p. 94). Special cast iron pans with hollowed out spheres are used to make octopus fritters (*tako-yaki*). All of these dishes share the same savory Worcestershire-like sauce and toppings of seaweed, bonito flakes and neon red ginger shards that I have come to love. This is without a doubt my favorite activity when I visit Japan.

The appetizers in this section are great for picnics or bento lunch boxes, and are perfect one-bite appetizers. The Beef and Asparagus Spirals (p. 61) are perfect for passing around. Although you can make a meal out of Mixed Yakitori Skewers (p. 62), a tray of these colorful skewers arranged like spokes on a wheel, can become the focus of a cocktail party.

When I serve a Japanese meal at home, I often adjust to the Western order of presenting food. In formal Japanese meals a variety of foods will be served together on one tray. Small bowls and plates are arranged for you to eat in an order or in combination. I like to serve as a starter course the refreshing and beautiful Salmon Roe with Grated Daikon in a Lemon Cup (p. 68) or the elegant Tofu Salmon and Avocado Appetizer (p. 69).

Chicken Balls in Teriyaki Sauce

Tsukune Dango

These chicken balls are a real crowd pleaser! They are a healthy low-fat alternative to beef meatballs and can be used in several different recipes. The seasoned ground chicken is rolled in cornstarch before cooking, this keeps them soft and helps thicken the glaze. Whether I set these out on sophisticated bamboo picks, add them to a *yakitori* platter, or tuck them into a lunch box, they are gone in a flash.

Junko Ogawa makes a batch and keeps them in a container in her fridge suspended in the ginger-scented cooking broth. This keeps them moist and at the ready when preparing her college-age daughter's bento box. She plucks a few and warms them up in a skillet with a sweet soy sauce glaze. Not only is the sauce delicious but it also acts as a preservative. Sometimes I will double the recipe and freeze the cooked, but unadorned balls (I make about 8 to a bag). They are also excellent in soup. Try them instead of the fish fillet in the recipe for Delicate Seafood Consommé (p. 79).

Makes about 24 balls
Prep Time 20 minutes
Cooking Time: 20 minutes in total

½ cup (65 g) cornstarch
1 lb (500 g) ground chicken (or turkey)
½ teaspoon salt
1 large egg white, beaten until foamy
2 teaspoons grated ginger
2 teaspoons sesame oil
¼ teaspoon pepper
2 green onions (scallions) or ¼ cup (15 g) chives, finely chopped
3 cups (750 ml) water
2 teaspoons dashi powder (optional)
Two ¼ in (6 mm) slices fresh ginger
½ cup (125 ml) Teriyaki Sauce (p. 32)
Japanese red pepper powder (*togarashi*) (optional)

1 Have on hand two large plates. Spread the cornstarch on one of the plates and set the other one aside.
2 Combine the ground chicken (or turkey) salt, egg white, ginger, sesame oil, pepper, and green onions in a medium size mixing bowl. The mixture will be very soft and a little difficult to handle.
3 Form the balls using two spoons. Scoop up about 1 tablespoon of the chicken mixture with one of the spoons and with the other spoon push the mixture off the end of the spoon and onto the plate of cornstarch. Using one of the spoons, roll the mixture in the cornstarch until it forms a ball. Carefully place the ball onto the clean plate. Repeat with the remaining chicken mixture.
4 Pour the water in a medium saucepan, and add the dashi powder (if using) and ginger slices. On medium heat, bring the water to a boil. Drop the chicken balls into the liquid. Stir them once or twice so they do not stick to the bottom of the saucepan. Once they are floating, turn the heat down and simmer for 5 minutes or until the chicken is cooked (the chicken mixture will be white when you slice into the ball).
5 Remove the chicken balls from the broth with a slotted spoon, and set on a clean plate. Set a wire mesh strainer over a bowl and pour the cooking liquid through the strainer. Reserve the liquid
6 Add the Teriyaki Sauce to the skillet. Bring the sauce to a boil over medium heat. Add the chicken balls and reduce the heat to low medium. Simmer for about 5 minutes or until the chicken is white on the inside and the chicken balls are nicely glazed.
7 Place 2-3 chicken balls on a small skewer or tooth-pick, then sprinkle on the Japanese red pepper powder, if using, and serve.

Salted Edamame in the Pod

One of the first Japanese pub foods I embraced while living in Japan was edamame. Go into any Japanese bar and the first thing they set before you are boiled and salted edamame in their fuzzy pods (the fuzzier they are, the tastier they tend to be). You place the pod in your mouth and suck out the beans. The combination of salt and the fresh taste of the soybean is sensational—and they're fun to eat.

Most American supermarkets carry shelled and unshelled edamame, in the frozen food section. They are great in salads, mixed in with steamed rice or just for munching. In Asian markets you can find them frozen in the pod. It is so much more fun to eat than potato chips!

Serves 8
Cooking Time: 10 minutes

1 lb (500 g) fresh or frozen edamame in the pod
1 tablespoon kosher or sea salt

1 Fill a medium saucepan with water. Add 2 teaspoons of the salt and bring to a boil.
2 Add the edamame and return to a boil. Lower the heat and simmer for 3 minutes.
3 Set a colander in the sink and drain the pods. Sprinkle on the remaining teaspoon of salt. When you set these out make sure you provide a bowl for the empty shells.

Soy Glazed Chicken Wings

These sweet and salty chicken wings couldn't be easier to make and are great with a glass of beer. Japanese moms wrap pieces of foil around the ends of little drumettes for easier handling at picnics and kids love them. Orange juice provides most of the sweetness with just a small amount of mirin added to give the sauce a glazy coating.

Serves 4
Prep Time: 10 minutes
Cooking Time: 15 minutes

8 chicken wings (1½ lb/750 g) split at the joint (16 pieces)
2 tablespoons soy sauce
2 tablespoons mirin
1 tablespoon oil
3 tablespoons orange juice

1 Place the chicken wings in a bowl. Add the soy sauce and mirin, and marinate for 10 minutes.
2 Heat the oil in a large skillet over medium heat. Add the marinated chicken wings and cook on both sides, about 3 minutes each side.

3 When the wings are browned, add the orange juice, and turn the heat to medium-high. Continue to cook, for another 8 minutes, turning the chicken pieces frequently until the sauce has been absorbed into the chicken. Cut into the thick part of a chicken piece to make sure there is no redness in the meat closest to the bone.

NOTE Try this with a boneless chicken breast. Keep the chicken breast whole while cooking. Increase the cooking time to ensure the chicken is cooked thoroughly. Slice the breast on the diagonal and serve on a bed of shredded lettuce.

Eriko's Onion, Clam, and Potato Fritters Kakiage

This home-style tempura is a real treat. The onion is the dominant flavor with bits of seafood and vegetables mixed in. It is an easy way to make tempura at home without frying endless ingredients separately. I learned the trick to making these from my Japanese sister, Eriko Ito. Eriko put the batter in one bowl and vegetables and seafood in another. She then sprinkled some flour and an egg onto the ingredients and stirred it together with her chopsticks. Eriko scoops some of the vegetable mixture into a shallow ladle and then spoons on the Tempura Batter. Ah ha! So that's how they maintain their shape—a batter within a batter! She tips this into the hot oil and with her chopsticks spreads the fritter a little bit. Soon the fritter is bobbing in the bubbling oil. Meanwhile, I grate the daikon radish, the classic accompaniment, and set it in bowls. Being from Boston, where fried clams (along with the universities and Red Sox, of course) are our claim to fame, I was drawn to Eriko's suggestion to use a mixture of clams and potatoes with the onions. You can create your own mixture, I've provided an alternative combination to inspire you. Make mini fritters for appetizers, medium sized ones for side dishes, or large ones to put on top of a bowl of rice.

Makes six to eight 3 in (7.5 cm) fritters
Prep Time: 25 minutes
Cooking Time: 20 minutes

8 oz (250 g) fresh chopped clams, drained
1 medium onion, sliced
1 medium potato, cut into matchstick strips
10 string beans, sliced down the center and cut into thirds
1½ tablespoons flour
1 large egg, beaten
3 cups (750 ml) oil

Tempura Batter
¾ cup plus 1 tablespoon (200 ml) ice water
1 egg yolk
⅔ cup (100 g) cake flour or white flour
1½ tablespoons cornstarch

For Dipping
4 oz (125 g) daikon radish peeled and grated
Lemon wedges
Soy sauce

Alternative Combination

8 medium shrimp, sliced along the back
1 onion, cut into matchstick strips
10 string beans, sliced down the center and cut into thirds

1 Add the clams, onion, potatoes, and string beans in a mixing bowl. Sprinkle on the flour and mix in the egg. Set aside.
2 To make the Tempura Batter, combine the ice water and the egg yolk in a bowl and mix thoroughly.
3 Sift in the flour and cornstarch by holding either a sifter or wire mesh strainer over the bowl with the egg mixture. Lightly whisk this together. It will have a few lumps.
4 Heat the oil on medium heat in a wok, or deep skillet, until it reaches 350°F (175°C). You will see a ripple on the top of the oil. Dip your chopstick into the Tempura Batter and drop a little batter into the oil. If it floats and turns light brown, the oil is ready.
5 Scoop up about ½ cup (125 ml) of the clam mixture with a ladle. Then add about ¼ cup (65 ml) of the Tempura Batter over the mixture and lightly mix

with your chopstick or fork.
6 Tip the mixture into the hot oil. The fritter will float. With a pair of chopsticks or two forks, gently pull apart the mixture so the ingredients are slightly separated. This will help everything cook evenly. Make a second fritter. Cook for about 2 minutes and carefully turn over. Cook for another 2 minutes or until nicely browned and crispy. Have on hand a wire rack on top of a baking sheet. With a slotted spoon lift the fritters out of the oil and set onto the wire rack.
7 Repeat the process using the remaining batter and clam mixture. They do not have to be served piping hot, but if you like, you can keep the fritters warm in a 300°F (135°C) degree oven until they are ready to serve.

TO SERVE Peel and grate the daikon radish. Pour the grated radish into a strainer and drain the liquid. Divide the radish into individual bowls. Squeeze in some lemon juice and a drizzle of soy sauce if you like. Alternatively serve with a dish of soy sauce and lemon wedges.

Stuffed Savory Pancake

Okonomiyaki

I was first introduced to Stuffed Savory Pancakes as a street food being served at the *matsuri* or summer festivals held at shrines all over Japan. Vendors mix piles of shredded cabbage, green onions (scallions), neon red ginger, and other tidbits into a batter and onto giant gas-fired griddles. They shellac the top of these pancakes with a piquant sauce and zigzags of mayonnaise. This followed with a shower of smoky-briny bonito flakes and shredded seaweed on top.

Everywhere in Japan there are restaurants devoted to letting customers design their own version of this humble pancake and make it on a griddle at their table. Everyone gets their own blunt edge spatula and starts cooking. *Okonomi* means "as you like it," so menus are filled with lists of seafood, vegetables, and meat that diners combine and add to the standard batter and cabbage. An electric skillet makes a great way to enjoy this as a communal meal at your own table at home.

Makes two 6-inch (15 cm) pancakes
Prep Time: 15 minutes
Cooking Time: 10-15 minutes

Batter

1 cup (150 g) flour
1 cup (250 ml) water
1 egg white, beaten until foamy

Fillings

2 cups (150 g) shredded cabbage
10 medium shrimp, peeled and deveined, tails off
2 oz (50 g) pork, thinly sliced into 3 in (7 cm) lengths
1 tablespoon pickled red ginger (*beni* or *kizami shoga*) (optional)
4 green onions (scallions) cut in half, lengthwise and then into 4 pieces
2 large eggs
2 tablespoons oil

Toppings

2 tablespoons dried seaweed shavings (*aonori*)
2 tablespoons dried shredded bonito flakes (*katsuo-bushi*)

Sauce

½ cup (125 ml) prepared Japanese Bull-Dog Sauce or Quick Tonkatsu Sauce (p. 32)

1 To make the Batter, combine the flour, water, and egg white in a large mixing bowl, then divide the batter into two medium bowls.
2 To make the filling, put half the cabbage, shrimp, pork, ginger, and green onions into each bowl. Make a well in the center and break an egg into the well.
3 Heat half the oil in a large skillet over medium heat until just hot, about 45 seconds.
4 Lightly mix the egg and filling of one bowl together until just blended. Pour the entire batter into the skillet to make one pancake. Cook on low-medium heat for 3 minutes, until the bottom is golden.
5 Flip the pancake and press all around to flatten. Cook for an additional 2-3 minutes. Flip the pancake 2 more times, cooking it for 1 minute on each side or until done.
6 Set the pancake on a plate and brush or drizzle on the Sauce. Add the mayonnaise if using. Sprinkle on the seaweed and fish flakes.
7 To serve, cut the pancake into wedges. Serve with extra sauce. Repeat with the remaining bowl.

Makes 12 pieces
Prep Time: 10 minutes
Cooking Time: 5 minutes

6 slices (4 oz/125 g) rib eye beef, sliced
    into ¼ in (6 mm) thick slices
Salt and pepper
12 asparagus spears, blanched or
    steamed, trimmed and cut into
    thirds
1 tablespoon oil
¼ cup (65 ml) Teriyaki Sauce (p. 32)

Beef and Asparagus Spirals

Like so many things in Japan, this comes in a beautiful package. The wrapping is thinly sliced rib eye rolled around asparagus spears and cooked in the sweet and salty Teriyaki Sauce (p. 32). The asparagus cooks just enough to remain bright, green and crunchy. The rib eye has just enough marbling to keep the meat tender and is very easy to chew. Instead of asparagus, you can use green beans and add carrot sticks (cooked) for color. It makes a great hot appetizer or is delicious cold and tucked into a bento for lunch—I love the versatility of these little spirals.

1 Lay out the beef slices on a cutting board or baking sheet. Sprinkle both sides of the beef with the salt and pepper.
2 Take 2 asparagus tips and lay them on the first third of the beef slice, with tips pointing out and extending about ¼ inch (6 mm) beyond the edge of the beef. Take 2 more pieces (not tips) and lay them next to each tip. Pick up the edge of the meat and fold over the asparagus. Continue to roll until the vegetables are completely enclosed. Set the beef roll, seam side down, on a tray. Repeat with the remaining slices of beef and asparagus.
3 Heat the oil in a medium size skillet over medium heat for 45 seconds. Set the beef spirals, seam side down, into the skillet, and fry for about 30 seconds. With a pair of tongs, turn the spirals over and cook for an additional 30 seconds. This will sear and seal the beef. Transfer the spirals to a clean baking sheet or plate.
4 Add the Teriyaki Sauce to the same skillet and increase the heat to high. Bring the mixture to a boil. Reduce the heat to medium. The sauce will still be bubbling.
5 Place the rolls back into the pan. Cook for an additional 2 minutes, turning frequently until the spirals are coated with a thick glaze.
6 Remove the rolls and place them on a clean cutting surface. Let them rest for a minute. Slice them in half on the diagonal and arrange on a platter. These can be served hot or at room temperature.

Grilled Mixed Veggie and Tofu Skewers Kushi-yaki

Kushi-yaki are tidbits of food threaded on a bamboo skewer and grilled over coals. Unlike kebabs with various ingredients on one stick, the Japanese version has multiples of the same ingredient on one stick. I have experimented with a *yakitori* soy glaze on tofu and vegetables. Well-drained, firm tofu works great on the sticks. If set in a grilling basket, these skewers can be grilled over coals, or placed directly into a cast iron ridged skillet on top of the stove. Even an electric George Foreman grill will do fine. Make sure the surface is large enough to hold the skewer flat.

Use small to medium size dark mushrooms that can be cooked whole, like the flavorful cremini or baby portabellas. Have all your ingredients laid out on a tray with the soaked skewers at the ready (everything can be prepared ahead of time). I begin cooking without putting on any sauce and then brush the glaze on when the vegetables are almost done. A trio of condiments: salt, Japanese red pepper (*togarashi*), and lemon are all the additional seasonings you'll need.

Makes 12 skewers
Prep Time: 15 minutes
Cooking Time: 10 minutes

Twelve 8 in (20 cm) bamboo skewers
1 block, about 14 oz (450 g) extra firm tofu, drained
6 green onions (scallions), cut into 4 sections
12 small brown mushrooms: cremini and/or portabellas
8 mini bell peppers, deseeded and cut in half, or ½ red or yellow bell pepper cut into 4 strips then cut into thirds
2 tablespoons oil

Sweet Soy Glaze
4 tablespoons soy sauce
4 tablespoons mirin
2 tablespoons sugar
4 tablespoons sake

Condiments
Sea or kosher salt
Japanese red pepper powder (toga-rashi)
Lemon wedges

1 Fill an 8-inch (20 cm) square cake pan half way with water. Set the skewers in the water and let them soak for about 15 minutes while you prepare the ingredients.

2 Set the tofu on a microwave safe plate and cook in the microwave for 1 minute. Drain the water from the plate. Cut the tofu in thirds horizontally and then cut section into 3 pieces to make a total of 9 pieces. Set a paper towel on a plate or cutting board and set the squares on the plate. This will help to absorb any additional moisture.

3 Wipe the surface of the mushrooms with a damp paper towel and set aside.

4 Take a skewer and carefully pierce the tofu from the bottom edge and come out at the top. Next add a piece of green onion. Repeat with tofu and green onion 2 more times. You should have enough for 3 skewers.

5 Use the mushroom and peppers on the same skewer with a green onion in between. You can prepare all of your skewers up to this point. Cover them with plastic wrap and refrigerate them until one half hour before cooking.

6 Bring to a boil the soy sauce, mirin, sugar, and sake in a small saucepan and then lower the heat to medium heat. Cook the sauce for another 3-5 minutes until it is reduced to a thick glaze. Turn off the heat.

7 Heat the grill pan for about 1 minute over medium high heat. When the surface of the pan is hot, brush on some oil and wait 30 seconds. Place as many skewers on the surface as the space will allow. Reduce the heat to medium. Cook for about 1 minute.

8 Turn over the skewers and let the other side cook for one more minute. Brush the glaze onto the tofu and vegetables with a pastry brush and turn over. Brush the glaze onto the other side and let this cook for one more minute. Turn the skewers and brush again. Let them cook for 30 seconds. Brush once more and turn the skewers a last time. Cook for 30 seconds. Turn off the heat and transfer the skewers to a serving platter.

RIGHT: **Yakitori, Grilled Mixed Veggie and Tofu Skewers**

Japanese Pot Stickers Gyoza

These dumplings, originally from China, are a favorite on the Japanese table. I have made hundreds of them over the years with friends pleating and folding while we chat. We would make dozens at a time and pack them in bags for the freezer. I was always sent home with a supply for my efforts. It took a bit of practice to learn how to make one in the palm of my hand, but now it comes naturally.

For practice, use a plate for the flat surface and if you don't want to pleat then just pinch the two sides together. Don't over-stuff! They will be hard to fold and will pop open during cooking. Make sure you have a flat underside because it creates the perfect surface for crispy bottoms. The filling can vary but is generally a mixture of ground pork, finely chopped vegetables, garlic chives and spices. My friend Yoshie Gordon, a fellow Bostonian via Tokyo, makes hers with ground turkey for a healthier dumpling. What a revelation! They are tasty, moist and delicious. In the winter, she makes a Yoshie's Gyoza Hot Pot (p. 104) where the dumplings are simmered in broth along with chunks of cabbage, tofu, and vegetables for a hearty but light meal.

TIP I like to use my hands to incorporate seasonings and rub marinades into meat and poultry, but I am not keen on raw meat on my hands, so I buy packages of plastic disposable gloves to use for this purpose. Sometimes I make extra filling to make mini logs that I wrap in plastic wrap and freeze. Defrost, wrap in parchment paper and cook in the microwave. Refrigerate, slice and use for an appetizer or in a bento lunch box.

Fried Dumplings

Makes about 36 dumplings
Prep Time: 45 minutes
Cooking Time: 20 minutes

1 cup (250 ml) water
¼ medium size (14 oz/400 g) Chinese (Napa) cabbage, coarsely chopped
8 oz (250 g) ground pork or turkey
3 green onions (scallions), both white and green parts, minced
2 oz (50 g) garlic chives, finely chopped or regular chives
2 teaspoons grated fresh ginger
½ teaspoon salt
1 tablespoon soy sauce
1 tablespoon rice wine
1 tablespoon sesame oil
36 gyoza or wonton wrappers
2 tablespoons oil
Water, for steaming

Dipping Sauce

2 tablespoons soy sauce
2 teaspoons vinegar (rice or white is fine)
Dash of hot chili oil (*rayu*) to taste

1 To make the filling mix all the ingredients together in a small bowl. Serve as dipping sauce with the dumplings.
2 Bring the water to a boil in a large saucepan and then add the cabbage, cover. Cook for 2 minutes until the cabbage is soft and wilted. Drain the cabbage into a colander. With your hands, squeeze out the excess water. Set aside.
3 Combine in a large mixing bowl the cabbage, pork, green onions, and chives.
4 Add the ginger, salt, soy sauce, rice wine, and sesame oil. Set aside.

To Assemble the Dumplings

Have on hand a small bowl of water and a baking sheet sprinkled with flour.
1 To make the dumplings, place one wrapper in your palm. Scoop a generous teaspoonful of the meat mixture into the center of the wrapper.
2 Dip the tip of your index finger into the water and moisten the rim of the wrapper around the mixture.
3 Pinch the wrapper on one side of the mixture into a pleat. Bring the bottom skin over the meat filling and press into the pleat. Continue pleating (three more times) and pinching the edges together.

Place the completed dumpling onto the prepared baking sheet. Repeat with the remaining wrappers and filling. (If you want to freeze the dumplings, this is the time to do so. Set the tray of prepared dumplings in the freezer for several hours until frozen. Place the dumplings in a gallon size zip top bag, label, and place back in the freezer. When you are ready to cook, no defrosting is necessary, but the cooking time will increase by a minute or two.) There are two ways to cook the dumplings: frying and boiling. The boiled dumplings, a healthier alternative, are called *sui gyoza*. The wrappers are soft and wrinkly, like wontons. They remind me of the Jewish soup dumpling, *kreplach*, that I grew up eating (without the pork!).

To Fry the Dumplings

1 Add the oil to a large skillet and heat over medium for 1 minute. Set the number of pot stickers, that will fit, flat side down, into the skillet. Fry for 2 minutes or until the bottom turns brown.

2 Pour ½ cup (125 ml) of the water into the pan. Cover and cook over medium heat for about 3 minutes. This will steam cook the dumplings.

3 Remove the cover and continue cooking until the water has evaporated, about 1 minute.

4 Loosen the dumplings with a long spatula and transfer them to a large plate. Repeat with the remaining dumplings.

5 Serve with the dipping sauce.

To Boil the Dumplings

1 Fill a medium saucepan with 6 cups (1.5 liters) of water and 1 teaspoon of salt. Bring to a boil.

2 Drop in 6-8 dumplings. After the dumplings rise to the top, cook for an additional 2 minutes.

3 Remove the dumplings from water with a slotted spoon, to a serving platter. Repeat with the remaining dumplings. Serve immediately with the dipping sauce.

Boiled Dumplings

AMEYOKO SHOPPING DISTRICT

The Ameyoko discount shopping district that stretches between Ueno and Okachi-machi stations is my favorite area to shop in Japan. In this deeply urban area, once home to a thriving black market after the second world war, the streets are lined chock-a-block with stalls of dried seaweed, rice crackers, teas, spices, fish mongers, clothing and golf clubs. I always stock up on dried goods, especially shiitake. Small informal eateries dot the street. Tucked among them is our favorite hole-in-the wall that specializes in jumbo dumplings. This is our first stop on any trip we take to Tokyo. Outside the shop a man in a white cap and once-white apron, scoops seasoned fresh ground pork from a vat and spreads the mixture onto a flour wrapper. In what seems like a blur of movements, he folds and pleats the dumpling in a matter of seconds. A line of customers snakes along the alley waiting for a seat at the crowded counter or to take out a package to cook at home. The gargantuan dumplings are fried and then steamed in the same pan. With crispy bottoms up, they are served 4 to a plate. On the counter are containers with soy sauce, vinegar and hot chili oil to make your own dipping sauce. My husband and I could eat a dozen—each!

Yakitori Party

Most of us know *yakitori* as Japanese kebabs—grilled juicy cubes of chicken and green onions (scallions) on skewers. All parts of the chicken are used on these sticks: chicken skin scrunched onto a skewer, gelatinous crunchy joint matter, dark meat, light meat, wings, and innards are all grilled over glowing coals. The cook twirls the skewers and either salts or coats the pieces with a delicious glaze. Although *yakitori* is eaten most often outside the home, you can make it using a cast iron ridged grill pan, a barbecue grill, or a broiler. Even a skillet will do—you just won't have the grill marks. I like to use the dark meat of chicken thighs, because it is moist and less likely to dry out. Remember that the food should be cut to the same size so it cooks at the same rate. Keep categories of food together for the same reason. Serve with little dishes of salt and Japanese red pepper powder. Make sure to soak the bamboo skewers in water before cooking so they will not burn. (If you are not a meat eater, check out the Grilled Mixed Veggie and Tofu Skewers, p. 62.)

Yakitori and Grilled Veggie Skewers

Makes 8 skewers
Prep Time: 25 minutes
Cooking Time: 15 minutes

1½ lb (750 g) boneless and skinless chicken thighs, cut into 2
  in (5 cm) chunks
2 tablespoons sake
Salt and pepper
6 green onions (scallions) cut into
  4 pieces each
Oil, for brushing on the skillet

Yakitori Glaze

Makes about 1 cup (250 ml)

¼ cup (65 ml) soy sauce, preferably low sodium
¼ cup (65 ml) mirin
¼ cup (65 ml) sake
2 tablespoons sugar

1 To make the Yakitori Glaze, combine the soy sauce, mirin, sake, and sugar in a medium saucepan. Bring the mixture to a boil over medium high heat. Cook for about 3 minutes until the sauce begins to thicken. Reduce the heat to medium low and cook for an additional 10 minutes until you have a thick glaze. You can refrigerate the glaze for future use. I like to keep a jar of this in the refrigerator to brush on a steak, fish, or add to a stir-fry.

2 Fill an 8-inch (20 cm) square cake pan half way with water. Set the skewers in the water and let them soak for about 15 minutes while you prepare the ingredients. Discard the water and set the picks aside.

3 Combine the chicken pieces, sake, salt, and pepper in a medium bowl. Set aside for 15 minutes.

4 Set the green onion pieces in a small bowl. Thread a piece of chicken onto the skewer; push the first piece toward the bottom, leaving about 1½ inches (3.75 cm) of exposed skewer. Next, thread a green onion onto the skewer, pressing it tightly down into the chicken. Repeat by scrunching each piece down close together until you have filled the skewer.

5 Heat a ridged cast iron skillet over medium heat for 1 minute. Add 1 tablespoon of oil and heat for 45 seconds. Make sure the pan is large enough to hold the whole chicken skewer when it lays flat. Flick a few drops of water onto the skillet. If the water beads and bubbles up the pan is hot enough.

6 Place the chicken into the prepared pan. Cook for 2 minutes and turn the skewers over and cook for another 2 minutes. Brush on the Yakitori Glaze and turn the chicken over. Cook for an additional minute. Brush the glaze on the other side, turn

Yakitori Rice Bowl

Yakitori Don

One day my friend Nobu Takeuchi and I were wandering through Nezu, a very old and traditional area of Tokyo to see the gorgeous sea of azaleas that bloom from April to early May at the Nezu Shrine. In the window of a *yakitori* restaurant we saw a big bowl filled with rice and on top was arranged succulent pieces of *yakitori* (off the skewers), a lettuce wedge, a few cherry tomatoes, and a poached egg. It was so appetizing we ducked under the *noren* and into the restaurant and ordered the *yakitori donburi*. We broke the yolk into the hot rice and mixed in the chicken with the dollop of mayonnaise. It was like a warm grilled chicken salad.

1 cup (200 g) cooked rice per person
4 oz (125 g) of cooked *yakitori* pieces
  per serving
1 poached egg
2 in (5 cm) lettuce wedge
Cherry tomatoes
Swish of mayonnaise
Roasted seaweed shreds (*yaki nori*)

Place the cooked rice in a bowl. Set the hot grilled chicken pieces on top of the rice. Add the lettuce and a few cherry tomatoes. Place one poached egg nestled next to the chicken. Add a dollop of mayonnaise and roasted seaweed shreds.

the skewer, and continue to cook for an additional minute. Brush one more time on each side and cook for an additional 45 seconds, per side or until the chicken is done.
7 Set the skewers on a platter and serve with small dishes of salt, Japanese red pepper powder and lemon wedges.

NOTE If you like chicken livers they make a very rich and delicious taste treat. Clean the livers and cut them in half. Thread only the livers onto the skewer. Cook them for half the time you would cook the chicken thighs.

Salmon Roe with Grated Daikon in a Lemon Cup

Airi Tamura, a family friend for more than 25 years, is a professor of Middle Eastern studies in Tokyo. One cold weekend in March we went to her weekend cabin at the foot of Mt. Fuji. The night we arrived we went to a local public bath fed by natural spring waters. After a cleansing dip in the indoor bath, we stepped out into the cold night air and slipped into the steaming waters outdoors (*rotemburo*). When we returned to the cabin, Airi threw together this refreshing appetizer of fresh salmon eggs (*ikura*), glistening like translucent jewels, nested on grated daikon radish, and set in a lemon cup. It has been a favorite of mine ever since. It is one of the easiest and most unique appetizers to put together and the refreshing daikon and salty eggs are a delightful combination. I squeeze the juice to make a Citrus Miso Sauce (p. 116), which I keep in the fridge for future use. Sometimes I add thin slices of raw scallops sprinkled with lemon juice, like ceviche, to the mix.

NOTE Salmon roe can be found fresh and frozen at Asian markets and at your local fish monger.

Serves 4
Prep Time: 15 minutes

2 lemons
½ cup (115 g) fresh salmon roe
8 oz (225 g) daikon radish
2 tablespoons fresh lemon juice
Soy sauce for drizzling

1 Halve the lemons and squeeze out the juice and reserve. With a spoon, scoop out the fruit and membrane and discard. Slice a small piece from the bottom of the lemon so that it will stay upright when set on a plate. Cut a few of these small slices into thin matchstick threads and reserve.
2 Peel and grate the daikon radish. Set a colander in the sink and pour in the daikon radish and drain the liquid.
3 Fill each lemon half with about 2 tablespoons of grated daikon radish. Drizzle on some of the lemon juice.
4 Spoon one tablespoon of the salmon roe onto the grated radish. Drizzle with the lemon juice and garnish with the lemon zest. Serve with the soy sauce.

Layered Tofu, Smoked Salmon, and Avocado Appetizer

When they came to Boston to teach a contemporary Japanese cooking class at my home, my friends Junko Joho and Emi Ono wowed my students with this "tofu tower." Emi had learned this at a class she had taken. They cut the tofu into 2-inch (5 cm) rounds with a biscuit style cookie cutter. The cutter acts as a mold to hold the stack together as they layered the tofu, salmon, and avocado. A small can (like one for deviled ham) works well too. Remove the top and bottom and press down any jagged edges with the back of a spoon. Capers, tomatoes, and edamame make excellent additions. I adapted this eye-catching recipe and hope you do the same.

Recipe makes 2 towers
Serves 2
Prep Time: 40 minutes

1 block (approx 1 lb/500 g) firm tofu
¼ lb (125 g) smoked salmon
2 tablespoons capers
3-4 tablespoons olive oil, or more to taste
3 tablespoons fresh lemon juice
Salt and pepper, to taste
1 ripe avocado
¼ cup (30 g) shelled edamame
2 cooked large shrimp, sliced in half along the back
2 sprigs of dill
8 cherry tomatoes, quartered
2 tablespoons soy sauce
1 tablespoon honey

1 Have on hand a deep 2-inch (5-cm) plain round cookie or biscuit cutter or any small can about the same size.
2 Place the tofu on a microwave safe plate and microwave for 2 minutes. Drain the liquid.
3 Set the tofu on a cutting board. You will be making 2 cylinders. Place the deep cookie cutter on the left side of the tofu and as close to the edge as possible.
4 Using a twisting motion cut into the tofu with the cutter making one large tofu cylinder. With a sharp knife, cut that cylinder horizontally into thirds. You will have 3 discs. Repeat with the remaining tofu. Lay a paper towel on a baking sheet and set the tofu discs on the paper towel.
5 Chop the salmon and 1 tablespoon of capers finely and put it in a bowl with 1 tablespoon of olive oil, 1 tablespoon of the lemon juice and a few twists of ground pepper. Drizzle on more olive oil if the mixture is dry and set aside.
6 Cut the avocado in half and remove the pit. Scoop out the flesh and place on a cutting board and chop the avocado. Combine the avocado with 1 tablespoon of the olive oil, 1 tablespoon lemon juice, salt, and pepper in a medium bowl.
7 Place 1 tofu disc into the cutter. With a spoon, add a ½-inch (1.25-cm) layer of the salmon mixture. Press it evenly with the back of the spoon. Top with a circle of tofu. Do the same with the avocado mixture. End with a circle of tofu. Carefully lift the biscuit cutter from the stack. Slip a small metal spatula under the bottom tofu and transfer to individual plate. For the second tower, repeat with the remaining ingredients.
8 Bring a saucepan of water to a boil. Once the water is boiling drop in the edamame. Cook for 1 minute. Drain, rinse with cold water, and pat dry with paper towels. Then garnish with the edamame, shrimp halves, and dill. Arrange the remaining capers and tomatoes around the tofu.
9 In a small bowl, whisk the remaining 2 tablespoons of olive oil with the remaining 1 tablespoon of lemon juice, soy sauce, and honey. Drizzle a little of the dressing on each stack and serve the rest separately. Serve with a fork and knife.

Chapter Three
Soups and Salads

Soups and salads are integral to traditional Japanese meals, but the way they are served and prepared is different from what we are accustomed to in western cuisine. The side dishes at a traditional Japanese meal are called *okazu*, which, for our purposes here, I call "salads." These salads typically arrive cooked, pickled, or dressed, and can be made up of seaweeds, vegetables, fish, and meat. Normally, they are presented in three to five plates or bowls, with just a few tablespoons mounded in the center. I have split the difference between the standard Japanese portion and American expectations, so to the Japanese eye the presentation won't seem too generous.

Many of these salads make great starters for a western-style meal. The salads range from rustic to elegant. Crabmeat and Seaweed Salad (p. 76) is a more refined *sunomono*, which I often use as a starter. Carrot and Daikon Salad (p. 77) can be marinated overnight and is a refreshing palate cleanser. Refreshing Tofu Salad (p. 73) is a western concept with Japanese ingredients: tofu and radish sprouts on a bed of greens topped with a piquant Soy Sesame Dressing.

Soup usually comes with or at the end of a Japanese meal. Dashi (Fish Stock) (p. 35), the building block for many Japanese soup bases (p. 33), is made from just two ingredients: bonito flakes (*katsuo*) and kelp (*kombu*) (It is also a base for dressings and sauces). I make a big batch, keeping a quart in the refrigerator for about one week, and freezing the rest. If you do not have time, however, pick up the convenient dashi granules and dashi packs that are widely available—and are widely used by great cooks. Many students ask me if they can use chicken stock or bouillon instead of bonito stock. Well, it isn't traditional, but why not? Chicken bouillon is strong and salty so I would use half stock/half water. Or try the Vegetarian Stock (p. 81) made with kelp (*kombu*) and dried mushrooms (shiitake). Chicken stock is used for some soups but not for miso or consommé.

Classic Miso Soup (p. 81), the entry level Japanese soup, can be part of a traditional breakfast, alongside rice, roasted fish, and pickles. White (*shiro*) miso paste, little cubes of tofu, and seaweed are cooked in Dashi (Fish stock) (p. 35) to make miso soup. A cousin of the standard miso soup is Eriko's Chunky Miso Chowder (p. 80), made with the more fermented red (*aka*) miso paste.

Soups served with a clear consommé base made from Dashi (Fish Stock) are often served in bowls with lids. The lid will have been "sealed" by the heat of the soup and requires the diner to gently squeeze the sides of the bowl in order to loosen the top. The reward is a whiff of the aromatic herb set on top of the broth for just this effect. My Japanese cooking teacher, Odagiri Sensei, taught us that this is the proper way to experience food: see, smell, and then taste. I find this most pronounced when having Japanese soup. And the perfect example is Delicate Seafood Consommé (p. 79), with its curl of lemon zest that releases a pleasant wisp of citrus.

Cherry Tomato Salad with Shiso and Basil

This simple little salad was a happy accident. I was picking *shiso* and basil from my garden and put both leaves in the same basket. Thinking I had separated them all, I stacked the leaves and rolled them into a tube to cut into a chiffonade and sprinkled the shreds over a bowl of multi-colored cherry tomatoes from the local Farmers Market. I was introduced to the combination, *shiso* and tomatoes in Japan and loved it.

    I tasted a spoonful and immediately realized I had mistakenly left some basil mixed in with the *shiso*. What a great blend of herbs. The anise-like flavor of the basil and the cilantro-minty taste of the *shiso* were a perfect match.

Serves 4
Prep Time: 15 minutes

12 oz (350 g) pints of cherry tomatoes, preferably multi-colored
½ teaspoon sea salt or kosher salt
¼ cup (65 ml) Kyoko's All-Purpose
  Dashi Soy Sauce Concentrate
  (p. 33)
1 tablespoon lemon juice
1 tablespoon olive oil
1 teaspoon sesame oil
8 *shiso* leaves, cut into shreds
8 basil leaves, cut into shreds
Freshly ground pepper

1 Cut some of the cherry tomatoes in half and others in quarters and pile in a serving bowl. Sprinkle on the salt and set aside.
2 Whisk together the Kyoko's All-Purpose Dashi Soy Sauce Concentrate, lemon juice, olive, and sesame oils in a small bowl until combined and toss with the tomatoes.
3 Scatter the *shiso* and basil over the tomatoes and serve at once.

Refreshing Tofu Salad

On a particularly steamy August evening in Tokyo, my husband and I were in search of a light meal when a life-size statue of a tanuki with his walking staff and straw hat at the entry of a pub caught our eye. The *tanuki*, a mythical badger in the anthropomorphic form of a country wanderer, is cunning and not always what he seems. Unwilling to walk one more step, we shuffled through the hanging curtains (*noren*) and practically collapsed onto the tatami mats. The pub was called Tanukichi, after the badger. The first thing we ordered with our two huge mugs of beer was this Refreshing Tofu Salad. Their mixtures of creamy tofu, spicy sprout, and cool cucumbers in a soy sesame vinaigrette and topped with my favorite herb, *shiso*—it was just what we needed. I re-created this dish at home and serve it as a starter or main course.

Serves 4
Prep Time: 25 minutes

1 head of soft leaf lettuce (Boston, red leaf), torn into bite size pieces
1 block of fresh tofu 16 oz (500 g), drained and cut into 2 in (5 cm) cubes (stir-fry the tofu in 1 tablespoon oil if you like)
12 oz (375 g) cherry tomatoes cut in quarters
2 mini cucumbers, sliced into ¼ in (6 mm) rounds
2 oz (50g) daikon radish sprouts (*kaiware*), spicy radish sprouts, or watercress
10 *shiso* or basil leaves, cut into shreds
¾ cup (200 ml) Akiko's Sesame Seed Dressing (p. 29)

1 Set the lettuce in a large salad bowl or platter.
2 Arrange the tofu, tomatoes, and cucumbers on the lettuce.
3 Pour one half of the dressing over the salad. Set the sprouts around the salad and top with the *shiso*. Add the remaining dressing to a pitcher and serve alongside the salad.

NOTE For a crunchy topping, place Japanese rice crackers (*sembei* such as soy flavored rounds and *kaki no tane*, spicy little crescents) in a plastic bag and lightly smash with a rolling pin. Serve in a bowl for diners to sprinkle on the salad.

Serves 4
Prep Time: 30 minutes
Cooking Time: 15 minutes

1 lb (500 g) fresh spinach or 10 oz (280 g) package of frozen spinach (defrosted)
2 cups (500 ml) water
10 oz (300 g) fresh bean sprouts
½ teaspoon salt
2 teaspoons sesame oil
½ cup (125 ml) Akiko's Sesame Seed Dressing (p. 29)
One 14-16 oz (500 g) cake of soft or medium tofu, drained
2 green onions (scallions) finely chopped

1 Fill a large bowl with cold water and set the spinach into the bowl and let the dirt settle to the bottom. Lift out the spinach and place it in a large saucepan with a lid.
2 Steam the spinach over medium heat with only the water clinging to the leaves, for about 2 minutes, or until the spinach has wilted.
3 Pour the spinach into a colander and rinse under cold water. Drain and squeeze out the water (if using frozen spinach, squeeze the excess water from the spinach). Place the spinach on a cutting board and cut into 2-inch pieces and place in a serving bowl.
4 Add 1 cup of water to the same pan with the bean sprouts and salt. Cover the saucepan and cook over medium heat for 3 minutes. Drain the bean sprouts and drizzle on the sesame oil. Set aside.
5 Crumble the drained tofu on top of the spinach and mix together.
6 Add the beans sprouts to the spinach mixture and toss well.
7 Just before serving, add the sesame seed dressing and mix until thoroughly incorporated with the vegetables. Garnish with green onions.

Spinach, Tofu, and Bean Sprout Salad

I have been making this salad for so long I honestly can't remember where I first learned it, but I put it on every menu I teach. My students love it, and it is always on my Japanese table. This cold dish is a delicious mishmash of several different recipes: spinach and both tofu and sesame dressings. When my Japanese "niece," Hideko Itoh, was in Boston to help with this cookbook, I served it to her. "*Oishii!*" she exclaimed (It's delicious!). She said it tasted familiar, but that she had never had it before. I sent her home with the recipe.

It is a cross between a salad and a side dish. I mix steamed spinach, crumbled tofu, and blanched beans sprouts in a sesame seed dressing. When I have the time, after toasting the sesame seeds, I crush them in my *suribachi*, a grooved bowl (mortar) with a *surikogi* (short thick wooden grinding stick). As you grind the seeds, you release the most delicious aroma. I like to keep a jar of this dressing in the fridge and scoop out a few tablespoons to dress up almost any vegetable.

Sweet and Spicy Celery Salad

Chef Masashi Ishida, a lively and very talented friend from Tokyo, created this dish while staying at our home for a week. He was here to cook at a program sponsored by the Japanese Consulate-General in Boston, and was kind enough to teach a few classes to my students. In Japan he works at a small maternity hospital where he creates sumptuous gourmet meals for lucky mothers who stay in the hospital for 5 days after giving birth. Rummaging through the vegetable bin in my fridge for something to make pickles with, he pulled out a bunch of celery. With the knife he brought with him from Japan, he sliced an entire bunch of celery into a pile of slivers in seconds and came up with this sweet and spicy celery condiment. Masashi simmered the celery until it was a tawny jammy mixture. I leave the celery in a crunchier state. The heap of celery is simmered in spicy red pepper, sugar, and soy sauce and cooked down into a glazy mound. It is great with rice, roast pork, and roast turkey. I call it the "constant condiment."

Prep Time: 15 mins
Cooking Time: 30 minutes

1 bunch (22 oz/650 g) celery
2 tablespoons canola oil
1 dried red pepper (*togarashi*), deseeded and minced (wear plastic gloves to protect your hands)
1 pitted and pickled plum (*umeboshi*), mashed (optional)
¼ cup (65 g) sugar
3 tablespoons soy sauce
1 teaspoon sesame oil
1 teaspoon toasted sesame seeds

1 Wash the celery and trim off the strings. Cut into very thin slices.
2 Add the oil to a large skillet over medium heat and stir-fry the red pepper for 30 seconds. Add the celery to the skillet and stir-fry on medium low heat for about 15 minutes.
3 Mix the pickled plum, sugar, and soy sauce together and pour onto the celery. Turn up the heat to medium and cook until the sauce begins to bubble. Reduce the heat back to medium low and cook until the liquid is almost completely absorbed and there is a light glaze over the celery. Sprinkle sesame oil and sesame seeds over the finished celery. It can be stored in an air-tight container in the refrigerator.

Crabmeat and Seaweed Salad

Sunomono is a class of vinaigrette salads served with nearly every Japanese meal. It provides a refreshing balance to simmered and fried dishes. This one was the first I learned to make at Odagiri Sensei's cooking class. I was hooked on the combination of soaked *wakame*, cucumbers, and crab—so simple, so tasty, so elegant. *Wakame* comes either in long thick threads or in little packages, pre-chopped. When re-constituted, the seaweed swells to almost 5 times its weight and is loaded with vitamin E (good for your hair growth and sheen). Japanese cucumbers have thin skins and are almost never peeled. Exchange them for the mini cucumbers, Armenian cukes, and the long English cucumbers you can find at most markets that you eat with the skin. Lightly salted, paper thin slices of these cukes add a crunchy contrast to the velvet smooth seaweed and the chunks of fresh crabmeat. For variation, use poached, shredded chicken. It is a little unconventional, but I sometimes spoon homemade sushi vinegar over the salad. This is still my favorite *sunomono*.

Crabmeat and Seaweed Salad (left),
Carrot and Daikon Salad (right)

Serves 4-6
Prep Time: 30 mins

½ cup (125 ml) *wakame*, reconstituted in 2 cups (500 ml) water for 10 minutes
1 teaspoon soy sauce
½ teaspoon sea salt or kosher salt
2 mini cucumbers or ½ English cucumber, sliced in ¼ in (6 mm) rounds (skin on)
1 tablespoon lemon juice
½ lb (250 g) crabmeat
5 tablespoons rice vinegar
2 tablespoons sugar
½ teaspoon salt
Toasted sesame seeds for garnish

1 Combine the *wakame* and water in a large bowl and soak for 10 minutes or until the seaweed has softened. Set a colander in the sink and drain the *wakame*. Rinse under cold water.

2. Set the seaweed on a cutting board and coarsely chop. Transfer to a mixing bowl. Add the soy sauce and mix well.

3 Sprinkle the salt on the cucumbers in a medium bowl and let sit for 5 minutes. Pick up a handful of the salted cucumbers and squeeze the liquid from the cucumbers. Add to the chopped *wakame* and mix until combined.

4 Divide the seaweed mixture among 4 (or 6) bowls and form a mound in the center.

5 Drizzle the lemon juice over the crabmeat and lightly mix. Take a generous pinch of the crabmeat and set on top of the seaweed.

6 Combine the vinegar, sugar, and salt in a small saucepan and heat over low heat for 1 minute or until the sugar and salt have completely dissolved. Alternatively, heat the dressing in the microwave.

7 Just before serving, spoon the dressing over the seaweed and crab. Sprinkle on the sesame seeds.

Carrot and Daikon Salad

This salad is part of the class of vinegared salads called *sunomono*. It is easy to make and refreshing to eat. By putting salt on the shreds of carrot and daikon radish releases their liquid, and kneading the vegetables creates icicle-like shards. They are usually marinated in a sweet-and-sour dressing, *amazu*, made with rice vinegar, sugar, and Dashi (Fish Stock). I often take a shortcut, and use the Sushi-zu Seasoning made from rice vinegar, sugar, and a little salt (p. 38). Make this ahead of time—even a day ahead of time—to let the flavors meld in the refrigerator. The salad is usually served on its own small plate. For a twist, though, toss it in a bowl with salad greens and enjoy your vegetables and dressing all at once. White daikon radish and the reddish carrot evoke the colors of celebration in Japan, so you will you find this on most New Year's tables. However, it's great to have any time.

Serves 4
Prep Time: 45 minutes

1 large carrot, peeled and cut into matchstick strips
½ lb (250 g) daikon radish, peeled and cut into matchstick strips
1 teaspoon salt
¼ cup (65 ml) rice vinegar
1½ tablespoons sugar
¼ cup (65 ml) water
Salt to taste

1 Combine the carrot and daikon radish matchsticks in a large bowl. Add the salt and toss lightly. Let them sit for 10 minutes. Then mix and lightly knead the vegetables with your hands. Working over a colander that is set inside a bowl, gather up the vegetables in your hands and squeeze out the liquid. Rinse and dry the bowl. Place the vegetables back in the bowl.

2 Mix the vinegar, sugar, and water in a microwave-proof bowl. Heat in the microwave for 1 minute or until the sugar dissolves. Alternatively, heat the mixture in a small saucepan. Cool to room temperature.

3 Sprinkle 1 tablespoon of the vinegar mixture onto the vegetables. Mix with your hand and then squeeze the liquid from the vegetables. Discard the liquid.

4 Add the remaining dressing to the vegetables. Cover and refrigerate for at least one hour until you are ready to use. It will keep for 2 days in the refrigerator.

Carrot and Celery Salad with Hijiki Seaweed

Hijiki is a sea vegetable that's rich in fiber, calcium, and Vitamin K. Sold in cellophane packages, it looks like little black wavy threads. Soak it in water to reconstitute it, and then cook this chewy, but not terribly briny seaweed. It swells to about 4 times its size. A quick stir-fry in sesame oil (or canola oil) adds depth. You can simmer with vegetables and sauce, and serve warm, but this preparation is for a cold salad with a light vinaigrette. I have exchanged the traditional component of deep fried tofu (*abura age*) for celery. If you wish, add firm tofu cut into strips and stir-fry until lightly browned.

Serves 4
Prep Time: 45 minutes
Cooking Time: 5 minutes

¼ cup (12 g) dried *hijiki* (reconstitutes to
   1 cup/100 g)
1 cup (250 ml) water
1 tablespoon sesame oil
1 carrot, peeled and cut into matchstick
   strips
1 large or 2 medium sized stalks celery,
   cut into ¼ in (6 mm) chevrons
2 tablespoons rice vinegar
1 tablespoon lemon juice
1½ tablespoons honey
1 tablespoon soy sauce, preferably low
   sodium
½ teaspoon salt

1. Add the *hijiki* and 1 cup of water to a medium bowl, and soak for 30 minutes. Set a colander in the sink and drain the seaweed.
2. Add half a tablespoon of oil to a skillet over medium heat and heat for 30 seconds. Add the *hijiki* and stir-fry for 2 minutes until the *hijiki* softens a bit. Transfer to a bowl and set aside.
3. Add the remaining oil to the same skillet and heat over medium heat for 30 seconds. Add the carrots and celery and stir-fry for 3 minutes until the vegetables are cooked but still firm. Add the vegetables to the *hijiki*.
4. Whisk together the vinegar, lemon juice, honey, soy sauce, and dash of salt in a small mixing bowl. Pour this dressing over the *hijiki* mixture and marinate for 30 minutes before serving.

Serves 4
Prep Time: 25 minutes
Cooking Time: 20 minutes

1½ cups (325 ml) water
8 pea pods
One half carrot, cut into matchsticks
½ lb (250 g) thick skinless white fish fillet (cod, haddock, halibut), cut into 4 pieces
1 tablespoon sake
3 cups (750 ml) Dashi (Fish Stock) (p. 35)
½ teaspoon salt
1 tablespoon soy sauce, preferably low sodium
2 teaspoons ginger juice
Four ¼ in (6 mm) pieces of lemon zest
1 green onion (scallion), cut into matchstick threads

1 Have on hand an 8 inch (20 cm) square piece of aluminum foil. Cut the fish into 4 equal pieces and place in a bowl. Sprinkle with sake and marinate for 5 minutes. Remove from the bowl and loosely wrap in the foil.
2 Fill a small saucepan with 1 cup (250 ml) water and a pinch of salt. Bring to a boil over medium heat.
3 Have a small bowl of ice water on hand. Add the pea pods to the boiling water for 30 seconds. Remove the pea pods with a slotted spoon and set in the ice water bath. Drain and dry on a paper towel. Set aside.
4 Add the cut carrots to the simmering water and cook for one minute. Remove with a slotted spoon to a plate. Discard the water.
5 Add the remaining ½ cup of water to a medium saucepan or skillet and bring to a boil. Reduce the heat to a simmer and add the fish in the foil packet. Cover and steam for about 10 minutes or until the fish is opaque. Remove the fish from the foil and set aside.
6 Simmer the stock and salt in a medium saucepan on medium low heat until it begins to steam.
7 Set out 4 bowls. Add 1 teaspoon of soy sauce and ½ teaspoon ginger juice to each bowl. Divide the Dashi (Fish Stock) among the bowls. Put one fillet into each bowl.
8 Arrange the carrots and pea pods on top of the fish. Garnish with a slice of lemon zest that's cut just before serving.

Delicate Seafood Consommé

Suimono is the consommé served at the end of a formal Japanese meal. The base of this refreshing clear broth can be a light Dashi (Fish Stock) or vegetarian stock. The soup is served in lacquer ware bowls, usually with fish or shellfish that have been cooked separately and assembled in the bowl just before serving. An aromatic herb or citrus skin is set on top and the bowl is covered with a lid.

The heat forms a seal and, when lifted, a wonderful scent greets you. I once met my former cooking students for lunch at a Tokyo restaurant, and they gave me these antique lacquer bowls specifically designed for this soup. Now they are treasured keepsakes.

This light soup is perfect regardless of the order in which is it served. You use one succulent clam per bowl, drop in a few of the uncooked Chicken Balls in Teriyaki Sauce (p. 56) or make it totally vegetarian with the Vegetarian Broth (p. 81) and slivers of shiitake mushroom, carrot and green onions (scallions). Make sure to pre-cook any of these substitutions.

> **NOTE** Another way to garnish this soup is with green onion curls. I learned this technique from Odagiri Sensei. Slice the green onion into matchstick strips. Fill a small bowl with cold water. Add one ice cube. Add the green onion threads to the water. While in the bowl, rub the green onion threads between your finger tips. The threads will begin to curl. Pour into a strainer and place the green onion rings on a paper towel to dry.

Eriko's Chunky Miso Chowder Ton Jiru

Eriko Itoh, my Japanese "sister," taught me to make this during one very cold January day. The darker, saltier, more fermented red miso paste dissolves in a flavorful broth with chunky vegetables and tofu. Its hearty, rustic presentation, with roll-cut vegetables, contrasts with the more refined *miso shiru.* Pick up the bowl and pluck the individual vegetables out of the soup with your chopsticks. The personality of each ingredient comes forth in every bite.

Serves 4
Prep Time: 30 minutes
Cooking Time: 15 minutes

1 block 14-16 oz (365-500 g) soft or medium tofu (*momen dofu*)
2 tablespoons canola oil
¼ lb (125 g) pork cutlet, sliced into ¼ in x 2 in (6 mm x 5 cm) pieces
2 carrots, roll-cut into 1 in (2.5 cm) pieces
1 large potato cut into 1 in (2.5 cm) pieces
5 dried shiitake mushrooms, reconstituted in 1½ cups (375 ml) liquid, reserved, sliced
1 whole pre-cooked bamboo shoot, cut into 1 in (2.5 cm) pieces (available in 1 lb/500 g tins)
1 medium onion, sliced
3 cups (750 ml) Dashi (Fish Stock) (p. 35)
½ cup (125 g) fermented red, white or a combination of both miso pastes (*awase* miso)

1 Set the tofu on a microwave-safe plate and microwave for 1 minute. Drain the liquid and set aside.
2 Add the oil to a medium saucepan and heat for 45 seconds over medium heat. Add the pork and stir-fry for 30 seconds.
3 Add the carrots, potatoes, mushrooms, bamboo shoot, and onions for 5 minutes, until the vegetables begin to soften.
4 Add the Dashi (Fish Stock) concentrate and reserved shiitake soaking liquid. Bring to a simmer, cover with a lid and reduce to medium low heat. Simmer for 5 minutes or until the vegetables are soft.
5 Combine the miso with a ladleful of broth in a small bowl. Mix until the miso is dissolved. Add the miso to the soup and gently stir in until combined.
6 Crumble the tofu in large chunks directly into the soup. Simmer for another 2 minutes. Serve immediately.

Eriko's Chunky Miso Chowder

Classic Miso Soup

This is the first Japanese soup I ever tasted and the first I learned to make. It was my initiation to a Japanese breakfast because it was served every morning in the cafeteria of our language study dormitory. I first had to get used to the idea of soup at breakfast, but soon grew to love the salty fermented taste, as well as the soft cubes of tofu and seaweed. I still enjoy a bowl of miso for breakfast from time to time. When we moved to our home stay family in Kyushu, I was taken under the wing of the elderly housekeeper we called *obaachan*, the endearment for grandma. She taught me how to scoop a ladle of miso paste from a pottery crock, dip it into simmering Dashi (Fish Stock) stock, and little by little with chopsticks, to dilute the miso into the soup. I watched as she set a block of tofu in the palm of her hand and, with a cleaver, sliced the tofu horizontally and then vertically, then using the knife to slide the perfect little cubes (still in the shape of a whole block) off her palm, tumbling them into the soup. After I dropped too much tofu onto the floor, *obaachan* set a bowl under my hand. When buying miso paste take care to read the labels. Some of the pastes include the Dashi (Fish Stock) flavoring. In this case you will only be adding the paste to water, not Dashi (Fish Stock). For an alternative to Dashi, try my friend, Joanne Rizzi's flavorful Vegetarian Stock. Dried shiitake mushrooms adds flavor to the liquid. Together, kelp and shiitake make a flavorful stock that I enrich with onions, carrots, and daikon.

Serves 4
Prep Time: 15 minutes
Cooking Time: 10 minutes

2 tablespoons dried wakame seaweed, reconstituted in 1 cup (250 ml) water for 10 minutes
4 cups (1 liter) Dashi (Fish Stock) (p. 35) (Vegetarian stock provided below is also very good)
4 tablespoons white miso
½ block 8 oz (250 g) soft tofu, cut into 1 in (2.5 cm) cubes
1 green onion (scallion), chopped finely

Joanne Rizzi's Vegetarian Stock

Makes 4 cups

5 cups (1.25 liters) water
One 2-in (5 cm) square kelp (*kombu*)
4 dried shiitake mushrooms
1 carrot, cut in half
¼ pound (125 g) daikon radish, peeled and cut in 8 pieces
1 small onion
3 sprigs parsley

1 To make the Vegetarian Stock (if using), add the water, kelp, and shiitake to a large saucepan and let sit for 30 minutes.
2 Over medium heat, bring the water and kelp to a boil. Add the carrot, daikon, leek and parsley. Return to a boil, remove the kelp, reduce the heat and simmer for 1 hour. Strain the vegetables from the stock. Keep aside. Refrigerate the shiitake and use in stir-fries.
3 Add the *wakame* and water to a large bowl. Set aside for 10 minutes or until the seaweed is softened. Set a colander in the sink and drain the seaweed. Rinse with cold water and coarsely chop. Set aside.
4 Bring the dashi concentrate or Vegetarian Stock to a simmer in a medium saucepan over medium heat, about 3 minutes.
5 Place the miso in a ladle. Submerge the ladle about one-third of the way into the hot stock. With a pair of chopsticks or spoon, dilute the miso, little by little into the stock until the miso is completely dissolved into the stock.
6 Add the tofu and seaweed and heat for about 2 minutes.
7 Turn off the heat. Add the green onion and serve immediately.

Chapter Four

Rice and Noodles

The centrality of rice in Japanese cuisine cannot be overstated. Besides the rice cooker that is busy every day, the Japanese kitchen is stocked with a variety of rice-based ingredients, like wine (*sake*), vinegar (*su*), and crackers (*sembei*).

Although Japan relies heavily on imports of other foods, it is self-sufficient in rice production thanks to government subsidies for the rice growers. Although rice production is now highly mechanized, you can still see stooped grannies wearing rubber boots, standing in water-filled paddies planting the shoots by hand. The medium and short grain variety of rice is known as *japonica* ("sticky rice" to Americans). Its texture allows it to be easily picked up with a pair of chopsticks. The more nutritious brown rice (*genmai*) an unpolished grain, is gaining in popularity, but white rice is still preferred for its taste.

Rice is a popular base for bento. Try Yoshie's Delicious Crab Fried Rice (p. 85) or learn how to make Stuffed Rice Balls (*Onigiri*) (p. 88) just like a Japanese mom. This chapter also offers four rice bowl (*donburi*) recipes. These rice bowls, with substantial toppings, are meals in themselves. The hot Chicken and Egg Rice Bowl (p. 84) has tender pieces of dark meat cooked in a stew-like sauce, absorbed by the rice below. Sweet Soy Beef and Onion Rice Bowl (p. 91) is a beef bowl of sweet and savory shreds of meat, popular with young men looking for an inexpensive and filling meal. The Fresh Tuna Rice Bowl with Cucumber, Avocado, and Spicy Mayonnaise (p. 86) is really a mixed sashimi salad—kind of like a deconstructed sushi roll, but a lot easier to make.

If you haven't seen the hilarious Japanese movie, *Tampopo*, directed by the late Juzo Itami, a comedy of manners and quest for the best ramen recipe, put it at the top of your list. Noodles are popular street fare and snacks, as well as the base for a simple meal. Udon Noodles with Everything (p. 92) is a thick *udon* noodle soup laden with vegetables, chicken, and fish in a Dashi (Fish Stock) (p. 35). The Mushroom Soba Noodle Soup (p. 93) was inspired by a chance meal on a cold winter afternoon at a *soba* shop in the famed restaurant supply area, Kappabashi. The added bonus was a *soba*-making classroom in the rear of the shop. What a find! For a snack or a meal, try our family favorite, Fried Noodles with Cabbage and Pork (p. 94). This standard festival fare of shredded pork and bits of cabbage covered with a savory sauce can easily be made at home. Round out your noodle repertoire with the hot weather favorite, Spring Rain Summer Noodle Salad, (p. 95) with its pretty glass noodles, the perfect foil for Japan's humid summers. And don't forget: in the case of soup noodles, slurping them and picking up the bowl to drink the soup is deemed polite at a Japanese table as it is considered evidence that one has enjoyed the meal.

Chicken and Egg Rice Bowl

Oyako Donburi

Even the Japanese are not sure which came first, the chicken or the egg. In this homey "mother and child rice dish," both get top billing. Chunks of dark chicken meat are simmered in a Dashi (Fish Stock) broth with soy sauce, sake, and mirin. Drizzle a blanket of lightly beaten eggs over the bubbling broth when the mixture is just about ready. The barely-set eggs will thicken the mixture. The stewy mixture is ladled over hot rice, flavoring the rice. In a twist on the traditional, and at the behest of my cooking students, I have tried substituting a light chicken broth for the Dashi (Fish Stock) while still using the same seasonings. The results are different, but also delicious.

Serves 4
Prep Time: 15 minutes
Cooking Time: 15 minutes

3 cups (750 ml) Dashi (Fish Stock) (p. 35) or low salt chicken stock
5 tablespoons soy sauce
3 tablespoons sugar
2 tablespoons mirin
1 onion, cut in ¼ in (6 mm) slices
¾ lb (350 g) skinless and boneless chicken thigh cut into 2 in (5 cm) pieces
4 shiitake mushrooms, (if using dried, reconstitute, then half the reserved liquid can be used for the soup stock) cut into ¼ in (6 mm) slices
3 green onions (scallions), sliced in half vertically and then cut into 4 pieces
4 large eggs, lightly beaten
4 cups (800g) cooked white or brown rice (see Preparing Japanese Rice on p. 31)
2 oz (50 g) *mitsuba* or celery leaves, chopped for garnish

1 Mix the stock, soy sauce, sugar, and mirin in a medium skillet or saucepan and cook over medium heat. Bring the mixture to a boil.
2 Add the onion and cook for one minute. Then add the chicken, mushrooms, and green onions. Continue cooking 5 minutes or until the chicken is just about done.
3 In a circular motion, pour the eggs over the surface of the chicken mixture and cook for 1 minute more. Turn off the heat and let the eggs set for an additional minute.
4 Place the hot rice into 4 bowls. Ladle the chicken mixture over the rice and garnish with *mitsuba* or celery leaves. Serve with a spoon.

Chicken and Egg Rice Bowl

Yoshie's Delicious Crab Fried Rice Chahan

This classic Chinese dish is a staple of Japanese home cooking. Everyone has their own fried rice recipe and, as my friend Yoshie Gordon says, it is really a great way to use left-over rice. Yoshie enhances her fried rice by adding a can of crabmeat. There are two secrets to making good fried rice. One is starting with day old cooked rice. Normally, Japanese rice doesn't go in the fridge, but in this case it's a good idea because the refrigerator dries out the rice, and the drier the rice the better it cooks. The second is cutting all your ingredients to the same size so they cook in the same amount of time. Stir-fry the rice and other ingredients in a combination of sesame and canola oils for an aromatic base. Use left over bits of shrimp, ground beef, tofu, a tablespoon of peas, and add them to the jumble.

Serves 4
Prep Time: 30 minutes
Cooking Time: 15 minutes

1 tablespoon sesame oil
1 tablespoon canola oil
1 small onion, chopped
1 carrot, diced
4 shiitake mushrooms, (or any mushrooms of your choosing) diced
1 stalk celery, diced
3 cups (600 g) cooked, day old short grain rice
One 6-8 oz (170 g) can of cooked crabmeat
½ lb (250 g) of baby shrimp or baked ham
½ cup (125 g) frozen green peas or shelled edamame
2 large eggs, beaten, with 1 teaspoon of sesame oil
1 tablespoon soy sauce
Salt and pepper, to taste

1 Heat a large skillet or wok over medium high heat. Add the sesame and canola oils and heat for 30 seconds. Add the onion, carrot, mushrooms, and celery and stir-fry for 1 minute.
2 Add the rice and break it up with a spatula. Toss the rice and vegetables together and continue tossing and flipping until everything is well blended. Add the crabmeat, shrimp, or ham and peas or edamame. Toss with the spatula.
3 Let the rice cook for about 2 minutes, pressing it into the bottom of the pan. With the spatula, push the rice toward the center, leaving about ⅓ of the wok closest to you, exposed. Drizzle on a little oil and heat for about 10 seconds.
4 Pour in the egg and sesame oil mixture and let it set for 20 seconds. With your spatula, begin to push the eggs into the rice a little at a time, until all the eggs have been incorporated into the rice.
5 Add the soy sauce, stir-fry for an additional minute. Taste the rice mixture and add salt and pepper if needed. Serve in bowls with spoons.

Fresh Tuna Rice Bowl with Cucumber, Avocado, and Spicy Mayonnaise

This recipe is a combination of two of my favorite fresh tuna dishes. The first is the tuna tartar set on top of rice under a coating of grated Japanese yam (*yamakake*); and the second is a striking appetizer of layered fresh tuna and avocado cubes with Spicy Mayonnaise dressing that I discovered with Miho Nakajima, once a teenaged neighbor and now an elegant banker in central Tokyo. Think of this tuna-topped rice as a deconstructed Spicy Tuna Roll. The rice is not seasoned, and the seaweed, instead of wrapped around the rice, is cut into shreds and placed directly on the tuna.

Serves 2
Prep Time: 30 minutes
Cooking Time: 30 minutes

2 cups (400 g) cooked white or brown rice
2 mini cucumbers or half an English cucumber (deseeded), cut into 1 in (2.5 cm) cubes
½ lb (225 g) sushi grade tuna, cut into 1 in (2.5 cm) cubes
1 avocado, cut into 1 in (2.5 cm) cubes
1 tablespoon fresh lemon juice
¼ teaspoon salt
2 tablespoons Spicy Mayonnaise (p. 28)
Roasted seaweed shreds (*kizami nori*)
Soy sauce, preferably low sodium, for drizzling
Wasabi, to taste

1 Divide the rice between 2 bowls.
2 Make a bed of cucumbers in a flat circle on the rice. Set the tuna cubes on the cucumbers.
3 Combine the avocado, lemon juice, and salt in a bowl and mix gently. Arrange the avocado around the tuna. Place a dollop of the Spicy Mayonnaise dressing in the center of the tuna with a dab of wasabi.
4 Sprinkle on roasted seaweed flakes or cut one-half sheet of roasted seaweed into shreds and add to tuna. Serve with soy sauce and wasabi.

Stuffed Rice Balls Onigiri

Onigiri are rice balls that can be made into the shape of a triangle or a ball and serve as the Japanese equivalent of a sandwich. *Onigiri* rice is unseasoned and naturally sticky. Also called *omusubi*, they can be eaten plain with a wrapping of seaweed or stuffed with a variety of fillings. I learned how to make Stuffed Rice Balls from Akiko Nakajima, our neighbor who took me under her wing and helped me navigate life as a young working mother in suburban Japan. Akiko filled a bowl of water and told me to wet my hands. She then sprinkled a little salt onto my palm, before scooping hot rice from the rice cooker onto it. Ouch! I tried to mirror her hand movements as she pressed, rotated and shaped the rice into a perfect triangle. My ball, or what was left of it, was a blob and the rest of the sticky grains ended up all over the floor and me. We had a good laugh, but there was lots of rice left in the cooker and she wouldn't let me off easy. By the end of the session my hands burned, but I managed to produce a few *onigiri* that didn't fall apart upon contact. This recipe is for rice balls stuffed with Spicy Tuna Salad (see below). I have provided several ideas for wrapping, stuffing, and sprinkling for a variety of options.

Makes 8
Prep Time: 30 minutes
Cooking Time: 30 minutes

1 recipe Spicy Tuna Salad (see below)
4 cups (800 g) hot steamed white or brown rice (see Preparing Japanese Rice on p. 31)
Sea salt or kosher salt
3 sheets roasted seaweed

1 Have on hand a small bowl filled half way with water.
2 Scoop up about ¼ cup of the rice and set it into a glass custard cup or rice bowl. With a spoon make a little indentation in the middle.
3 Add one tablespoon of the Spicy Tuna Salad. Now add another ¼ cup of the rice to the top of that.
4 Lightly wet your palms. Sprinkle on a little salt. Turn the rice onto your cupped left palm (if you are a righty!). With even pressure mold the rice into a ball until it stays together. With your right hand cupped over the top of the rice press the rice together to form a ball. Apply enough pressure to keep the rice from falling apart, but not too much that will crush it. Rotate the rice forward with your right hand, ¼ turn. Com-

press the rice ball again. Repeat several more times until a firm ball/triangle has been formed. Set the ball aside on a tray. Cover with a sheet of plastic wrap. Repeat with the remaining rice and tuna until you have 8 balls.
5 To cut the seaweed without using scissors, fold sheets of roasted seaweed in half, just like a piece of paper. Press the crease to ensure the sheets have separated. You will hear a little crunching sound and have 4 pieces. Fold it in half again. You now have 8 pieces.
6 If you are serving immediately, set the seaweed under the bottom of the rice ball and bring the sides of the seaweed up onto the rice. The seaweed will adhere naturally to the rice. Make larger pieces of seaweed if you prefer to have more covering the surface of the rice. If you are serving later, you can wrap the seaweed around the rice at this point or wrap the cut seaweed in plastic wrap, then everyone can wrap their own. It will keep the seaweed from becoming too moist.

Spicy Tuna Salad

2 cans (5 oz/150 g each) solid white or light tuna in water, packed in water
3 tablespoons mayonnaise
2 teaspoons dark sesame oil
1-2 teaspoons Sriracha sauce

1 Drain the tuna in a colander to remove all excess liquid. Place in a medium bowl.
2 Add the mayonnaise, sesame oil and Sriracha sauce and mix well. Keep refrigerated until you are ready to use.

Other suggested fillings
Grilled Salmon, flaked into 1 in (2.5 cm) pieces
Pitted pickled plum (*umeboshi*)
¼ cup (3 g) shredded *katsuo* + 1 teaspoon soy sauce mixed together

Wrap with Roasted Seaweed
Shiso leaves

Roll in or mix with Commerical Furikake: Seaweed and *Katsuo* or *Yukari* (*shiso* and plum)
Sesame Seed Salt (*goma shio*): 1 tablespoon sesame seed + 1 teaspoon kosher salt (black sesame seeds or toasted white sesame seeds)

How to Form the Rice Balls

1. Place a plain or stuffed rice ball into your dampened hands, with the left palm forming a flat surface and cupping the right hand over the top of the rice to form a triangle.

2. Rotate the rice ball ¼ turn forward and lightly compress the rice as you go. Repeat several times.

3. Roll the rice ball in the rice seasonings.

Rice Bowl with Three Toppings

Oyako Donburi

This tasty rice bowl is a snap to make. All the ingredients are cooked in a single skillet, one after the other. Ground beef, scrambled eggs, and a green vegetable are seasoned, cooked and cover the rice like a colorful striped blanket. Its crumbly texture and bright topping make it a favorite among young children. Substitute ground turkey or firm tofu for the beef. This is a very popular option for a bento lunch.

Serves 4
Prep Time: 20 minutes
Cooking Time: 15 minutes

1½ tablespoons canola oil
1 lb (500 g) ground beef, turkey or medium-firm tofu
1 tablespoon sugar
3 tablespoons soy sauce
2 tablespoons mirin
2 tablespoons water
3 large eggs
¼ cup (65 ml) Dashi (Fish Stock) (p. 35) or water
1 teaspoon sugar
½ teaspoon salt
½ lb (225 g) green beans (or peas), cut on a diagonal into ½ in (1.25 cm) pieces
4 cups (800 g) cooked rice

1 Heat 1 tablespoon of the oil in a medium skillet for 45 seconds. Add the ground meat and stir-fry for three minutes or until it loses its pink color.
2 Sprinkle the sugar over the meat and stir-fry for another minute. Then add the soy sauce, mirin, and water and continue cooking until most of the liquid has been absorbed into the meat. Transfer the mixture to a bowl and set aside. Wipe out the skillet with a paper towel.
3 Beat the eggs, Dashi (Fish Stock) or water, sugar, and salt together in a medium bowl. Add the remaining oil to the skillet and heat on medium for 45 seconds. Pour the eggs into the skillet and scramble them until they are set but still soft. Transfer to a bowl and set aside. Wipe out the skillet with a paper towel.
4 Fill the skillet with 1 inch (2.5 cm) of water and salt and bring to the boil. Add the green beans (or peas) and cook for about 3 minutes. Set a colander in the sink and drain the vegetables. They should be bright green.
5 Divide the rice among the 4 bowls. Arrange the meat, eggs, and vegetables on top of the rice, covering the entire surface. Serve with a spoon.

Rice Bowl with Three Toppings

Sweet Soy Beef and Onion Rice Bowl Gyudon

If rice balls are the peanut butter and jelly sandwiches of Japanese cuisine, the beef rice bowl is the hamburger—complete with its own fast food chain. Just like McDonalds' golden arches, Yoshinoya's orange steer horn logo is the beacon for hungry Japanese seeking a heap of shredded beef on top of rice—an inexpensive and filling meal. Like a good burger, this sweet and savory rice bowl can be made at home. Use a good quality shaved steak now readily available in the meat section of your supermarket. Alternately, get a good piece of sirloin steak and freeze it for ninety minutes. You will be able slice (almost shave) this better cut of meat. The butchers in the meat department might even do the slicing for you. I learned this meat-tenderizing trick from my friend and co-author of *The Korean Table*, Taekyung Chung. Add some grated apple, kiwi, or pineapple to the beef and marinate; this adds a sweet taste and helps tenderize the meat.

Serves 4
Prep Time: 25 minutes
Cooking Time: 25 minutes

1 lb (500 g) shaved beefsteak
6 tablespoons soy sauce, preferably low sodium
½ apple, grated (skin on)
2 teaspoons sugar
1 tablespoon oil
1 large onion, thinly sliced
½ teaspoon salt
3 tablespoons sugar
4 tablespoons rice wine (sake)
1½ cups (375 ml) water
3 large eggs, lightly beaten
4 cups (800 g) steamed white or brown rice (see Preparing Japanese Rice, p. 31 and 32)
2 oz (50 g) *mitsuba* leaves or celery leaves (optional)

1 Combine the beef, 2 tablespoons of the soy sauce, grated apple, and sugar in a mixing bowl. Set aside to marinate for 10 minutes.

2 While the meat is marinating, heat the oil in a saucepan or skillet over medium heat. Add the onions and sprinkle on the salt. Stir-fry on medium low heat until the onions are just wilted.

3 Add the marinated beef to the onions and stir-fry for about 2 minutes until the meat begins to lose its pink color.

4 Sprinkle on the remaining sugar, soy sauce, and sake. Turn the heat up to medium high and add the water. Bring the mixture to a boil. Reduce to medium and cook for an additional 3 minutes. This will reduce the liquid.

5 Have the beaten eggs at hand in a small bowl. In a circular motion, add the eggs to the top of the beef. Turn off the heat and let the eggs set for about 2 minutes.

6 Divide the rice among 4 bowls. Spoon the beef over the rice. Pour any remaining liquid over the beef. Sprinkle on the greens.

Udon Noodles with Everything

Nabe Yaki Udon

I love this thick, chewy, noodle hot pot—it really has it all. Served in individual clay pots with lids, its Dashi (Fish Stock)-based broth is enriched by the simmered vegetables, fish, and meat toppings. It is brought to the table bubbling hot, and when you lift the lid, you'll find one perfectly poached egg. Break into the egg and watch little ribbons form in the soup. *Kamaboko*, a steamed fish cake with a pretty pink border is a common ingredient. I substituted imitation crab legs, as they are available at all supermarkets and add a similar flavor to the stock and color to the pot. Find the noodles in the refrigerated or frozen food section of Asian markets. I have recently seen prepared *udon* in individual packets and, of course, dried udon is in the Asian section of western supermarkets. I usually buy several packages of the fresh noodles and keep them on hand in the freezer.

Serves 2
Prep time 20 minutes
Cooking time 10 minutes

3 cups (750 ml) Dashi (Fish Stock) (p. 35)
2 tablespoons soy sauce
1 tablespoon mirin
1 tablespoon sugar
½ teaspoon salt
1 tablespoon sake
1 leek, top removed, cleaned, split in half and cut into 4 pieces
½ lb (250 g) fresh or dried *udon* noodles
8 oz (250 g) fresh spinach, washed and trimmed
4 shiitake (if using dried, reconstitute)
4 sticks imitation crabmeat, cut in half
1 (¼ lb/125 g) skinless and boneless chicken thigh, cut into 2 in (5 cm) cubes
1 large egg
Japanese red pepper powder (*togarashi*) for sprinkling

1 Add the Dashi (Fish Stock) stock, soy sauce, mirin, sugar and salt in a "stove to table" casserole pot. On medium heat, bring the stock to a boil. Add the sake and leek. Reduce the heat to medium and cook for an additional 2 minutes.
2 Prepare the dried *udon* noodles according to package instructions. If using fresh noodles remove them from the package.
3 Add the *udon* to the soup.
4 Arrange the spinach, mushrooms, imitation crab and chicken on top of the noodles. Over medium low heat, simmer the noodles and toppings for 5 minutes or until the chicken is done.
5 Crack the egg into the soup. Cover the casserole with a lid and turn off the heat. Let the noodle soup sit for one minute.
6 Bring the casserole to the table and set it on a hot pad or trivet. Divide the soup, noodles and toppings between 2 bowls. Sprinkle on the Japanese red pepper powder (*togarashi*).

Mushroom and Soba Noodle Soup

This dish was inspired by a bowl of handmade noodles I had on a very cold January day. My friend, Takako Suzuki, and I were shopping in the restaurant supply district, Kappabashi, in Tokyo. Laden with purchases, cold and hungry, we saw a noodle shop with a sign that said " *te uchi* " (handmade) *soba*, and looked no further. An elderly couple was eating bowls of delicious-looking hot soup with mushrooms heaped atop the brownish noodles. "We'll have what they are having," I said. It was a great choice. It turned out the owner of the shop, Koichiro Morihana, gave *soba* making classes right in the back of the shop, of course we signed up for them.

You can find *soba* noodles packed like pasta in a supermarket or in a package of individual-serving size (100 g) banded bundles at Asian grocers. In this recipe, I serve them hot in a soup so I rinse them in warm water before adding them to the bowl. Put together a variety of Asian and Western mushrooms and stir-fry them in butter with a dash of soy sauce, then add cooked and drained *soba* noodles to the hot stock, the result will be a wholesome combination of buckwheat noodles and earthy mushrooms for a comforting dish on a cold day.

Serves 4
Prep Time: 20 minutes
Cooking Time: 20 minutes

1 cup (250 ml) Kyoko's All-Purpose Dashi Soy Sauce Concentrate + 3 cups (750 ml) water
2 tablespoons soy sauce
2 tablespoons mirin
1 tablespoon sake
2 lb (1 kg) mushroom mixture: *shimeji*, *himeji*, *enoki*, shiitake, oyster, white mushrooms, or trumpet mushrooms
1 teaspoon sea salt or kosher salt
2 tablespoons butter
1 lb (500 g) soba noodles, cooked according to instructions on the package
1 tablespoon soy sauce
2 green onions (scallions), finely chopped
Japanese red pepper powder (*togarashi*)

1 Heat Kyoko's All-Purpose Dashi Soy Sauce Concentrate and water in a medium size saucepan if using, or make the soup by combining the stock, soy sauce, mirin, and sake in a large saucepan. Simmer on medium heat for 15 minutes. Turn the heat to low and keep warm.
2 With a wet paper towel, wipe off the mushrooms. Cut the mushrooms with larger surfaces, into ¼-inch (6 mm) slices. Break the *shimeji*, *enoki*, and *himeji* bunches into small bundles.
3 Heat the butter in a large skillet over medium heat until it is melted. Add the mushrooms and sprinkle on the salt. Stir-fry for 3 minutes, until the mushrooms are just wilted. Turn off the heat.
4 Cook the soba noodles according to the instructions on the package. Set a colander in the sink and drain the noodles. Set a large bowl in the sink and add the noodles. Rinse the noodles under warm running water and divide among 4 bowls.
5 Turn the heat to high under the mushrooms. Add the soy sauce, toss and cook for one minute. With a pair of chopsticks or tongs, divide the mushrooms onto the top of the noodles.
6 Ladle the soup stock around the *soba* noodles and garnish with green onions. Serve with Japanese red pepper powder (*togarashi*).

Fried Cabbage and Pork Noodles

Yakisoba

We brought this noodle dish back from Japan, and it soon became a family favorite that fed crowds of hungry teenage boys. At the team dinners I hosted before their high school soccer matches, Brad and Alex's teammates inhaled platefuls of what they playfully called "Yucky Soba." Along with Teriyaki Steak Tips (p. 98), this was their most requested dish.

This tangle of noodles, pork, dried shrimp and cabbage is tossed in a savory Worcestershire-based sauce. As the clear packages of noodles with their telltale Chinese borders suggest, *yakisoba* has Chinese origins, but today it is thoroughly Japanese, thanks to the addition of seaweed and bonito flakes.

Serves 4
Prep Time: 25 minutes
Cooking Time: 15 minutes

1 lb (500 g) fresh Chinese style noodles
2 tablespoons oil
¼ lb (125 g) pork, sliced into match-stick strips
½ head of small cabbage (250 g) cut into 1½ in (3.75 cm) pieces
8 oz (250 g) bean sprouts
3 tablespoons dried shrimp (optional)
Red ginger (optional)
½ cup (125 ml) Bull-Dog Sauce or ½ cup (125 ml) Quick Tonkatsu Sauce (p. 32) plus more for drizzling over the finished dish.
2 tablespoons shaved seaweed, (*Aonori*)
3 tablespoons shredded bonito flakes

1 Bring to a boil a large pot of water. Add the fresh noodles and cook for 3 minutes, until the noodles are cooked but firm. Set a colander in the sink and drain the noodles. Let sit for several minutes so the noodles can dry out a bit.
2 Heat the oil in a large skillet over medium heat. Add the pork and stir-fry for 2 minutes.
3 Then add the cabbage, bean sprouts, and dried shrimp, if using, and stir-fry for another 3 minutes until the cabbage begins to soften. Add the sauce and bring to a boil.
4 Add the noodles to the cabbage mixture and toss together until the mixture is thoroughly combined. Heat the noodles through about 2 more minutes. Transfer the noodles to a serving platter.
5 Drizzle on the remaining sauce. Scatter on the pickled ginger, seaweed shavings, and a generous pinch of shredded bonito flakes.

Spring Rain Summer Noodle Salad

Harusame

Japanese summers are intensely humid, even after the torrential rains called *tsuyu*. Everyone carries around handkerchief-size towel hankies, merchants give out rounded summer fans, dishes change from solid pottery to glass, and if there is any breeze, glass wind chimes tinkle. All of this is designed to help you think cool, but the heat can crush your appetite. Few things are more refreshing than this cold plate of Spring Rain Summer Noodle Salad. The translucent noodles tossed in a light vinaigrette are perfect for perking up your appetite and attitude. It can be prepared in advance and set on the table with a glass of chilled barley tea. It is a great salad anytime, so you needn't wait for a heat wave to enjoy this dish.

Serves 4
Prep Time: 30 minutes
Cooking Time: 20 minutes

1 package or 8 oz (250 g) bean thread noodles (*harusame*) or rice stick noodles
16 pea pods
½ teaspoon salt
3 lemon slices
16 extra large cooked shrimp
6 dried shiitake mushrooms, reconstituted in 2 cups (500 ml) water and cut into strips (reserve 1 cup soaking liquid)
1½ tablespoons sugar
1 tablespoon mirin
1 cup (250 ml) soaking liquid
1½ tablespoons soy sauce
2 mini cucumbers, cut into matchsticks
2 large eggs, made into an omelet and cut into strips

Dressing
½ cup (125 ml) rice vinegar
3 tablespoons sugar
2 teaspoons sesame oil
½ teaspoon salt

1 In a small bowl, whisk all of the ingredients for the Dressing in a small bowl until the sugar is completely dissolved.

2 Have on hand a large platter or tray to set the vegetables, shrimp, and egg strips on as they are prepared.

3 Bring a large saucepan of water to a boil. Place the noodles in a large bowl and pour the boiled water over the noodles. Let the noodles sit for 10 minutes or until the noodles are softened but still firm. Then drain and rinse the noodles with cold water in a colander. Transfer the noodles to a large shallow serving bowl. Pour on half the dressing and toss with the noodles.

4 Fill a bowl with cold water and keep it on hand. Bring the water and salt to a boil in a medium saucepan filled halfway. Add the pea pods and blanch for 30 seconds. Remove with a slotted spoon and set in the bowl of cold water. Remove the pods from the water (reserve the water) and set on a cutting board. Cut the pea pods in half on a diagonal and set on the platter.

5 Bring the water back to a boil. Add the lemon slices and shrimp and cook for 3 minutes or until the shrimp is opaque. Remove the shrimp with a slotted spoon and set in the bowl of cold water. Remove the shrimp from the cold water and set them on the tray.

6 Combine the mushrooms, sugar, mirin, and the soaking liquid from the mushrooms in a small saucepan and cook for about 3 minutes over medium high heat. Add the soy sauce and continue cooking until almost all of the liquid is absorbed. This takes about 8-10 minutes in total. Transfer to a dish to cool.

7 Scatter the cucumber shreds over the top of the noodles. Next, add the mushrooms, followed by the shrimp, then the peapods. Drizzle the remaining Dressing over the noodles, and garnish with the egg strips.

Chapter Five
Meat and Poultry

Whether due to the early adoption of Buddhist teachings that ruled out meat consumption or due to the late arrival of Western cuisine, the eating of beef, pork and poultry has largely played second fiddle to the fish and vegetable-based Japanese diet. But with world famous dishes like beef *sukiyaki*, chicken *yakitori*, and *tonkatsu* pork cutlets, Japanese cuisine is justifiably as renowned for its meat and poultry as it is for its many other delights.

As a typical western omnivore, shopping for meat and poultry in Japan was a puzzling experience for me. In the first place, everything seemed downsized. And it was. I couldn't find packages of meat larger than 100 grams—less than a quarter of a pound. Moreover, the packages contained pre-sliced meat in categories I did not recognize. What was I going to do with so few thin strips of, what looked to me to be, stringy beef and fatty pork? And would it be enough to feed my family? I soon learned that these cuts and these volumes were delicious and perfectly suited for recipes I was learning from my friends.

Consider chicken. It is still rare to find a whole bird in a Japanese supermarket. Instead, the markets are laden with packages of chicken parts: breasts, thighs, drumettes, wings, and offal are all on offer. Japanese recipes rarely mix these parts together. The juicy dark meat of the chicken thigh is particularly popular, and is sold in convenient packages of pre-cut chunks. Japanese Fried Chicken (*Kara age*) (p. 107), tasty fried chicken nuggets marinated in ginger and garlic, is made with dark thigh meat. Try this cut even if you prefer white breast meat. Cooking times are relatively short and the meat stays moist.

Ground pork is also popular, especially when it is stuffed into Japanese Pot Stickers (*Gyoza*) (p. 64). Fried Pork Cutlets (*Tonkatsu*) (p. 104) served with piles of shredded cabbage,are also favorites in Japanese homes and specialty restaurants. My friend, Eri Kunimatsu's version of the Sliced Pork with Ginger (*Shoga Yaki*) (p.106), everybody's favorite dinner standby, is a honey sweet and ginger sharp stir-fry.

Sukiyaki Hot Pot (p. 101) is the iconic cooked meat dish of Japan. Japanese chefs have elevated the dish by using *wagyu* (*wa* refers to Japan and *gyu* means beef), the product of pampered cows living short but high quality lives. It was at first shocking to see the highly marbled slab of meat. I thought, "Where's the beef?" But the flavor lives in the fat and melts into the simmering dish. *Wagyu* is too rich for me to eat as a 12-ounce steak, but is perfect for the paper-thin slices of beef that cook almost instantaneously in a rich, simmering sauce. The price is dear, but a little bit goes a long way. One pound of this *wagyu* beef can feed eight as part of a Sukiyaki Hot Pot that includes copious amounts of vegetables and tofu. In the States, I substitute rib eye steak for *wagyu*.

You will see in the recipes in this chapter that I have followed the lead of Japanese butchers and cooks who make it easy to eat meat with chopsticks. They slice the chicken, meat, and pork into bite-sized pieces before serving. No knives or forks are needed.

Teriyaki Steak Tips

Teriyaki ("luster grilling") Sauce became familiar outside Japan long before sushi did. I consider it the "Swiss Army Knife" of Japanese sauces, as it works with meat, chicken, fish, and vegetables. In this recipe I use it not only as a glaze, but also to marinate the strips of sirloin. My Korean friend and co-author of *The Korean Table*, Taekyung Chung, showed me how to add grated fruit to meat to tenderize the tougher cuts. I use grated apple here.

   I make them in the oven and finish them off by giving them a minute or two under the broiler. When Dick's grad students came to the house for an end of the year party, these were on the menu again, this time on the barbecue. I make the marinade early in the morning and put the tips in a plastic zippered bag and keep them refrigerated until the grill was hot. The smell of grilling steak and soy sauce is like a siren's call. The hungry students hovered around their professor, offering to "help," and as soon as he set a platter of the grilled tips on the table, they were gone. There are never any leftovers.

Serves 8-10
Prep Time: 20 minutes plus 5 hours for marinating
Cooking Time: Approximately 20 minutes

1 cup (250 ml) Teriyaki Sauce (p. 32)
4 lb (2 kg) sirloin steak tips
1 small apple or Asian pear, grated (about 2-3 tablespoons)
3 green onions (scallions), cut in 4 pieces and crushed

1 Trim the steak tips of any excess fat and, with a two-prong carving fork, prick the strips, just piercing the surface. Divide and store the tips split between two 1-gallon (3.75 liter) plastic zip top bags.

2 Pour half the Teriyaki Sauce into each bag. Add the grated apple and green onions. Compress the air from the bag as you zip the top closed. Massage the sauce into the meat, turning the bag over several times to evenly distribute the sauce. Refrigerate for 5 hours or up to 1 day. Remove the meat from the refrigerator 20 minutes before you are ready to cook.

3 Set the oven at 425°F (220°C). Cover a baking sheet with heavy-duty aluminum foil. Pour the marinade from the bag into a small saucepan. Bring to a boil and turn down the heat. Simmer for 5 minutes. Discard the green onions. Pour the sauce into a bowl and set aside.

4 Place the steak tips on the prepared sheet and set on the middle rack of the oven. Cook for 5-8 minutes on one side. With a pair of tongs, turn over the meat and baste with the sauce. Cook for an additional 5-8 minutes. Cut into the meat to check for doneness by cutting into the center of one strip. Continue to cook in one-minute increments until the meat is done to your liking. Cooking times will vary depending on the thickness of the steak tips.

5 To further brown the steak tips, remove them from the oven. Baste them with the sauce and pan drippings. Turn on the broiler and set them back in the oven about 6 inches (15 cm) below the broiler. Cook for 1 minute on each side.

6 Lay the tips on a cutting board and cut them in half. Slice the meat against the grain and arrange on a serving platter. Brush the slices with the sauce. Pour the remaining sauce in a bowl.

7 If cooking on a grill, prepare your gas or charcoal grill for direct grilling. Set the tips on the preheated grill. Brush with the boiled sauce and cook to your liking. The meat is delicious hot or cold.

Japanese Style Fillet of Beef

Red meat can be so expensive in Japan. You may have heard about *wagyu*, the marbleized beef that comes from Japanese steers that live in near spa-like conditions until their demise. In Japan it is sold in 100 gram (4 oz) increments and can go for over $120.00/ lb. Forget 14 ounce (650 g) steakhouse portions; a few slices of the best beef you ever tasted is quite satisfying. Although I am not recommending breaking the bank, do buy the best cut of beef you can afford.

My friend, Etsuko, gave me this recipe for stove top "Japanese Rare Beef." Cooking it this way is fail-proof. Sear the beef first to give it an appetizing border and then cook it in the soy-based sauce with green onions (scallions) and ginger for just 8 minutes. That is not a typo—give it 4 minutes each side. Turn off the heat, cover the pot with a lid, and walk away for an hour. Use a fillet about 4 inches (10 cm) in diameter, and keep it under 1½ pounds (750 g), or else it will not "cook" through. Heat the gravy separately and drizzle it over the rosy petals. Serve with freshly grated ginger.

Serves 4
Prep Time: 10 minutes
Cooking Time: 10 minutes, Resting Time: 1 hour

1¼ lb (625 g) beef tenderloin roast fillet (or other high quality cut)
1 tablespoon canola oil
½ cup (125 ml) sake
½ cup (125 ml) soy sauce
½ tablespoon sugar
3 slices ginger, cut into matchstick strips
1 tablespoon mirin
1 clove garlic
2 green onions (scallions), finely chopped

Toppings
2 green onions (scallions), finely chopped
2 tablespoons grated ginger

1 Put 1 tablespoon of canola oil in a saucepan (with a lid) that's large enough to hold the beef and heat it over medium heat for 45 seconds.
2 Add the beef and sear for 20 seconds on all sides. Remove from the pan and set it on a plate.
3 Add the sake, soy sauce, sugar, mirin, ginger, and garlic to the saucepan. Bring to a boil for 1 minute.
4 Reduce the heat to medium low and return the beef to the saucepan. Cover and cook for 4 minutes. Turn the meat over, cover and cook for an additional 4 minutes.
5 Turn off the heat. Add the chopped green onions. Place the cover back on and let sit for one hour.
6 Remove the beef, reserving the sauce from the pan and set on a cutting board to rest for 10 minutes before slicing. (If you want to serve it cold you can cover the roast with aluminum foil and refrigerate at this point.) Cut into ½-inch (1.25 cm) slices and arrange on a platter in overlapping circles.
7 To serve, (hot or cold) bring the sauce to a boil. Simmer on medium high and heat until the sauce is reduced slightly and thickened.
8 Drizzle the sauce over the meat and scatter on additional green onions. Set the grated ginger in the center of the platter.

Sukiyaki Hot Pot

If ever there was an iconic cooked Japanese dish it would be the Sukiyaki Hot Pot. This is what most Japanese natives serve foreigners when they visit their homes because it is meat-based. The preparation is done before guests arrive, and cooking and eating Sukiyaki is a social activity.

I have had this dish dozens of times over the years, but the most memorable time was at the home of cookbook author and teacher, Keiko Hayashi. She, and her husband Jiro, invited us to dinner to share some very special meat that arrived unmarked, from an undisclosed source. She arranged the paper-thin beef on a platter in concentric circles, placing a thick pat of suet in the center. Hayashi Sensei plucked the suet with her long chopsticks to grease the hot cast iron pan. She provided a raw egg for each guest's bowl. Crack, swish—we dipped the cooked beef bathed in the egg for a sweet finish.

When the ingredients are more important than the cooking technique they had better be top notch and for Sukiyaki Hot Pot it is all about the beef. Thin slices of highly marbleized beef are cooked with a sweet sauce. Vegetables, clear noodles, and grilled tofu are continuously added, enriching the pot. The slightly bitter chrysanthemum leaves (*shungiku*) are commonly used for this hot pot. Not always available or easy to find, my friend Keiko Kanda, who has lived in Boston for over 30 years, recommended watercress as a good substitute.

Fat is where the flavor lives and makes meat tender. I am fortunate to live near several Asian markets that carry beef pre-sliced for Sukiyaki Hot Pot. However, I have asked butchers at supermarkets to slice rib-eye steak on their machine. If that isn't possible, freeze the beef until it is semi-frozen (about 1-1½ hours), take your sharpest knife from the drawer, and slice it as thinly as possible.

Serves 4-6
Prep Time: 45 minutes
Cooking Time: Approximately 30 minutes total

1 lb (500 g) rib eye beef, thinly sliced in ⅛ in (3 mm) slices

8 green onions (scallions) cut in quarters (white and green part) on the diagonal

2 bunches of watercress or chrysanthemum leaves

8 fresh shiitake mushrooms

1 block (1 lb/500 g) broiled tofu (*yaki dofu*), or plain firm tofu, cut into 8 pieces

16 ounces *shirataki* noodles or 8 oz (250 g) dried clear *harusame* noodles reconstituted

1-2 tablespoons oil

1 lb fresh *udon* noodles (dried *udon* noodles can be used if cooked first according to package instructions)

½ cup (125 ml) soy sauce

½ cup (125 ml) sake

2 cups (500 ml) water

2 tablespoons sugar

1 Arrange the beef on a platter, in overlapping fashion, so that it will be easy to lift each slice and set it into the skillet.

2 On a separate platter, arrange the green onions, watercress, tofu, and *shirataki* in piles.

3 Mix the soy sauce and sake in a small bowl or pitcher and set aside. Have the water in a separate pitcher next to the soy and sake mixture and the sugar in a bowl on hand.

4 Heat an electric skillet or if you are using a table top burner heat your pan over medium heat. Add the oil.

5 With a pair of chopsticks or a long fork, add one quarter of the meat to the hot skillet. Sprinkle on a spoonful of sugar and stir-fry until the meat begins to lose its pink color.

6 Pour ¼ cup of the soy and sake mixture and ½ cup of the water over the meat. Cook for 30 seconds and push the meat to one side of the pan and begin adding one quarter of the vegetables, tofu, and noodles. Let the sauce come to a boil and reduce the heat to a simmer.

7 Each diner will serve themselves from the skillet into individual bowls.

8 As the ingredients are depleted, continue to add more of everything including the sauce and water. This is going to make a very delicious and rich sauce.

9 Add water to the remaining sauce if necessary and bring to a boil. Add the udon noodles to the sauce. Since the noodles are already cooked they will need to heat for only 2 minutes or so. Everyone helps themselves to these sauce soaked noodles.

Sweet Soy Beef and Vegetables

Niku Jyaga

Niku Jyaga means "meat and potatoes," and is a comfort food for many Japanese. My Japanese friends say it evokes their mother's home cooking or *ofukuro no aji*, (literally, but endearingly, *"flavors of the bag"*) a phrase often used by men. After all, it does include the classic Japanese seasonings: soy sauce, mirin, sugar, and sake, simmered with wafer thin meat. So you can use good quality shaved beefsteak if you like. In the Japanese kitchen, a flat wooden lid, an inch or so smaller than the saucepan (*otoshibuta*), is set directly on top of the food while it is cooking. This keeps the liquid from evaporating, helps the vegetables hold their shape and concentrates all the sauce into the ingredients. You can use a piece of cooking parchment, cut to the size of the bottom of your saucepan, and set it directly on top of the simmering ingredients. I have my own *niku jyaga* for comfort food when I live away from the states—meatloaf and mashed potatoes!

Serves 4
Prep Time: 20 minutes
Cooking Time: about 15 minutes

Parchment paper
½ lb (250 g) sirloin or rib-eye meat, thinly sliced or shaved beefsteak
1 tablespoon canola oil
3 tablespoons soy sauce
3 tablespoons sake
1 medium onion, thinly sliced
8 small white potatoes or 2 medium size potatoes
1 large carrot
1 onion, thinly sliced
2 tablespoons sugar
1 cup (250 ml) Dashi (Fish Stock) (p. 35) or 1 cup water (250 ml) plus ½ teaspoon dashi powder

1 Select a medium size saucepan. Take a piece of parchment paper and a pencil. Set the pan on the paper and trace the bottom of the saucepan. Cut the circle out and set aside.
2 Combine the meat, 1 tablespoon soy sauce, and 1 tablespoon of sake in a small bowl and marinate for 15 minutes.
3 You are going to trim the edges on the potato for both decorative and practical reasons. If using small white boiling potatoes, then cut them in half. If you are using a regular potato, cut them into 2-inch (5 cm) chunks. Using a paring knife or vegetable peeler, trim around the potatoes to create beveled edges. This will help the potatoes hold their shape during the cooking process.
4 Peel the carrot and set the carrot on a cutting board and cut a 1-inch (2.5 cm) piece of carrot on the diagonal. With your palm on the carrot, roll the carrot towards you ¼ turn. Continue rolling and cutting on the diagonal. This is called *ran giri*, *butsu giri*, or triangular cut.
5 Add the oil to the saucepan and heat on medium for 45 seconds. Add the carrots, onion, and potatoes to the saucepan. Mix with a wooden spatula until the vegetables are completely coated.
6 Add the meat and continue cooking and stir-frying for one minute, until the meat loses its pink color.
7 Add the Dashi (Fish Stock) stock and remaining 2 tablespoons of soy sauce, 2 tablespoons of sake, and bring the mixture to a boil until most of the liquid is absorbed and the vegetables are just tender but not too soft. Remove the parchment paper and cook for an additional minute. Serve in individual bowls with rice on the side.

Debra's Home-style Korean BBQ Yaki Niku

Yaki Niku is Japanese for Korean barbecue. Owned by both Japanese and by Korean residents of Japan, *yaki niku* restaurants are immensely popular and found all over Japan. Some are local neighborhood joints, while others are very upscale establishments. Tables are outfitted with braziers in the center and have room for the platters of seasoned beef, seafood, and vegetables that are cooked at leisure by the diners. Garlic, soy sauce, sesame oil, and green onions are some of the classic Korean seasonings used to marinate the beef. The Kai family, our neighbors in the Tokyo high-rise we lived in near the Tsukiji Fish Market, introduced us to *Yaki Niku*. Kai-san was then the manager—and later the owner—of Dai-Ichi En, a small grill house in a corner of the Ginza in central Tokyo. The original owner, Mrs. Wang, who was Korean, adopted us and loved holding our infant, Brad. Over the years my husband entertained colleagues and hosted students at their low tables, groaning with seasoned meat and side dishes (*banchan*). When my kids were growing up I often made a version of this on weekends. To make this easy for you, I use the Teriyaki Sauce as a base for the marinade and add sesame oil, garlic, and green onions. On a non-stick tabletop griddle, I combine several elements of the meal. One section of the griddle is reserved for the savory beef, another for chopped Chinese (Napa) cabbage, and a third for bean sprouts drizzled with sesame oil. We scoop the saucy beef and vegetables on top of a bowl of rice and enjoy a leisurely meal as we catch up on the week's activities. Don't forget to get a jar of kimchi to accompany the Korean barbeque—just like they do in Japan.

Serves 4   Prep Time: 40 minutes
Cooking Time: 25 minutes

1 lb (500 g) boneless short ribs or sirloin steak, cut into
    2 x 3 in (5 x 7.5 cm) slices
½ cup (125 ml) Teriyaki Sauce (p. 32)
2 green onions (scallions), finely chopped
2 green onions (scallions) cut on the diagonal into 2 in
    (5 cm) slices
2 cloves garlic, minced
1½ tablespoons sesame oil
12 oz (350 g) bean sprouts
1 small head Chinese (Napa) cabbage, cut into
    3 in (7.5 cm) chunks
½ teaspoon Korean red pepper flakes (optional)

1 Combine the beef, Teriyaki Sauce, chopped green onions, garlic and ½ tablespoon sesame oil in a medium bowl. Marinate for 30 minutes. Remove the meat to a platter and reserve the marinade.
2 Heat a non-stick tabletop skillet or stovetop skillet over medium for 1 minute. Add half the beef and sliced green onions to the center of the skillet. Stir-fry for one minute. Push the meat over to one side and add half the bean sprouts to one section of the skillet and half the cabbage to the other. Drizzle one teaspoon of sesame oil over the cabbage and sprouts. Sprinkle the red pepper flakes over the bean sprouts if using.
3 Stir-fry the meat and vegetables in their own sections.
4 When the meat and vegetables are ready, each diner takes what they want from the skillet and puts it into their individual platters. Replace the meat and veggies and continue cooking. Add the sesame oil and marinade as you cook. Serve with rice and, of course, kimchi.

Yoshie's Gyoza Hot Pot

After learning from Yoshie Gordon about using ground turkey instead of pork in making dumplings (*gyoza*), she also told me that she used them to make a healthy hot pot. That sounded like a winter-time winner so I set to work that night creating my own. *Oishii!* Delicious!

If you don't have time to make your own, you can use commercially prepared gyoza. I always have a big bag of them in my freezer.

Serves 4

6 cups (1.5 liters) water or broth (chicken or beef)
½ head Chinese (Napa) cabbage, cut into 2 in (5 cm) chunks
2 carrots, cut on the diagonal in 1 in (2.5 cm) slices
8 shiitake, (if using dried, re-constitute) cut in half
1 leek, cut on a diagonal into 1 in (2.5 cm) slices
4 oz (125 g) daikon radish, cut into 1 in (2.5 cm) rounds
1 package *harusame*, glass noodles, reconstituted according to package instructions (optional)
1 block firm tofu cut into 8 pieces
24 dumplings (gyoza)

1 Bring to a boil 4 cups (1 liter) of broth in a large tabletop skillet or a large pot.
2 Add half the cabbage and cook for 2 minutes.
3 Add half the vegetables, noodles and tofu and cook for another 2 minutes.
4 Add 12 dumplings and cook for 3 minutes. Serve in individual bowls with dipping sauce.
5 Replenish the hot pot with remaining ingredients. Make sure to bring the stock to a boil before adding the dumplings.

Fried Pork Cutlets Tonkatsu

One of our favorite haunts, while living near Meguro Station in Tokyo in 2000, was a neighborhood restaurant, Tonki Tonkatsu, known for their Fried Pork Cutlets. There was a large sign high on the side of the building with a smiley pig logo (what was he so happy about?). Dick and I would sit at the long blonde wood counter dotted with pots of thick brown Worcestershire-like sauce. We either ordered the lean pork loin (*hire*), or the fattier, tastier, and expensive cutlet (*roosu*). The pork cutlet, coated with coarse Japanese bread crumbs (*panko*), is deep-fried and sliced so that it can be easily picked up with chopsticks. It is set against a backdrop of finely shredded green cabbage (free refills!) and served with a dab of hot yellow English-style mustard.

Panko is now very popular outside Japan and is widely available in most supermarkets. Although these cutlets are most delicious when deep-fried, most of my friends just heat up some good oil and cook them in a skillet. To make this a smooth process you want to have all of your ingredients at hand so you can dip, coat, and fry with little fuss. These cutlets, when cold, make great sandwiches for a bento meal (p. 150).

2 large eggs
1½ cups (105 g) *panko*, Japanese style bread crumbs
½ cup (75 g) all-purpose flour
4 boneless pork cutlets (1¼ lb/625 g) (about 1½ inches/3.75 cm thick)
2 cups (500 ml) canola oil (if deep frying)
Salt and pepper
¼ wedge each, red and green cabbages, shredded
½ cup (125 ml) Bull-Dog Tonkatsu Sauce or Quick Tonkatsu Sauce (p. 32)
English style yellow mustard (*karashi*)

1 Set up your assembly line first. Break and lightly beat 2 eggs in a shallow plate, one that's large enough to hold one cutlet at a time. In two other similar-sized and separate dishes, pour in your *panko* and flour. Set them on the counter.
2 Lay the pork cutlets on a cutting board. With the blade of a chef's knife, lightly chop the surface of the cutlets. Turn the cutlets over and do the same thing on the other side. This will help the cutlets to cook evenly. Have on hand a baking sheet with a wire rack set on top.
3 Dip a cutlet into the flour first, coating both sides. Then dip it into the egg and finish with a thick coating of *panko*. Set the breaded cutlet on a

Fried Pork Cutlets

plate. Repeat with the remaining cutlets.
4 Add the oil to a large skillet and heat over medium heat for about 1 minute. Add the cutlets and cook for about 2 minutes, or until one side is lightly browned. Turn the cutlets over with a pair of tongs or a long fork and fry for an additional 2 minutes. Turn over and cook for an additional minute on each

side. The total time will depend on the thickness of the cutlet. The cutlet is done when the center is no longer pink. Total time should be about 8-10 minutes. Place the finished cutlet on the wire rack. Do not place directly on a paper towel, this will only absorb the oil not drain it away from the cutlet.
5 Repeat with the remaining 2 cutlets.

When the cutlets cool slightly, slice each cutlet on a diagonal into about 6 pieces.
6 Make 2 piles of red and green cabbage on the plate. Set the sliced cutlet in front of the cabbage. Drizzle the Tonkatsu Sauce onto the cutlet. Serve with extra sauce for dipping on the side.

Sliced Pork with Ginger

Shoga Yaki

If you like the taste of fresh ginger, you are going to love this dish. When she was living in Boston, Eri Kunimatsu, a former cooking student, spent a day with me and my foodie friend, Elsa Tian, teaching us to make decorative sushi rolls. We painstakingly colored rice and stuffed skinny rolls into fat ones to create beautiful flowers and animals. That was an experience I am glad to have had—once. I asked Eri, a busy mom now with two little girls, for a family favorite recipe to include in this book and she didn't hesitate to offer her unique recipe for this very simple pork and ginger stir-fry (shoga yaki) dish.

In Italy, rosemary is often used in pork dishes, but in much of Asian cuisine, the refreshing and spicy ginger is the aromatic that's used when cooking this tasty, white meat. Eri makes her sauce with honey, adding sweetness to the heat. And, if she ever finds the time, she probably will include those cute decorative sushi rolls with any leftover ginger pork for her kids' bento.

Serves 4
Prep Time: 10 minutes
Cooking Time: 10 minutes

2 tablespoons flour
¾ lb (350 g) pork cutlet, thinly sliced into ½ in (1.25 cm) pieces
2 tablespoons canola oil
2 tablespoons soy sauce, preferably low sodium
1 tablespoon sake
2 tablespoons honey
1 tablespoon ginger, grated

1 Put the flour in a shallow mixing bowl and dredge the pork slices in it. Set the floured pork on a plate.
2 Heat the oil in a large skillet or wok over medium heat for 45 seconds. Add the pork slices and stir-fry for one minute on each side. Transfer to a plate.
3 In a small bowl, mix the soy sauce, sake, honey, and ginger. Pour it into the skillet and heat for one minute. Return the pork to the skillet and cook it in the honey ginger sauce for an additional 3 minutes or until the pork is done. Serve with rice.

Classic Chicken Teriyaki

Classic Chicken Teriyaki has long since become a part of western cuisine; you'll see it used as a pizza topping or stuffed in pita pockets. You have probably bought the sauce in a jar at your local supermarket, but you can easily make your own by boiling soy sauce, mirin, sake, and sugar into a thick syrup and then brush it on as a glaze to finish your cooking. I like to add the sauce to chicken breasts about half way through to add more flavor. In this recipe, I prefer to use breasts with skin on, this keeps them from drying out while cooking. Slice the breasts on the diagonal for visual appeal and set them on a bed of shredded iceberg lettuce with a slice of lemon. If you have any left over, for lunch the next day, stuff the slices in pita pockets with some shredded lettuce, carrots, and sprouts; then drizzle on the Teriyaki Sauce as a dressing.

Serves 4
Prep Time: 15 minutes
Cooking Time: 15 minutes

4 boneless chicken breasts, (24 oz/750 g) skin on
Salt and pepper
2 tablespoons canola oil
½ cup (125 ml) Teriyaki Sauce (p. 32)
¼ cup (65 ml) water
One half head iceberg lettuce (9 oz/250 g), cut into shreds
1 lemon, cut into 4 wedges
1 tablespoon toasted sesame seeds

1 Rinse and pat dry the chicken with paper towels. Sprinkle the salt and pepper on both sides of the breasts.
2 Lay the breasts, skin side down on a cutting board or work surface. Fold one end of the chicken breast to the center. Fold over the other end so that it overlaps.
3 Heat the oil in a medium skillet over medium heat for 45 seconds. Set the chicken breasts into the skillet with the seam side down and cook for 2 minutes. Turn the breast and cook for another 2 minutes. This will sear the chicken and seal the seam.
4 Pour the Teriyaki Sauce over the chicken breasts and bring to a boil. Reduce to medium-low heat and simmer for 1 minute. Turn the chicken over and simmer an additional minute. Do this two more times or until the center of the chicken is done. Transfer the chicken breasts to a platter.
5 Increase the heat to medium and cook the sauce until it is reduced to a thick glaze, about 1-2 minutes. Cut each chicken breast on the diagonal into 1-inch (2.5 cm) slices.
6 Divide the shredded lettuce among 4 plates. Set one whole sliced breast on each plate and brush the sauce over the top. Set a lemon wedge next to the chicken and sprinkle on the sesame seeds.

Japanese Fried Chicken Kara-age

Colonel Sanders arrived in Japan about the same time we did, in the early 1970s, but the country already had terrific fried chicken (*kara-age*). These chunks of moist chicken thighs marinated in soy sauce and mirin, with fresh ginger and garlic, are enjoyed for dinner or picnics, in lunch boxes; even at *izakaya* pubs. Instead of a thick flour-based batter, like another popular fast food import, the chicken nugget, the chicken is tossed in a dusting of potato starch (*katakuriko*) and then deep-fried. Cornstarch works fine too. Unlike nuggets, no dipping is necessary; all you need is a spritz of lemon.

Serves 4
Prep Time: 25 minutes
Cooking Time: 15 minutes

1 lb (500 g) skinless boneless chicken
   thighs cut into 2 in (5 cm) pieces
2 tablespoons soy sauce
1 tablespoon sake
1 tablespoon mirin
1 tablespoon grated ginger
2 cloves garlic, minced
¾ cup (90 g) cornstarch or potato starch
2 cups (500 ml) oil for frying
1 lemon, cut into wedges

1 Cut chicken into 2-inch (5 cm) pieces and place in a medium bowl.
2 Add the soy sauce, sake, mirin, ginger, and garlic. Marinate for 15-30 minutes.
3 Place the cornstarch in a small bowl. Take a few pieces of chicken at a time from the marinade and dredge them in the cornstarch. Place on a platter. Repeat until all the chicken has been coated.
4 Have on hand a baking pan with a wire rack set on top. Heat the oil in a skillet over medium heat for about 1 minute or until the surface of the oil begins to ripple. Add half the coated chicken pieces and fry for about 2 minutes or until the pieces begin to brown. Turn the chicken over and cook for another 2 minutes. Cook until browned. Turn once again for one minute on each side. Transfer the cooked pieces to the wire rack. Repeat until the remaining pieces are done.
5 Serve with a lemon wedge.

Shoko's Summer Sesame Chicken Salad

One summer day in Tokyo, deep in August, we were invited to the home of our Japanese "brother," Shingo Oishi, his wife, Shoko, and their sons, Banri and Moro. It was only a ten-minute walk from the train station, but by the time we had arrived we had wilted from the heat. We greedily drank down ice-cold glasses of roasted barley tea, and Shoko had almost completed making a gorgeous cold chicken dish. The sliced, ginger-scented chicken lay on a bed of lightly crushed chunks of cucumbers, surrounded by skinned tomato wedges and topped with a heaping mound of chopped green onions (scallions). Shoko had saved the drama of dressing preparation for last. She filled a soup ladle with dark sesame oil and held it just above a low flame. When the oil began to bubble, she withdrew the ladle and poured it directly over the chicken. The crags in the smashed cukes held the dressing. Sizzling hot oil met cold chicken and green onions (scallions). Wow! What an appetite trigger! I like to shred the poached chicken breasts and serve the whole dish on top of a bed of shredded lettuce along with the tomatoes and cucumbers.

Shoko's Summer Sesame
Chicken Salad

Serves 4
Prep Time: 30 minutes
Cooking Time: 30 minutes

4 cups (1 liter) water
4 slices of ginger, ¼ in (6 mm) thick
1 medium onion, sliced
3 boneless chicken breasts (1 lb/500g)
4-5 mini cucumbers or 1 English cucumber, unpeeled (or 1 Kirby cucumber, peeled and deseeded)
2 large tomatoes, cut into eighths
6 green onions (scallions), finely chopped
¼ cup (65 ml) sesame oil
Salt and fresh ground pepper, to taste

Vinaigrette

¼ cup (65 ml) light soy sauce
1 tablespoon lemon juice
1 tablespoon rice vinegar
2 teaspoons sugar
1 teaspoon whole peppercorns, lightly crushed

1 To make the Vinaigrette, mix the soy sauce, lemon juice, vinegar, sugar, and peppercorns in a microwave-safe bowl. Heat for one minute and set aside.

2 Bring the water, ginger, and onion to a boil in a medium sized saucepan over medium heat. Lower the heat to a simmer and add the chicken breasts. Cook for 15 minutes.

3 Turn off the heat and let chicken sit in the hot liquid for 10 minutes. Remove the chicken from the stock, and when it is cool enough to handle, shred the chicken with your hands. Place the chicken back into the stock in a bowl and refrigerate until you are ready to use.

4 Lightly scrape the skin of the mini or English cucumbers with a paring knife.

5 If using mini cucumbers cut them into 1½ inch (3.75 cm) chunks. If you are using an English or Kirby cucumber cut them in half lengthwise, and then into 1½ inch (3.75 cm) chunks.

6 Place a chunk of cucumber under the broad part of a kitchen knife. With your fist, hit the top of the blade once, and lightly crush the cucumber. Repeat with the remaining pieces.

7 Arrange a layer of the crushed cucumbers around a large serving platter. Remove the cold chicken from the stock and place it down the center of the platter. Surround the chicken with the tomato wedges and top it with green onions.

8 In a stainless steel ladle or small pot, heat the sesame oil over a low flame until bubbles appear, approximately one minute. Turn off the heat and pour the oil evenly over the green onions and chicken. Strain the Vinaigrette and drizzle it over the chicken and vegetables. Add salt and pepper to taste.

Red Miso Chicken and Vegetables

This is another oft-used recipe attached to an index card with yellowing tape that lives on my kitchen counter in a banged up red metal recipe box. Every time I think I am going to transcribe them to my computer files, I find a long-gone relative's handwritten notation or, in this case, a stain that evokes a food memory worth keeping. This stir-fry combines chicken, vegetables, and miso. I switch out the vegetables with whatever is in season, but prefer bamboo, broccoli florets, and bell pepper chunks. Marinate the chicken in soy sauce, sake, and cornstarch, which acts both to tenderize the meat and thicken the sauce. I am pretty sure that the stain on the recipe card is an ancient splash of miso.

Serves 4
Prep Time: 15 minutes
Cooking Time: 15 minutes

¾ lb (375 g) chicken thighs, cut into 2 in (5 cm) cubes
1 teaspoon soy sauce
1 teaspoon sake
1 teaspoon grated ginger
2 tablespoons cornstarch
3 tablespoons + 1 teaspoon canola oil
1 small head (8 oz/250 g) broccoli broken into florets and blanched in boiling water
1 tin of cooked bamboo shoots (15 oz/425 g), cut into 2 in (5 cm) pieces
2 green onions (scallions), cut into 2 in (5 cm) lengths
1 clove garlic, minced
1 dried hot red pepper, roughly chopped
¼ cup (65 ml) water, if needed

Sauce

2 tablespoons red miso
1½ tablespoons soy sauce
1½ tablespoons sugar

1 Prepare the Sauce by mixing the miso, soy sauce, and sugar in a bowl. Set aside

2 Place the chicken, soy sauce, sake, and grated ginger in a bowl and marinate for 30 minutes.

3 Pour the cornstarch into a plastic bag and take a few pieces of chicken at a time and toss in the cornstarch. Remove from the bag and set on a clean platter.

4. Add 1 tablespoon of oil to a large skillet or wok and on medium high heat stir-fry the broccoli and bamboo shoots for 3 minutes. Set aside.

5 Add 2 tablespoons of oil to the skillet and heat for 1 minute. Add the chicken pieces and fry for about 2 minutes each side. Transfer to a platter.

6 To the same skillet add the last teaspoon of oil and stir fry the green onion, garlic, and red pepper for one minute. Add the Sauce and heat until it begins to bubble.

7 Pour the vegetables and chicken into the Sauce and mix until thoroughly coated. Cook for 2 minutes. If the mixture is too dry add the water. Cut into the chicken to check that the center is done. Serve with brown rice.

Chapter Six
Fish and Seafood

Japan is an island nation that long has looked to the sea for nutrition. The ocean's bounty includes endless varieties of fish, shellfish, seaweed, and minerals. Fish is still the mainstay of the Japanese diet, and is eaten daily in a variety of forms, starting with Dashi (Fish Stock) (p. 35), the base of most soups, made with smoked and shaved bonito (*katsuo*). Eating fish in season is particularly important to get the maximum flavor and nutrition. In the fall, the Japanese eat Pacific saury (*sanma*), a type of mackerel; in the winter, yellow tail (*buri*) is prized; in the spring, it is sea bream (*tai*), a close cousin to red snapper; and in the summer, freshwater eel (*unagi*) is a favorite to help restore flagging appetites and loss of energy (*natsubate*) that many people experience during muggy hot summer days. Fish is often purchased, cooked, and eaten whole—head to tail—a custom with which many Americans are still not comfortable. A fabulous Asian super-market opened just minutes from my home in suburban Boston, and there the fish and seafood counter is laden with whole fish—gleaming eyes, scales, and all. One day I overheard two simultaneous conversations while standing at the fish counter. One from an Asian woman thrilled that she could finally buy a whole fish in the suburbs and another from a lady who had a look of horror on her face and said she wasn't going to eat fish for a year. I think I could get her to try the mild tasting Whole Red Snapper Steamed in Parchment (p. 123), a whole fish baked in parchment paper.

There is no end to the creativity built into Japanese fish fixing. Seafood in Japan is eaten dried, preserved, pickled, roasted, fried, boiled, steamed, baked, simmered, glazed, grilled, pressed, breaded, ground, and of course, eaten raw. No single chapter can survey the rich range of Japan's seafood kingdom. I will provide you here with a sampling, a small tidal pool, of my favorites. When I serve raw fish it is often tuna (*maguro*) or salmon (*sake/shaké*) that I get from a trusted fishmonger or from a market that sells "sushi grade" fish. Proper handling and chilling is essential to the quality of the fish. As we now are finding out, blue fin tuna is becoming endangered from over fishing and we may need to be looking to other species to satisfy our collective craving. To be suitable for sashimi, a fish must be handled with special care from the time it is caught to the time it is sold. Large fleets have flash ("super") freezing equipment to maintain their catch at prescribed temperatures in order to kill any parasites. So, although the fish may appear to be fresh when you see it, it actually may have been previously frozen. In this case, that is a good thing! I often buy the fish in frozen blocks and keep it in my freezer so at anytime I can make the Fresh Tuna Salad with Herbs and Crunchies (p. 112), a refreshing mixture of basil, *shiso*, coriander leaves (cilantro), and cornflakes. Yes, cornflakes.

Dark-flesh fish like mackerel are popular in Japan for their nutritious fatty acids and strong flavor. The flesh stands up well to simmering in miso or soy based sauces. Mackerel is not always available, and its strong flavor is often unappreci-ated. But as this is such a delicious preparation, I substituted bluefish for mackerel in the Soy Simmered Bluefish Fillets (p. 115). Salmon fillets are terrific with Teriyaki Sauce (p. 32), so try the Succulent Salmon Teriyaki (p. 119) and tuck any leftovers into a bento lunch box the next day. The Mixed Seafood Hot Pot (p. 120) is like a miniature ocean of seafood, shellfish, and vegetables cooking at your table and is my favorite cold weather dish for entertaining. We think of Jumbo Shrimp Tempura (p. 114) as restaurant fare. After all, deep-frying can be intimidating. But it can be done at home with great results. A successful deep-fry requires good quality oil heated to the right temperature and something worth fry-ing, like Jumbo Shrimp Tempura. Serve them on skewers with just a spritz of lemon and a sprinkling of *matcha* salt.

Fresh Tuna with Herbs and Crunchies

Tuna (*maguro*) is the best entry-level sashimi for those of us who didn't grow up eating raw fish. At least I had eaten smoked salmon on top of a bagel when I was a kid. So, I was almost prepared for the texture when I took my first bite of sashimi in the home of Chie Kikuchi, an outgoing teenager who adopted two bewildered American students at a train station in the early 1970s. She showed us how to add wasabi to soy sauce before dipping the thick red slice of tuna. Whoosh, a blast of wasabi went through my head.

Tuna has variations in color from red to pink. The lighter the color (and the higher the fat content), the more tender and expensive is the fish. The most common sushi-grade tuna (and this must be sushi grade) in western markets has red flesh. Most tuna is super-frozen on the fishing vessels immediately after being caught. It isn't, and should not be, inexpensive.

I learned about this surprising fresh tuna "salad" while studying home-style cooking in Tokyo. My instructor cut *shiso* leaves into slivers (my favorite herb). Everything seemed normal until she pulled out a box of corn flakes and told me to crush them. Corn flakes? Turns out the buttery-salty crunch complements the soft texture of the tuna beautifully. Fried Chinese noodles are a good substitute for the corn flakes making this Chinese-style sashimi. *Shiso* was hard to get when I came back to the States, so I used fresh basil with great results. Now I make a mixture of *shiso*, basil, and coriander leaves (cilantro) for an herby flourish. I enjoy the look of surprise on their faces when guests ask what that crunchy topping is and I tell them that it's corn flakes.

Fresh Tuna with Herbs and Crunchies

Serves 6-8 as an appetizer
Prep Time: 30 minutes

1 lb (500 g) fresh tuna, sliced into ¼ x 1½ in rectangles (6 mm x 3.75 cm)
2 green onions (scallions) minced
¼ cup (15 g), chives finely chopped
Salt and freshly ground pepper, to taste
10 *shiso* leaves, cut into shreds
10 basil leaves, cut into shreds
½ cup (30 g) coriander leaves (cilantro), finely chopped
1 cup (35 g) corn flakes, crushed

Dressing
1 tablespoon soy sauce
1 teaspoon wasabi paste
2 tablespoons rice vinegar
2 tablespoons canola oil
2 teaspoons sesame oil

1 If you are using a chunk of tuna from your fishmonger cut it in half so you have a block approximately 2 x 4 in (5 x 10 cm) long. This makes it easier to cut one-bite pieces of tuna.
2 Slice the tuna with your knife at a slight angle, against the grain and on the diagonal. Arrange the slices in overlapping concentric circles on a large plate. Reserve 3 slices. Make a rosette by twisting one slice into a tube. Wrap the next slice around the tube and finish with the third slice. Set in the middle of the platter.
3 Scatter the green onions over the surface of the tuna.
4 Snip the chives into tiny pieces over the tuna with a pair of scissors.
5 Make the Dressing by whisking together the soy sauce, wasabi, vinegar, canola, and sesame oils in a small bowl. Drizzle over the tuna. Sprinkle on the salt and pepper.
6 Combine the *shiso*, basil, and coriander leaves in a small bowl and mix with your hands. Scatter the herbs over the tuna.
7 Spread the crushed cornflakes over the surface and serve.

TIP Instead of cornflakes try crushing: Chinese thick fried won-ton like noodles. They come in cellophane bags in the Asian section of most supermarkets.

Fried Oysters Kaki Furai

Panko, the coarse Japanese breadcrumbs now so popular in Japanese and western restaurants, are widely available in most supermarkets. These little dry nibs of bread make a crunchy coating for a variety of ingredients. This is the first recipe my friends turn to during oyster season in Japan. Instead of rinsing the oysters under water, they set them in a bowl of grated daikon, which helps draw out impurities and enhances the oysters' taste. After coating and frying these delectably slippery bivalves, they dip them lightly in Bull-Dog (brand) vegetable and fruit sauce. You can substitute large shrimp and leave out the daikon radish rinse.

Yield about 16 oysters
Prep Time: 10 minutes
Cooking Time: 3-5 minutes

1 lb (500 g) fresh oysters, drained
4 oz (125 g) daikon radish, grated
1 large egg, beaten
¾ cup (100 g) flour
1½ cups (100 g) *panko*
2 cups (500 ml) canola or other neutral oil
Bull-Dog Tonkatsu Sauce for Dipping or Quick
  Tonkatsu Sauce (p. 32)

1 Combine the oysters and grated daikon in a medium size bowl and mix gently. Set aside while preparing the other ingredients.
2 Place the flour, eggs, and *panko* in separate shallow bowls.
3 Meanwhile, set a wok or large skillet over medium heat and add the oil. Heat until the oil reaches 350°F (175°C) or when you add a few *panko* flakes to the oil little bubbles form around them.
4 Remove the oysters from the daikon radish and pat dry with paper towels.
5 Coat 4 oysters in the flour and then dip them into the egg. Finally roll the oysters in the *panko* and set on baking sheet. Repeat with the remaining oysters.
6 When the oil is ready, slip the oysters into the hot oil. Fry for about 3 minutes, turning them frequently. Remove them with a slotted spoon and set on a wire rack placed on a baking sheet. Repeat with the remaining oysters.
7 Serve with individual bowls of Bull-Dog Sauce for dipping and lemon wedges.

Wrapping thin slices of *maguro* to make a sashimi "rose."

Jumbo Shrimp Tempura

Makes 12 Jumbo (Colossal) Shrimp
Prep Time: 25 minutes
Cooking Time: About 5-8 minutes

Shrimp tempura is a versatile fritter. It can be served on its own, as part of a platter, on top of noodles, on top of rice, or as a crunchy ingredient in a fancy sushi roll. After dipping the shrimp in a batter of flour, egg yolk, and ice water then fry it in hot oil. Nothing is more important in making tempura than the quality and temperature of the oil.

Our friends, Noriyasu Tsuchiya, a potter, and his wife, Setsuko, took us to a jewel of a tempura restaurant, Ohtsubo's, in the Ginza. We walked up narrow stairs and entered the small 12-seat restaurant. As we arrived, Chef Ohtsubo plucked a crispy shrimp (sans head that was served separately later) from the bubbling oil and set it on one of Tsuchiya-san's dishes. All the pottery dishes, pitchers, and condiment holders were made by Tsuchiya-san and hand-picked by Ohtsubo-san. We were sitting between two artists. Over the next several hours we enjoyed a procession of vegetables and fish, each served individually for us to dip in flavored salts, spicy red pepper, or to spritz with lemon.

Buy colossal or jumbo shrimp (shell and tail on), as they hold up well in the hot oil. Remove the shell but leave the tail on. Slash the under belly of the shrimp to keep them from curling during frying. When I serve them as appetizers or use in sushi rolls, I thread a skewer through the body from tail to top and fry them on the stick, ensuring they maintain a straight shape. Cooking time for the shrimp will vary according to the size of the shrimp. Keep the finished fritters hot by placing on a foil-lined baking sheet in a 300°F (150°C) oven. Tempura is usually served with, a Tempura Dipping Sauce (p. 32) and grated daikon. I usually just use lemon, sea salt, and a *matcha* salt mixture. Sesame oil is often added to the vegetable oil for an additional delicious flavor. Putting in too many skewers at a time will lower the temperature of the oil and make for greasy shrimp, so I put in no more than 4 skewers into the oil at a time.

NOTE You can use the same oil if you are making vegetables and fish tempura. Fry the vegetables before the fish so the oil doesn't absorb the flavor of the fish. Oil can be re-used 3 times. Filter the oil and pour into a jar. Store the oil in the refrigerator for up to 3 months.

12 Jumbo Shrimp
12 bamboo skewers, soaked in water for 30 minutes
3 cups (750 ml) canola oil or other non-flavored oil

Tempura Batter
¾ cup (200 ml) ice water
1 egg yolk
⅔ cup (100 g) cake flour or regular white flour
2 tablespoons cornstarch
1 lemon cut into 8 wedges
1 tablespoons sea salt or kosher salt for sprinkling
Matcha salt
1 teaspoon *matcha* (powdered green tea)
1 tablespoon sea salt or kosher salt

1 Remove the head and shell from the shrimp, while leaving the tail intact.
2 Rinse and pat dry. Devein the shrimp by removing any dark waste.
3. Turn the shrimp over and make 2 horizontal slashes along the belly. This will help keep the shrimp flat. Pat dry. Insert the skewer through the tail and straight through the body of the shrimp emerging at the top about 1 inch (2.5 cm).
4 Make the Tempura Batter by adding the water and egg yolk to a large mixing bowl. Whisk until frothy. Add the flour and cornstarch, then whisk until combined but not smooth.
5 Mix the *matcha* powder and salt in a small bowl and set aside.
6 Add the oil to a wok or large saucepan and heat on medium heat until you see ripples on the surface and the oil reaches 360°F (180°C).
7 When you think the oil is ready, dip a chopstick or fork into the batter and drip the batter into the hot oil. The drops should sizzle and float.
8 Pick up the skewer and dip it into the batter. Set it into the hot oil. Add 3 more skewers. Fry for about 3 minutes or until the shrimp is a light brown. Turn with a pair of metal tongs. Cook for an additional 2 minutes. Remove the shrimp and set on the rack.
9 Repeat until all the shrimp are done. Serve with salt, *matcha* salt, and lemon wedges.

Jumbo Shrimp Tem

Soy Simmered Bluefish Fillets

The Japanese use mackerel (*saba*), an intensely flavored fish, for this dish. I have exchanged equally dark-fleshed, but milder, bluefish for the mackerel because it is more widely available and because they have a piece of the skin on the underside that holds the fillet together allowing it to stand up well in a simmered sauce. To keep that entire delicious flavor concentrated in the fish, a piece of parchment paper lays atop the fish while it is cooking. The bluefish remains moist, and its natural juices mingle with the sauce, which is reduced to a jellied glaze.

Serves 2
Prep Time: 10 minutes
Cooking Time: 15 minutes

1 lb (500 g) bluefish fillets or mackerel cut in 4 pieces
3 tablespoons sake
Parchment paper
½ cup (125 ml) Dashi (Fish Stock) (p. 35) or ½ cup (125 ml) water + ¼ teaspoon dashi powder
1 tablespoon mirin
2 tablespoons soy sauce
1 in (2.5 cm) fresh ginger, peeled, and cut into matchstick strips

Variation

This sauce is also delicious for braising the fish

3 tablespoons miso
2 tablespoons sake
2 tablespoons mirin
¾ cup (175 ml) water or Dashi (Fish Stock) (p. 35)

NOTE Fish fillets often taper off into thin pieces. Tuck the thinner flat end under to create an even and thick section.

1 Set the fish on a plate and sprinkle with 1 tablespoon of sake. Set aside for 10 minutes.
2 Now you will make your own drop lid (*otoshibuta*). Set the saucepan you'll be using for the fish on a piece of parchment paper and, with a pencil, trace the bottom onto the paper, and cut out the circle. This will give you the size for the paper to fit directly onto the ingredients. Set aside.
3 Add the Dashi (Fish Stock), mirin, remaining sake, soy sauce, and ginger to a medium saucepan over medium heat. Bring to a boil, reduce the heat to medium low and simmer for 2 minutes.
4 Add the fillets to the saucepan, skin side down. Spoon some of the sauce over the fish and cover with the piece of parchment paper and simmer for about 5 minutes.
5 Remove the parchment paper and set aside. Slip a metal spatula under the fish and carefully turn the fish over. Replace the paper and continue cooking for another 4 minutes.
6 Cut into the fish and check that the center is opaque and the thickest part of the fish is firm to the touch. Transfer the fish to a platter.
7 Continue to cook the sauce for about 1 minute more until it is a thick glaze. Spoon or brush the sauce over the fillets.

Scallops with Citrus Miso Sauce

Scallops, like lobsters, are a rich distinctive shellfish that need little enhancement. Actually, one of the best ways to eat scallops is as sashimi, but that's not for everyone. This simple preparation lets the briny bivalve take center stage. Sear them in butter and then finish with a glaze of Citrus Miso Sauce under the broiler. Be careful when removing the scallops from the oven, they will be bubbling hot from the caramelized miso. The rich flavor of the scallop goes well with the salty, sweet miso sauce.

Serves 4
Prep Time: 15 minutes
Cooking Time: 12 minutes

1½ lb (750 g) large sea scallops
1 tablespoon canola oil
2 tablespoons butter
1 tablespoon fresh lemon juice
Lemon or lime zest for garnish
Lemon wedges

Citrus Miso Sauce

10 tablespoons white miso (or 6 tablespoons red miso + 4 tablespoons white miso)
2 tablespoons sake
4 tablespoons mirin
2 tablespoons fresh lemon juice
4 teaspoons grated lemon zest

1 Make the Citrus Miso Sauce by mixing the miso, sake, and mirin, in a small saucepan.
2 Over medium heat bring to a simmer for one minute. Turn off the heat and add the lemon juice and lemon zest. Mix thoroughly. Set aside.
3 Rinse and pat dry the scallops. Set a paper towel on a baking sheet and place the scallops on the paper towel for 5 minutes. Remove the scallops, discard the paper towel, and dry the baking sheet. Brush the oil on the baking sheet and set aside.
4 Melt 2 tablespoons of butter in a large skillet over medium heat. When the butter begins to brown and bubble add the scallops to the skillet using a pair of tongs.
5 Sear the scallops on medium heat for 1 minute. Turn the scallops over and sear for another minute. Drizzle on the lemon juice. Set the scallops on the prepared baking sheet.
6 Set the oven to 475°F (200°C)
7 Brush the scallops with the Citrus Miso Sauce. Set the cookie sheet on a rack in the upper third of the oven. Cook for 1 minute or until the Citrus Miso Sauce begins to caramelize and bubble.
8 Remove from the oven and divide the scallops among the individual plates. Garnish with lemon or lime zest. Serve with a lemon wedge.

2 cups (425 g) short grain rice (this is an American cup measurement it is the equivalent of 3 rice cooker cups or 3 *go*)
One 2-in (5 cm) piece of kelp (*kombu*)
1 cup (250 ml) Dashi (Fish Stock) (p. 35) or water
3 tablespoons soy sauce
3 tablespoons sake
2 tablespoons mirin (or sugar)
1 teaspoon salt
4 dried shiitake mushrooms, reconstituted in 1½ cups (375 ml) water, ½ cup (125 ml) liquid reserved
1 potato (125 g), cut into 2 in (5 cm) cubes
¼ cup (35 g) fresh, frozen, or canned corn kernels
¼ cup (35 g) peas (fresh or frozen)
½ lb (250 g) skinless fresh salmon fillet (or other firm flesh fish)
2 tablespoons butter
Roasted seaweed shreds or chopped parsley for a garnish

1 Rinse and drain the rice 3 times and soak in 3 cups (750 ml) of water for 20 minutes. Pour the rice into a colander and drain. Let the rice sit in the colander for 20 minutes.
2 Add the rice to the rice cooker with the Kelp, Dashi (Fish Stock), or water, ½ cup (125 ml) mushroom liquid, soy sauce, sake, mirin, and salt. Mix gently.
3 Rinse the reserved mushrooms and cut into quarters. Add the mushrooms, potatoes, and corn.
4. Place the whole salmon fillet on top of the mixture. Close the lid and turn on the rice cooker.
5 When the rice cooker indicates it is done, open the lid and sprinkle on the peas and add the butter. Close the lid and let sit for 10 minutes.
6 Open the lid and, with a rice paddle, gently flake the salmon and fold into the rice.
7 Serve in bowls with shredded seaweed or chopped parsley.

Salmon Rice Cooker Casserole

Takikomi Gohan

This family favorite has vegetables, chicken, or fish that is cooked along with the rice in a seasoned Dashi (Fish Stock) stock. Turn on the rice cooker and 40 minutes later you've got dinner. This one-pot meal came from lively Elsa Tian, a dear friend, and extraordinary cook. Elsa came to the United States over 40 years ago from Indonesia. She worked at Massachusetts Institute of Technology and, along with her husband, Jan, were a host family to legions of lucky young graduate student couples whose families were far away. Many of her "kids," as she calls them, were Japanese, and this recipe has been adapted from one of them, Kiri Izumi.

Set the raw salmon fillet on top of the rice and vegetables. When the rice is done, the cooker will ping. Gently flake the salmon and fold it into the rice with a wooden paddle. Change the vegetables with the season. This dish can also be made with chicken. Cut the chicken into 2-inch (5 cm) chunks.

Succulent Salmon Teriyaki

My first meal in Japan included a sweet soy glazed yellowtail (*buri*) fillet. It came on a small plate with a mandala of miso soup, rice, and pickles. I ate this nutritious meal for breakfast almost everyday for a month, while studying intensive Japanese. The *buri* was fine, but the sauce was always chopstick-licking good (but don't lick your chopsticks!). Teriyaki glaze complements the salmon's orange flesh and buttery rich taste in this simple baked fish recipe. Get thick fillets with the skin on the bottom if possible. There is a layer of fat between the skin and the flesh that adds great flavor to the fish. Baste the fillet with the sauce while baking; this will result in fish tender enough to pull apart with chopsticks.

Serves 4
Prep Time: 10 minutes
Cooking Time: About 10-15 minutes

1 tablespoon canola oil
Four 6 oz (750 g) thick salmon fillets
2 tablespoons sake
Salt and freshly ground pepper
½ cup (125 ml) Teriyaki Sauce (p. 32)

1 Set the oven to 375°F (175°C). Line a baking sheet with aluminum foil. Brush the canola oil on the foil and set the salmon fillets on the pan.
2 Sprinkle the fillets with sake and the salt and pepper. Set aside for 10 minutes.
3 In a small saucepan over medium heat add the Teriyaki Sauce and bring to a boil. Reduce the heat to low.
4 Place the fillets in the oven and bake for 5 minutes. Brush the sauce over the fillets. Continue to baste with the sauce every 5 minutes, for about 20 minutes or until the salmon is firm and opaque when a knife is inserted into the center.
5 Heat the sauce on medium for 1 minute. Drizzle extra sauce over the fish if desired.

Mixed Seafood Hot Pot Yosenabe

The word *oshare* usually refers to someone who is fashionably dressed, but I have also heard it exclaimed over a particularly gorgeous display of food. For me, there is nothing more "*oshare*" than this Mixed Seafood Hot Pot. This is a one-pot wonder, mixing seafood, chicken, tofu, glass noodles, and vegetables. Once the preparation is done, you are home free—the cooking happens at your table (or stovetop). Fish fillets with the skin on helps the fish to hold its shape. Whole clams, succulent scallops, and giant shrimp give the broth a briny undertone, and the tofu and glass noodles absorb the flavors from the stock. A communal earthenware pot is set in the middle of a table alongside the beautifully displayed platter of raw ingredients. A citrusy soy sauce with a generous dollop of grated daikon sprinkled with red pepper flakes sits in individual bowls for dipping. Diners leisurely make their way through a platter, replacing whatever has been removed from the pot. This communal style of eating around a hot pot on a tabletop burner is a favorite way to entertain or gather around the table. I use a deep two-handled stainless steel electric skillet that looks beautiful and does a great job. At the end of the meal, thick chewy *udon* noodles are added to the tasty broth and served hot. This is served in soup bowls.

Serves 6-8   Prep Time: 40 minutes
Cooking Time: 40 minutes

6 cups (1.5 liters) water
One 3 in (7.5 cm) kelp (*kombu*)
4 chicken drumsticks
¾ lb (350 g) salmon fillet, skin on
¾ lb (350 g) white flesh fish, skin on
   one side (red snapper, halibut,
   or cod)
8 hard shell clams (little necks or
   cherrystones)
8 fresh shiitake mushrooms
1 block firm tofu 14-16 oz (500 g),
   drained and cut into 8 pieces
1 large carrot, peeled and sliced
   on the diagonal into 2 by ¼-inch
   pieces (5 cm by 6 mm)
One half medium Chinese (Napa)
   cabbage, (12 oz/350 g) cut into 3 in
   pieces (7.5 cm)
1 bundle *enoki* mushrooms, trimmed
   and separated into small bunches
2 leeks, cleaned and sliced, on the
   diagonal into 8 pieces
3 tablespoons soy sauce
3 tablespoons mirin
1 tablespoon sake
12 extra large shrimp, deveined and
   peeled with tail-on
8 sea scallops
4 green onions (scallions), sliced into
   4 pieces
4 oz (125 g) *harusame* (potato starch)
noodles (or rice stick noodles)
8 oz (250 g) cooked *udon* noodles
can be simmered in rich broth at
the end of the meal.

Dipping Sauce
½ cup (125 ml) soy sauce
2 tablespoons lemon juice

Mix together and serve in a small pitcher.

Condiments
8 oz (250 g) daikon radish, peeled
Japanese red pepper powder (*togarashi*)

Grate the daikon on the smallest holes of a box grater to get a slushy mixture. Serve in individual bowls. Sprinkle on the red pepper powder for an added kick.

1 Put the water and kelp in a large, deep electric skillet, or stovetop casserole and let sit at room temperature for 30 minutes. Remove the kelp and set aside.
2 Add the chicken drumsticks to the *kombu* stock. Bring to a boil and skim the foam from the surface of the stock. Reduce the heat and simmer for 10 minutes. Continue to skim the foam from the broth until completely clear. Remove the chicken and set aside. Turn off the stock.
3 Cut each of the fillets into 6 pieces. Set on a serving platter.

4 Rinse the clams and soak in water for 10 minutes. Drain and set on a platter with the other ingredients.
5 Remove the stems from the shiitake mushrooms and wipe the tops with a wet paper towel. Incise an X on the mushroom cap. Set on the platter.
6 Add the tofu, carrots, cabbage, *enoki*, leeks, and green onions to the arrangement.
7 Follow the instructions to reconstitute the potato starch noodles. Drain and add to the platter. Your beautiful display is done.
8 Add the soy sauce, mirin and sake to the prepared chicken and seaweed stock and bring to a boil. Lay the chicken, bone ends toward the center, to the hot stock. Add half of the fish, shrimp, scallops, vegetables, and clear noodles, in their clusters to the pot but alternating the groups. Set 4 clams, bottom side down, around the dish and tucked in among the ingredients. Cover and reduce to a simmer. Cook for 3 minutes or until the clams open. Remove the cover and cook for another minute.
9 Each diner helps themselves to the fish and vegetables. Everyone pours a little of the dipping sauce into a separate small bowl. Add a spoonful of the spicy daikon mixture and begin dipping the cooked food into the sauce.
10 Bring the stock back to a simmer. And repeat until all the ingredients have been used.

Whole Red Snapper Steamed in Parchment

Sea bream (*tai*) is a member of the red snapper family. It is a mild sweet fish with white flesh and beautiful red scales. The Japanese serve it on celebratory occasions because *omedetai* is Japanese for "congratulations" and the Japanese are fond of word play. The fish is often served simply steamed or roasted with salt and set on a footed plate as the centerpiece for the celebration. Roasting fish can smell up your house for days and most of us don't have steamers large enough for a whole fish, so here is my happy compromise: Bake the fish in parchment paper to simulate steaming, and then finish it under the broiler to crisp the skin. Shred fresh ginger and green onions (scallions), and pile on top of the fish before enclosing in the parchment paper.

Most of us here in the United States are not used to cooking a whole fish and prefer the boned fillets. I hate bones in my fish as much as I hate shells in my scrambled eggs, but I urge you to give this a try. Have your fishmonger remove the scales and clean the fish for you. And make sure your fish isn't giving you the hairy eyeball! The eyes should be clear and will turn an opaque white when cooked. To serve, slice the fish along the top spine, and lift the flesh off the bones. Use this same cooking method for fillets. Your cooking time will be much less, depending on the thickness of the fillet.

Serves 2-4
Prep Time: 15 minutes
Cooking Time: About 15 minutes

1 whole 2½ lb (1.5 kg) red snapper, scaled, gutted, and side fins removed
Parchment paper, cut two and one half times the size of the fish
2 teaspoons sea salt or kosher salt
One 2 in (5 cm) piece of fresh ginger, peeled and cut into matchstick pieces
3 green onions (scallions), white and green part, cut into matchstick pieces
1 tablespoon soy sauce, preferably low sodium
½-1 tablespoon fresh lemon juice

1 Set the oven to 350°F (175°C). Rinse off the fish and pat dry with paper towels. Make 3 diagonal slashes about ¼ inch (6 mm) into the skin, on both sides.
2 Take the cut piece of parchment paper and lay on a shallow baking sheet. Set the fish in the center of the paper. Sprinkle salt on both the outside and inside of the fish.
3 Take a few shreds of the ginger and green onion and place inside the cavity of the fish.
4 In a small bowl toss the rest of the ginger and green onion together and pile it onto the fish, spreading it out along the surface but keeping a mound in the center.
5 To wrap the fish up in the paper, roll the short ends of the parchment paper forward several times. Then bring the long sides together and fold over several times leaving plenty of room between the surface of the fish and the paper, but not so loose that the juices will seep out.
6 Set the fish in the oven for 15 minutes. Pull the fish out and carefully open the top of the parchment to check to see if the fish is done. The flesh will be opaque and firm to the touch; if it is not, put it back for another 3 minutes and check again.

7. When the fish is done open the parchment paper carefully. The steam being released will be very hot. Pour the juices into a small saucepan. Set the fish on a platter still in the parchment paper. Then carefully rip the paper into quarters and slide them from underneath the fish. Discard the paper.
8 Pour the soy sauce and lemon juice into the saucepan with the fish juices and heat for 1 minute over medium heat. Drizzle over the fish and serve immediately.

NOTE If you want to crisp the skin on the fish, leave the fish on the baking sheet and remove the parchment paper. Remove the ginger and green onions and set aside. Turn on the broiler and set the fish on the 2nd rack down from the heat source. Broil for 1 minute and check the fish. If you would like a darker surface, put back under the broiler for 30 seconds or until you have reached the desired crispy texture. Do not leave the parchment paper under the fish when using the broiler! Your fish and house might go up in smoke! What a way to ruin a dinner.

Chapter Seven
Vegetable and Tofu Dishes

"Tt-t-t-toot. Tt-t-t-toot. T-t-t-Tofu!!"

A wiry grandpa, hauling a covered container balanced on the back of his bike, rode through the streets of my neighborhood tooting a small horn to announce his arrival. We crowded around him as he scooped blocks of tofu from their bath of crystal clear water into a plastic bag.

Once there were small tofu shops in every Japanese neighborhood, mostly mom and pop operations, many multi-generational. The smell of cooking soybeans wafted into the street. The owners wore knee high rubber boots to ford the steady stream of running water at their feet. A kerchief-wearing lady sold fresh and fried tofu cakes through a window. With that kind of access to fresh tofu it was hard not to become a tofu lover.

Today, these shops and peddlers are disappearing, but gleaming supermarkets everywhere have high quality tofu available. Some of their tofu is even made on the premises. Fresh tofu comes in different textures, but unless there is an Asian grocer near you, you are limited to but a few styles. "Cotton" (*momen*) tofu is firm and "silken" (*kinu*) tofu is smoother, softer, and moister. This non-animal source of protein is low in fat and calories—a boon to vegetarians and omnivores alike. Fortunately, the quality of tofu available in western supermarkets has improved dramatically.

If you are looking to introduce a dish to the tofu-phobic, try the Tofu and Vegetable Scramble (p. 132)—a sort of scrambled eggs with vegetables simmered in a sweet soy sauce. If you are already a lover of tofu, the Tofu Hot Pot with All the Trimmings (p. 138) is a great way to enjoy the pure form. Tofu dishes appear in other chapters in this book as a part of the supporting cast instead of the star.

The other stars of this chapter are the vegetable dishes that have also long been central to Japan's diet. Multiple side dishes (*okazu*) are served at a Japanese meal and can make up the bulk of an bento lunch (See Chapter 8). I have not included some of the more difficult-to-find vegetables like burdock root (*gobo*) or the Japanese long potato (*nagaimo*) even though I love them. They are hard to find outside an Asian market, and, the quality has been disappointing. When I think of vegetable preparation, two guidelines come to mind: seasonal and minimal. Most here are simmered in the Dashi (Fish Stock) (p. 35), but you can also use the Vegetarian Stock (p. 81).

Daikon radish is one of several simple boiled or steamed veggies that are tossed with a tasty dressing. Try the String Beans with Crunchy Toasted Peanuts (p. 126) or the Simmered Daikon with Citrus Miso (p. 127). Steamed Fresh Asparagus with Soy Mustard Dressing (p. 133) and Okra with Umeboshi and Katsuo Shreds (p. 137), are all steamed up and served with wasabi soy sauce. Eriko's Simmered Eggplant (p. 131) is a soft, flavorful, and traditional side dish. For a contemporary treatment of Japanese mushrooms, try the Japanese Mushroom Mélange with Butter and Soy Sauce (p. 135). And if you want all your Japanese vegetables in one pot, try the classically flavored Shoko's Simmered Vegetables with Chicken (p. 128).

We may never hear the tofu peddler's horn or run into the wisecracking green grocer again, but we still have plenty of chances to continue making and enjoying Japanese tofu and vegetables.

String Beans with Crunchy Toasted Peanuts

Ingen no Peanutsu Ae

Any boiled green vegetable with this nutty dressing becomes something special. Regardless of the variety, toasting a nut before grinding brings out its flavor. If I don't feel like getting out my mini food processor, I place the warm peanuts on a cutting board, place a paper towel over them and, with a rolling pin, lightly smash them before rolling the pin back and forth over the covered nuts to give them a crumbly, but crunchy texture. This dish is served at room temperature, so it can be made ahead of time. When served as part of a Japanese meal, it is placed in individual bowls. I serve them in this rustic dish made by our friend Noriyasu Tsuchiya, a potter from Shizuoka. You can see that the salad is mounded in the center, but doesn't fill the entire bowl. The circular patterned design and subtle purples and browns of the glaze are all visible. Admiring the vessel is as much a part of the meal as tasting the food.

Serves 4
Prep Time: 15 minutes
Cooking Time: 5 minutes

1 lb (500 g) green beans
½ cup (about 50 g) toasted, unsalted peanuts
2 tablespoons Dashi (Fish Stock) (p. 35) or water
2 tablespoons sugar
4 tablespoons soy sauce, preferably low sodium
1 tablespoon dried shredded bonito flakes (optional)

1 Wash and trim the beans. Fill a medium saucepan half way with water and ½ teaspoon salt. Set over medium heat and bring to a boil.
2 Add the beans and bring back to a boil. Lower the heat to medium and cook for 3 minutes until the beans are cooked through but remain crisp.
3 Fill a large mixing bowl half way with water and 1 cup of ice. Set a colander in the sink and drain the beans. Plunge the beans into the ice water and stir with your hands until the beans are cool to the touch. Drain the beans in the colander and set aside.
4 Add the peanuts to a food processor and pulse until coarsely ground. Transfer to a small mixing bowl. Or finely chop the nuts on a cutting board.
5 Add the Dashi (Fish Stock), sugar, and soy sauce and mix thoroughly into a thick paste.
6 Toss the dressing with the beans. Top with bonito flakes if using.

Serves 4
Prep Time: 10 minutes
Cooking Time: 30 minutes

1 medium daikon, about 1½ lb (750 g)
3 cups (750 ml) Dashi (Fish Stock) (p. 35) or Vegetarian Stock (p. 81) or water
3 tablespoons white miso
1 tablespoon mirin
1 tablespoon sake
2 teaspoons lemon juice
1 teaspoons grated lemon zest
Lemon zest for topping

1 Peel and cut the daikon radish into 2-inch (5 cm) circles. Trim around the top and bottom edges of the radish circles to create a beveled edge using a paring knife or vegetable peeler.
2 Add the Dashi (Fish Stock) stock or water to a medium-size saucepan and bring to a boil over medium heat. Add the chunks of daikon so they sit in one layer on the bottom of the pan.
3 Reduce the heat and simmer the daikon for 25-30 minutes or until the tip of a knife pierces the daikon through the center. There should be no resistance.
4 Continue cooking until the liquid is almost completely gone but be careful not to burn the bottoms. With a slotted spoon, transfer the chunks to a serving platter.
5 Add the miso, sake, and mirin to a small saucepan and place over low heat. Stirring constantly, cook the sauce for 2 minutes. Take the miso off the heat and add the lemon juice and grated lemon zest.
6 With a spoon or pastry brush, add about ½ tablespoon of the sweet miso paste to the top of each chunk.
7 Cut a sliver of lemon zest for each radish. Just before setting the zest on top of the miso, gently twist to release the aroma and natural lemon oil into the miso.

Simmered Daikon with Citrus Miso Sauce

The daikon radish is almost two vegetables in one. When it is eaten raw and grated, it is sharp and spicy; when simmered in water or Dashi (Fish Stock), it becomes soft and sweet. You would barely recognize it as the same vegetable. I recommend using Dashi (Fish Stock) as it does add a soft but distinct flavor to the daikon. For this recipe, cut the root vegetable into 2-inch thick (5 cm) rounds. But, don't forget, there is cutting and then there is cutting Japanese-style. Trim or shave the edges of the circle with a knife to round them slightly, creating a "beveled edge," as Elizabeth Andoh, the celebrated cookbook author, describes in her detailed book on Japanese cuisine, *Washoku*. This is not just for aesthetics; it also helps the daikon hold its shape over long simmering times. Like a good boiled potato, this preparation brings out the best in the vegetable. Top off the tasty chunk with a swirl of sweet miso. When you slice the lemon zest, the natural oil in the zest releases a citrusy aroma enhancing the whole sensory experience.

Shoko's Simmered Vegetables with Chicken Chikuzen Ni

"This is real 'obaasan no aji,'" says Shoko Oishi—my Japanese "sister-in-law." She is offering the high praise of "grandmother's flavoring," a pure, old-fashioned taste. Her sons, Banri and Moro, don't like it, but I love it. Her sons prefer wafu-style cuisine, a mixture of Japanese and Western ingredients and cooking styles and, of course, McDonald's!

This dish embodies Japanese cuisine to me. Crunchy lotus root, small starchy Japanese potatoes, meaty shiitake, and soft bamboo shoots cook in Dashi (Fish Stock) stock, sugar, soy sauce, mirin, and sake. All the vegetables and chicken are cut to similar sizes for even cooking. Shoko sets a wooden lid directly onto the simmering vegetables, ensuring that the sauce is absorbed.

She is married to our "brother," Shingo, a doctor who was a middle-school student when we first lived at his home in rural Japan. The still stylish Shoko is a veteran flight attendant, and brings all the efficiency and speed of her career training to her kitchen as well. We started to make the dish together when Shoko realized she had forgotten to soak the shiitake. In a flash, she set the mushrooms in a dish, added water, and sprinkled on a little sugar. She zapped them for 2 minutes in the microwave and said "Shoko Point!" They were ready.

If you can get a hold of them in your Asian market, use fresh pre-cooked lotus root and bamboo shoots. They come in plastic pouches. Look for them in the frozen food section or in cans if fresh are not available, both ingredients are optional. Keep cans or bags of these vegetables on hand, so that every recipe does not require a field trip. We used little chunks of chicken but make it vegetarian-style if you like.

"Shoko Point"—If you are in a hurry to soak the dried mushrooms add 1 teaspoon of sugar to the water and put in a microwave for 2 minutes.

Serves 4
Prep Time: 45 minutes
Cooking Time: 30 minutes

Parchment paper
4 dried shiitake mushrooms, soaked in 1 cup (250 ml) water, liquid reserved
1 large potato
1 large carrot
1 bamboo shoot, (boiled or from a tin about 8-12 oz/225-375g), cut into 2 in (5 cm) chunks
4 oz (125 g) cooked lotus root
2 chicken thighs, (7 oz/200 g) cut into 2 in (5 cm) pieces
2 tablespoons canola oil
1½ cups (375 ml) Dashi (Fish Stock) (p. 35)
2 tablespoons sake
1 tablespoon mirin
1 tablespoon sugar
2 tablespoons soy sauce, preferably low sodium
12 pea pods
½ cup (125 ml) water
¼ teaspoon salt

1 Cut a piece of parchment paper to the diameter of the bottom of a medium size saucepan and set aside.

2 Cut the mushrooms in half and set aside.

3 You are going to trim the edges on the potato for both decorative and practical reasons. Cut the potatoes into 2-inch (5 cm) chunks. Trim around the potatoes to create beveled edges using a paring knife, or a vegetable peeler. This will help them hold their shape during the cooking process.

4 Peel the carrot and set the carrot on a cutting board and cut a 1-inch (2.5 cm) piece of carrot on the diagonal. With your palm on the carrot roll the carrot towards you ¼ turn. Continue rolling and cutting on the diagonal. This is called ran giri (wild cut).

5 Cut the bamboo shoots into 2-inch (5 cm) pieces. Slice the lotus root into 1-inch (2.5 cm) slices.

6 Add the canola oil to a medium saucepan over medium heat. Add the chicken pieces and cook for 2 minutes.

7 Then add the bamboo shoots and stir-fry for 1 minute. Add the carrots and potatoes and stir-fry for 1 minute. Next add the lotus root and finally the mushrooms and stir-fry for another 2 minutes.

8 Add the reserved mushroom liquid, Dashi (Fish Stock), sake, mirin, and sugar. Place the parchment paper on top of the chicken and vegetables and cook for 10 minutes.

9 Add water and salt to a small saucepan and bring it to a boil. Place the pea pods in the water for 30 seconds. Remove the pea pods with a slotted spoon, drain the water from the pot and refill with cold water. Add the pea pods to stop the cooking. Drain and set aside.

10 Remove the parchment paper and add the soy sauce. Set the parchment paper back on and cook for an additional 8-10 minutes until the vegetables are done and the stock has been almost completely absorbed into the vegetables. Transfer the simmered vegetables and chicken to a serving bowl and garnish. Toss in the pea pods and mix well. Reserve a few pea pods for a garnish.

Grilled Eggplant with Sweet Miso Sauce Nasu Dengaku

The meaty flesh of the eggplant and the sweet salty topping of *Dengaku* make a perfect match. Japanese eggplants are petite and, for this dish, often cut in half horizontally, maintaining their curvy shape. The sauce is brushed over the surface of the cooked eggplant passed under a broiler to create a caramelized crust. It isn't easy to find the smaller Japanese eggplants, so I cut Italian eggplants into rounds. The sauce can be made with either white or red miso. The white is milder than the saltier, more fermented red. You can even combine the two for a mixed miso (*awase miso*).

Vary the flavor of the sweet miso sauce by adding different aromatics, like lemon zest or green onions (scallions). The miso/ green onion (scallions) combination is brushed on plain rice balls (*yaki onigiri*) to make a very popular bar snack.

Serves 4
Prep Time: 20 minutes
Cooking Time: 20 minutes

3 tablespoons white miso
1½ tablespoons sugar
1 tablespoon mirin
1 tablespoon sake
¼ teaspoon salt
3 Japanese or Italian eggplants, cut into 2 in (5 cm) rounds
3 tablespoons canola oil for frying
Toasted sesame seeds for garnish

1 Combine the miso, sugar, mirin, sake, and salt in a small saucepan over low heat. Stir constantly with a spoon, for about 2 minutes until the sauce begins to bubble. Turn off the heat and set aside.
2 Have on hand a baking sheet covered with a paper towel. Rinse the eggplants and pat them dry with a paper towel. Set the rounds on the baking sheet. With the tip of a knife, score the flesh of the eggplant in a hatch mark pattern. Turn the eggplant over and repeat.
3 Add the oil to a large skillet and place over medium heat for 45 seconds. Add the eggplant, in a single layer, and fry for two minutes. Loosen the eggplant with a spatula and turn them over.
4 Fry on the other side for an additional two minutes. Insert the tip of a knife into the center of the eggplant. If it is soft on the inside the eggplant is done. Set a wire rack on top of a baking sheet to drain. Transfer the eggplant rounds to the rack to drain.
5 Remove the wire rack from the baking sheet and spread a piece of aluminum foil on the sheet. Set the eggplant rounds on the foil and brush each one with the miso sauce.
6 Set the oven to broil. Place the oven rack one third of the way down from the broiler coils and place the baking sheet on the rack. Broil for 30 seconds to a minute. Remove the eggplant from the oven and arrange on a serving platter. Sprinkle with toasted sesame seeds.

Variation

Tofu Dengaku

In Japan, a two pronged pick, which helps to keep the tofu intact, is inserted into tofu rectangles and sweet miso sauce, *Dengaku*, is swirled over the top. The mini skewers are grilled, broiled and decorative aromatic garnishes is set atop each piece. I have adapted this by setting the tofu on a baking sheet and broiling the tofu instead of grilling. Slip a spatula under the bars of tofu and set on a plate with 3 of your favorite aromatics.

1 block firm tofu

1 Set the tofu on a microwave safe plate and place in the microwave for 2 minutes.
2 Drain the water from the plate and pat the tofu dry with a paper towel.
3 Cut the tofu in half horizontally. Cut each half into 6 rectangles. Pat them dry with a paper towel.
4 Pour cornstarch on a small plate. Dip each rectangle into the cornstarch and coat each side. Set on a plate. Proceed cooking as with the eggplant, frying both sides.
5 Brush the top with the *Dengaku* sauce and set under the broiler, as with the eggplant for 30 seconds or until a light caramelized crust forms.

Eriko's Simmered Eggplant Nasu no Nimono

I love eggplant. It is my favorite vegetable and my favorite color. Even my kitchen cabinets are purple! I adore every shade from lavender to the deep royal *aubergine*. My friend Junko Joho "J.J." calls it "Debbie-color." My dear Japanese "sister," Eriko, taught me how to make this dish. The small eggplants are initially cooked in a bit of oil and then sprinkled with sugar, forming a caramelized crust. They are then simmered in Dashi (Fish Stock) and seasonings with dried red pepper, until they are as soft as feather pillows. A drop lid cover (*otoshibuta*) is set on the simmering eggplants to keep the liquid concentrated towards the vegetables. A piece of parchment or aluminum foil will work as well. Japanese eggplants are small and slim, and their skins are tender. This matters because in this recipe the vegetable is not peeled. They most closely resemble Italian eggplants in length and Chinese eggplants in width. Use either variety for this recipe.

6 Japanese or Italian eggplants (small and
   narrow)
3 cups (750 ml) water
2 teaspoons salt
3 tablespoons canola oil
1½ tablespoons sugar
1 small dried red pepper, chopped or ¼
   teaspoon red pepper flakes
1 cup (250 ml) water
2½ tablespoons soy sauce
Parchment paper or aluminum foil

1 Cut eggplant in half length-wise. Lightly score the skin side with lattice marks.
2 In a large bowl add water and salt. Add eggplant and soak for 10 minutes.
3. Remove eggplant and dry thoroughly with paper towels.
4 In a large sauce pan, heat the oil over medium heat.
5 Place skin side down and fry for 2 minutes until skin begins to separate and turn light brown. Turn over and cook an additional 2 minutes.
6 Add sugar and continue to cook the eggplant, turning once, until crust begins to form.
7 Add 1 cup (250 ml) of water and the dried red pepper.
8 Bring to a boil and place aluminum foil or parchment paper directly on the eggplant. Lower the heat and simmer for 10 minutes, until the eggplant is soft.
9 Remove the foil and add the soy sauce.
10 Raise the heat, returning it to a boil and cover with foil again.
11 Cook for an additional 5 minutes or until most of the liquid is absorbed.
12 Serve hot or cold with remaining sauce.

Tofu and Vegetable Scramble Iri Dofu

This is Tofu 101, folks. When people tell me they don't like tofu, I always recommend this dish. In the early nineties, during one of our extended stays in Tokyo, I spent several afternoons cooking alongside a highly-skilled Japanese home cook, who shared several recipes with me—though all in Japanese! After arduously translating her recipes, I began to make them at home for my family. Over the years many of them have become favorites, this one being at the top of the list. I include this in every introductory Japanese cooking class I teach. Tofu simmers alongside carrots, shiitake, and green beans in a sweet stock, absorbing the flavors of the cooking liquid, like a sponge. Finally, beaten eggs blanket the surface before being folded into the sumptuous mixture. I have "westernized" the texture and look of this dish by making all the ingredients a bit chunkier than the Japanese original; I like the mouth-feel of these larger pieces. This is Japanese comfort food. Maybe it is one of the reasons I like it so much, scrambled eggs are my comfort food. My friend, Grace Niwa, must have also appreciated the homey and somewhat rustic feel of this dish because, after helping prepare this dish one day, the first thing she said after tasting a spoonful was, "I'm making this for my kids!" Music to a teacher's ears!

Serve this as the main course in a vegetarian meal with tofu as the protein along side a bowl of brown rice and Classic Miso Soup (p. 81). Your course work is complete!

Tofu and Vegetable Scramble

Serves 4
Prep Time 30 minutes
Cooking Time 15 minutes

3 dried shiitake mushrooms, reconstituted in 1 cup (250 ml) water, reserve the soaking liquid
One 16 oz (500 g) block firm tofu
1 tablespoon canola oil
1 large carrot, cut in matchstick strips
8 green beans, blanched, sliced diagonally into 3 pieces (½ cup edamame, green peas, or pea pods)
2 tablespoons soy sauce
2 tablespoons sake
4 tablespoons sugar
½ teaspoon salt
2 large eggs, beaten

1 Soak the shiitake mushrooms in water for 20 minutes or until soft. Remove and rinse the mushrooms and slice into matchstick strips. Reserve the soaking liquid.
2 To drain water from the tofu, place on a microwaveable plate or bowl and heat for 2 minutes. With a slotted spoon or spatula transfer the tofu to a medium size bowl and discard the liquid. With your fingers, break the tofu into large chunks and set aside.
3 Add the oil to a medium size skillet, and place over medium heat. Add the carrots and mushrooms. Stir-fry for one minute. Add the tofu and continue to stir-fry for another 2 minutes. The tofu will break apart into large "crumbs."
4 Carefully pour ½ cup (125 ml) reserved mushroom liquid into a bowl,

Steamed Fresh Asparagus with Soy Mustard Dressing

Preparing these vegetables is a very simple thing. Set a few steamed spears on a dish, with their stalks peeled, and drizzle on a wasabi soy sauce (what I call the "little black dress" for steamed vegetables). The bright green color of the asparagus will be set off by a puddle of brown soy sauce seasoned with wasabi. I first had a dish like this during a springtime visit to a country inn in the mountainous Nagano prefecture. The innkeeper served the dressing on *zenmai*, wild fiddlehead ferns with long stalks and coiled tops. I look forward to the brief season for fiddlehead ferns in New England and make this dish as often as I can.

You can also use a flavored butter, seasoned with wasabi and soy sauce to create a richer sauce. I keep a small log of this in my refrigerator and use it when broiling fish, on top of boiled potatoes, or on any steamed vegetables.

Serves 4
Prep Time: 15 minutes
Cooking Time: 5 minutes

1 lb (500 g) fresh asparagus, trimmed
　　and stalks peeled
2 cups (500 ml) water
1 teaspoon sea salt or kosher salt
½-1 teaspoon wasabi powder + 2 tea-
　　spoons water or wasabi paste to taste
2 tablespoons soy sauce
2 teaspoons toasted sesame seeds

1 Cut off the tough part of the asparagus stalk and discard. Peel the stalk with a vegetable peeler. This extra step has everything to do with the mouth feel and chewing experience. It does make a difference—try it.
2 Put 1 cup water and salt in a large skillet with a lid and bring to a boil over medium heat. Add the asparagus and cover the skillet. Reduce the heat to low and cook for 2 minutes. Turn off the heat and let the asparagus steam for another minute. Cooking time will vary with the thickness of the stalk.
3 Have a bowl of 1 cup ice water on hand. With a pair of tongs, remove the asparagus from the cooking liquid and plunge into the water to stop the cooking. This will retain the beautiful green color. Set paper towels on a baking sheet. Remove the spears from the water and drain on the paper towel. Arrange on a platter. Whisk the mustard and soy sauce together in a bowl and drizzle.

Wasabi Soy Sauce Butter

I was inspired to make this after reading about flavored butters on the website for Plugra European-Style Butter. I had a small jar of the Wasabi Soy Sauce Butter in the fridge and all I had to do was add it to softened butter for a new dimension to seasoning vegetables, broiled fish, and pasta. Unlike wasabi *joyu*, which can be added, like a dressing, to cold or room temperature vegetables, flavored butters should be added while the food is hot.

1 stick (½ cup/125 g) unsalted butter
　　softened
2 teaspoons wasabi paste or powder
　　or to taste
1 tablespoon soy sauce

Combine the softened butter, wasabi, and soy sauce in a small mixing bowl. Mash together with a fork. Form into a log and wrap in plastic wrap or wax paper. Chill for several hours in the refrigerator. Cut desired amount from the log, toss with hot asparagus or fiddleheads and serve immediately.

leaving behind the sediment. Add soy sauce, sake, sugar, and salt. Mix until dissolved. Pour this over the tofu and vegetables. Cook for one minute until the liquid is bubbling. Add the green beans.
5 Turn the heat to medium high and continue cooking until almost all of the liquid has been absorbed and the green beans are just done.
6 Drizzle the egg over the entire surface. Cook for one minute and turn off the heat. Gently fold the egg into the tofu. Serve hot or at room temperature with short grain white or brown rice.

Sweet Potato Tempura Fritters

Japanese sweet potatoes are great for making vegetable *tempura*. They have a rosy red skin and a sweet flesh that cooks in minutes. It is almost always part of a vegetable tempura display. The western sweet potato or yam, with its bright orange flesh, is just as attractive, and makes a caramel-y and rustic substitute. The Tempura Batter is a light coat of crunch. Although we always think of tempura as hot-out-of-the-pot fare, it often is included as an element in bento lunch boxes.

Yield 8-10 pieces
Prep Time: 15 minutes
Cooking Time: 3 minutes each batch

Oil for deep-frying
1 large sweet potato or yam, cut into 2 in (5 cm) rounds

Tempura Batter
¾ cup (200 ml) ice water
1 egg yolk
⅔ cup (100 g) cake flour or regular white flour
2 tablespoons cornstarch

For Sprinkling
1 tablespoon sea salt or kosher salt for sprinkling
Matcha salt

1 Have on a hand a wire cake rack set on a baking sheet. Make the Tempura Batter by whisking together the ice water and egg yolk in a large mixing bowl until frothy. Add the flour and cornstarch and whisk until combined but not smooth.
2 Pour the oil in a wok or large sauce pan and heat over medium heat until you see ripples on the surface and the oil reaches 350°F (175°C).
3 When you think the oil is ready, dip a chopstick or fork into the batter and drip the batter into the hot oil. The drops should sizzle and float.
4 Pick up a slice of sweet potato with a pair of chopsticks, tongs or long fork and dip the sweet potato slice into the batter and slip it into the hot oil. Repeat with 4 or 5 more slices. Fry for about 3 minutes, turning the sweet potato periodically until it turns light brown.
5 Set the sweet potatoes on the wire cake rack.
6 Repeat until all the potatoes are done. Serve with plain or *matcha* salt.
The batter can be used for most vegetables—try green peppers, shiitake, and *shiso* leaves.

Japanese Mushroom Mélange with Butter and Soy

Patricia Gercik, the life of any party, was hosting a Japanese dinner soirée at her home in Cambridge, Massachusetts. I provided the fixings for hand rolled sushi and she did everything else. Pat grew up in postwar Japan, shadowing the family cook and learning to speak fluent Japanese.

We enclosed a mélange of Japanese mushrooms dotted with butter and soy sauce, in an aluminum packet and popped it in the oven. When ready, as I opened the packet, the rich smell of mushrooms and soy sauce rose up with the steam. We tipped the mushrooms and their juices into one of Pat's antique *imari* bowls and set it on the table. Her work still brings her to Japan, and when I asked her about this recipe she told me that she charmed it out of the chef in an elegant Tokyo restaurant. That's so Pat!

Mushrooms, a natural source of glutamates, provide that savory fifth taste, *umami*. I mix mushrooms with a variety of textures and shapes (they don't need to be all Japanese): Use *enoki*, with its long, thin, white stems and diminutive tops; *shimeji* and *himeji*, with little caps and thicker stems that grow in clumps; meaty shiitake mushrooms; and the now standard baby portabellas and white mushrooms. When they are available, I also use any of the exotics, like Trumpet (*eringhe*) or Oyster Mushrooms. Some of these varieties are thought to have healthful qualities that aid in circulation, digestion, and disease prevention.

This is a hard dish to plan because you never know when you are going to find such a rich variety of mushrooms. Bake them in the oven in parchment paper or aluminum foil. Open the packet and "ooh-mami!" The natural juices mingle with the butter and soy sauce for an intense, earthy, burst of aroma. Spoon the mushrooms over tofu, salmon, or just plain rice.

Serves 4
Prep Time: 10 minutes
Cooking Time: 20 minutes

2 lb (1 kg) of mushroom mixture: *enoki*, *shimeji*, fresh shiitake, baby portabella, white, trumpet, oyster
2 tablespoons unsalted butter
1-2 tablespoons soy sauce
Salt, to taste

1 Set oven to 350°F (175°C). Take a 10 by 13-inch (25 x 32.5 cm) piece of parchment paper or aluminum foil and set on a baking sheet.
2 Trim the thick ends of the *enoki*, *shimeji*, and oyster mushrooms leaving most of the length of the stem intact. Gently pull them apart leaving them in small clumps. For the shiitake, white, and portabella mushrooms, remove the stems. Wipe the caps with a damp paper towel and cut the large ones in quarters and the smaller caps in half.

3 Pile the mushrooms together in the center of the foil. Cut the butter into 1-inch (2.5 cm) cubes. Dot the mushrooms with the butter and drizzle on the soy sauce.
4 Take the long sides of the parchment paper and bring together up over the mushrooms and fold closed. Roll each end toward the center crimping the edges as you go, enclosing the packet.
5 Place the cookie sheet on the middle rack of the oven and bake for 15 minutes.
6 Remove the mushrooms from the oven. Carefully unfold the packet at the top and check to see that the mushrooms are soft.
7 Serve the mushrooms and their juices over tofu as a side dish to grilled fish or eat with brown or white rice.

Pumpkin Rounds Kabocha no Chakin

This looks like pure Americana but I got this recipe from Takako Suzuki, the wife of the former Consul-General of Japan in Boston. While I was teaching a Thanksgiving cooking class to an International Women's group, Takako showed us how to shape mashed pumpkin into the shape of a *chakin* (purse) using a piece of plastic wrap. She twisted the wrap around the mashed vegetable, making a pumpkin! She took a green pea, set it on top, and everyone "oohed." *Kabocha* means both pumpkin and is a variety of squash. In the States we often see it labeled as *kabocha* pumpkin—"pumpkin pumpkin," as it were. It is difficult to peel, but the flavor is worth the effort. The traditional way to serve *kabocha* is in wedges with a bit of skin left on, and simmered in a sweet Dashi (Fish Stock) broth. The deep orange flesh has less moisture, making it perfect for this preparation.

I have tried this with butternut squash, which has higher water content, and found it difficult to handle. Acorn squash is too stringy. If you can't find *kabocha*, use the buttercup variety, but you will have to continue cooking it after it is mashed to evaporate the moisture. This recipe also works with sweet potatoes or yams. It is great for your Thanksgiving table or a bento lunch box but is delicious anytime of the year.

Pumpkin Rounds

Makes about 12 3-inch (7.5 cm) rounds
Prep Time: 45 minutes
Cooking Time: 25 minutes

1 kabocha, 1½ lb (750 g) (about 2 cups pureed)
1½ cups (375 ml) Dashi (Fish Stock) (p. 35) or kelp (*kombu*) stock
½ cup (125 ml) water
1 tablespoon sugar
½ teaspoon salt
1 tablespoon butter
1 teaspoon soy sauce
12 edamame or green peas, cooked

1 Cut the *kabocha* in half with a chef's knife. With a spoon, scoop out and discard the seeds.
2 Cut into large chunks. Set the flat side of a chunk on a cutting board, and carefully slice away the tough skin. (Alternatively you can cook this with the skin on and scoop out the flesh after it is cooked through.)
3 Add the stock, water, sugar, and salt in a medium saucepan. Add the *kabocha* pieces and bring to a boil.
4 Reduce the heat to medium low and continue cooking until all the liquid is absorbed and the *kabocha* is fork tender.
5 Turn the *kabocha* into a mixing bowl and add the butter and soy sauce. With a potato masher, mash the flesh until soft. A ricer or food mill will also work.
6 Tear off a 3-inch (7.5 cm) square of plastic wrap.
7 Scoop ¼ cup (65 ml) of the mashed *kabocha* and place it in the center of the wrap.
8 Bring up all the sides and gently twist until you have a round pumpkin shape. You should see vertical indentations. Open the package and set the pumpkin on a serving platter. Continue to use the plastic wrap for the remaining *kabocha*. If it becomes too messy, tear off another piece.
9 Garnish each with a cooked edamame bean or a pea.

Okra with Umeboshi and Katsuo Shreds

I came across this recipe about ten years ago while flipping through a Japanese women's magazine called *Orange Page*. I was attracted to the combination of the sour pickled plum (*umeboshi*) and okra. The green pods are blanched to loosen the seeds and all that gooey goodness.

Serves 4
Prep Time: 10 minutes
Cooking Time: 3 minutes

12 okra pods
¼ teaspoon salt
1 Japanese pitted sour plum (*umeboshi*)
¼ red bell pepper, finely chopped
1 tablespoon shredded bonito flakes (*katsuo-bushi*)
1 teaspoon soy sauce

1 Trim the top of the okra. Be careful not to cut into the pod.
2 Fill a medium saucepan half way with water and add the salt. Over medium heat, bring the water to a boil. Add the okra and lower the heat. Simmer for 3 minutes.
3 Set a colander in the sink and drain the okra. Rinse under cold water. Slice the okra into ¼-inch (6 mm) rounds and set in a mixing bowl.
4 Cut the sour plum in half and remove the pit. Mash with a fork and combine with the okra. Add the red bell pepper and bonito flakes with a dash of soy sauce. Divide among 4 small bowls for individual servings.

Sliced Okra with Wasabi Soy Dressing

Prep Time: 15 minutes
Cooking Time: 3 minutes

½ lb (250 g) okra pods
1 teaspoon salt
2 tablespoons soy sauce
1 teaspoon wasabi paste or more to taste

1 Trim the top of the okra, and slice into ¼-inch (6 mm) rounds. Fill a small saucepan half way with water. Add the salt and bring to a boil.
2 Add the okra to the boiling water. Reduce the heat to medium. Cook for 3 minutes or until the okra loses its raw texture but is still crunchy.
3 Set a colander in the sink and drain the okra. Place the okra in a mixing bowl.
4 Combine the soy sauce and wasabi paste in a small bowl, whisk together until smooth. Pour over the okra and mix.

AN ODE TO OKRA

I know, I know—you either hate okra or you love it. Personally, I love the textured combination of the crunchy green pod and viscous insides, as well as the pretty star-shapes when it's sliced—okra has so much character. Both of these little salads can be served as accompaniments, or as a topping for rice or stir-fried tofu. You can use frozen pre-cut okra.

Tofu Hot Pot with All the Trimmings Yudofu

Tofu has become my comfort food. If I find myself on my own with no one to cook for, I almost always make a tofu dish. Since tofu is the star of this show, make sure to get the highest quality available. While living in Japan I had access to fresh tofu just steps from our apartment. I ate it right out of its bath of water—nothing could be more pure. In the summer, I prepare it cold and uncooked in a dish called Cold Tofu and Toppings (*Hiyayakko*) (see inset below), and in winter I make the hot pot, as *Yudofu*.

Use the silken (smooth) or a medium-firm texture. I strongly prefer fresh tofu or an Asian brand, like the Japanese House Brand or the Korean Pulmuone. However, the quality and options of tofu available in general supermarkets is getting better. The Japanese Mori-nu Company makes a shelf-stable tofu that comes in a carton and in a variety of textures. Buy a few boxes so you can always have some on hand. I have seen this on the shelf of my local supermarkets in Boston.

Tofu simmers in a kelp (*kombu*) broth in a clay pot (*nabe*) set on a table top burner. It needn't be Japanese. I picked up this earthenware, *muqueca*, for $20 at a Brazilian market in Boston. Although it is supposed to be used for a seafood pilaf—it's perfect for this homey dish!

The tofu can be cooked on its own without any additions, but for a more filling and tasty version use leeks and Chinese (Napa) cabbage. Set a bowl before each diner with small dishes of condiments of grated ginger, feathery bonito fish flakes, minced green onions (scallions), and soy sauce dressing, to add to your tofu canvas. A deep electric skillet will also work or make this in your stovetop casserole and bring it piping hot to the table

Serves 4
Prep Time: 30 minutes
Cooking Time: 20 minutes

4 cakes medium tofu (about 2 lb/1 kg), sliced into 4 pieces each for a total of 16 pieces
1 small head (1½ lb/750 g) Chinese (Napa) cabbage, cut into quarters, and then 3 in (7.5 cm) pieces
3 leeks, rinsed and sliced on the diagonal into 2 in (5 cm) pieces
4 cups (1 liter) cold water
3-in (7.5-cm) piece kelp (*kombu*)

Toppings

½ cup (5 g) shredded bonito (*katsuo*) flakes
2 tablespoons grated ginger
4 green onions (scallions), minced
Japanese red pepper powder (*togarashi*) or Shichimi 7 Spice Powder

Sauce

4 tablespoons low sodium soy sauce
2 tablespoons Dashi (Fish Stock) (p. 35)
2 tablespoons mirin

1 Put the ingredients for the Sauce mixture into a small saucepan over medium heat, bring the mixture to a boil. Divide Sauce into 4 bowls.
2 Set the toppings into individual serving dishes for each diner.
3. Arrange the tofu, cabbage and leeks on a large platter and set on the table.
4 Add the water and *kombu* to a large tabletop casserole or pot and let it sit for 15 minutes. Add half of the leeks to the casserole and cook over medium-low heat for 15 minutes.
5 Add 8 pieces of tofu and half the Chinese cabbage to the casserole. Increase the heat to medium and let the dish come to a boil. Reduce the heat to medium low and simmer for 5 minutes.
6 As the ingredients are ready, each diner serves themselves by placing the tofu, Chinese cabbage, and leeks into individual bowls. Add the toppings and drizzle on the Sauce.
7 Replenish the tofu, cabbage, and leeks to the pot until done.

Cold Tofu and Toppings (*Hiyayakko*)
A warm weather remedy for flagging appetites, *Hiyayakko*, is the purest way to enjoy tofu. Soft or silken tofu is the best texture for this dish. Cut 1 block of soft or silken tofu into 4 pieces and arrange and set in 4 bowls. Top with grated ginger, minced green onions (scallions), and shredded *katsuo*. Drizzle soy sauce over the top and serve.

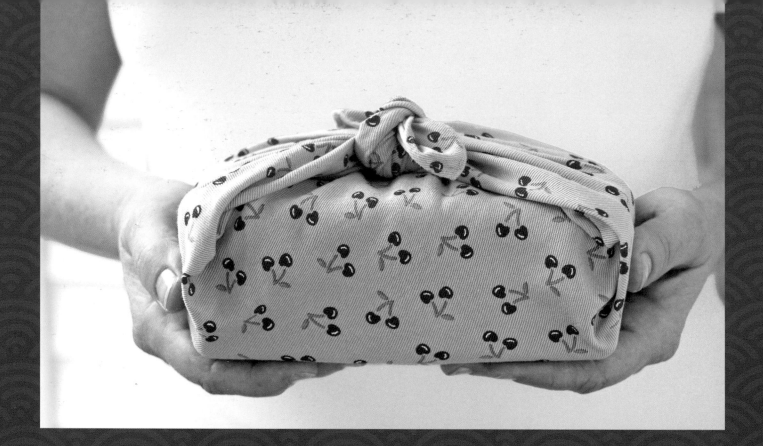

Chapter Eight

Bento

She undoes the decorative knot carefully and lets the crisp pink cotton cloth unfurl around the box. Lifting the lid, she smiles at the beautiful arrangement of delicate bites. A bright red tomato cup is set in a corner with tuna salad tucked into its center. Resting next to it is a flower carved from a carrot, its leaves are made from a cucumber. Pinwheels of bread, cheese, and ham nest against a bundle of steamed asparagus tips set in a lemony dressing. Blueberries cluster around juicy watermelon orbs and a sprig of mint gives off a pleasant aroma. High tea at an upscale restaurant? Nope. Just standard lunchtime fare for many school age children in Japan.

These aesthetics are not lost on a five-year-old. To the contrary, the Japanese box lunch (bento) is a powerful symbol of culture and values, like effort and obligation. The person who prepared the meal made the effort; the one who it was made for is obliged to appreciate that and is expected to eat the meal in its entirety. The planning and execution of a bento is the same for a 5-year-old as it is for a 50-year-old. Nutritional and caloric needs are always considered, the contents are always arranged in an eye-catching fashion, and the yum factor is always high. *Bento bako*, the compartmentalized box, and all of the accompanying accoutrement, is big business in Japan. From kitschy to streamline; made from plastic or wood, there is a box that can fit every design and dietary desire. The boxes usually have two tiers, with dividers for separating food and controlling portion sizes. Unless you fill both layers with chocolate, it is hard to over eat. When you are done with the meal, the box, like a Transformer toy, collapses back into a single layer. Pure genius. There are molds in the shapes of flowers, cartoon characters, soccer balls, animals, and fans for making attractive rice balls and sandwiches. Fancy toothpicks, silly toothpicks, and mini containers for soy sauce and dressings are part of the clever cache of items all designed to be an inviting part of the mealtime experience.

Ready made bento is available at all convenience stores, railway stations (*eki-ben*), and food emporia. Even busy restaurants offer this classy take-out. Books and magazines, with endless recipes, tips, and short cuts, are devoted to the subject and take up shelf space in bookstores and newsstands. A mom might make lunch for her school age or adult children, her husband, and herself—all before leaving for work. There are magazine and books aimed at single men encouraging them to prepare their own bento instead of the less nutritious bowl of noodles for lunch. Historically a simple bento used to consist mostly of rice or rice balls, (*onigiri* or *omusubi*) wrapped in roasted seaweed and accompanied by some pickles—the perfect portable meal. Elegant and sumptuous repasts were prepared for the upper classes for a flower-viewing picnic. Today however, I like to think of bento as a food sampler. Rice still may take up a fair amount of real estate in an bento but it is the colorful side dishes that, taken together, make the whole. Bento is a state of mind that emphasizes variety with balance and presentation. A properly constructed bento involves selecting foods of five different colors—red, black, yellow, green, and white—that are associated with the five elements—wood, fire, earth, metal, and water—and that correspond to five important human organs—liver, heart, stomach, lungs, and kidney and the five tastes—sour, bitter, sweet, hot, and salty. As you can see, this system is more complicated than our "food pyramid," but it serves the same function, ensuring a balanced meal.

Wondering how best to depict this system of balance for a western audience, I happened on an exhibit in an elegant Tokyo mall sponsored by the Japan Association of Graphic Designers called *Tabemono no Nuno* (food cloths). There, to my surprise and delight, the very first item I encountered in a creative exhibit of cloths used to wrap bento boxes was one that literally depicted this five-color concept (p. 143). How serendipitous! The artist, Shoji Morishige, designed this cloth so that when his son went to college he would be reminded what constitutes a good meal. Morishige-san said he has very fond memories of going fishing as a kid and sitting on a rock, legs dangling toward the ocean, and opening his simple bento lunch and feeling his mother's love.

One key to a good bento is having good leftovers. Another is time for a bit of planning. I spent a day with Junko Ogawa who shared several tips for making great bento lunches. She moved swiftly, using containers of her own sauces, homemade pickles, and meatballs, and salads from her refrigerator. She put up the rice cooker, and in minutes we had an assembly project. Junko reminded me that bento food must taste good hot or cold and that a variety of cooking methods is important: grilled, steamed, fried, etc. This is a thoughtful process.

Like Japanese anime, bento has gone global. Hundreds of recipe-sharing websites are devoted to bento in many languages and "chara-ben," or character bento, be it a samurai or Spiderman, is an art form for all ages. Books are widely available in English, and Asian grocers carry bento boxes. But you can also find perfectly suitable substitutes with built in dividers, tops with cubbies to stash utensils, and ice packs in your local supermarkets, kitchen shops, and camping outfitters thanks to what I call the Japanification of our plastic ware. Add a few extras, like silicon baking cups and mini containers, to fill out this improvised bento-ware collection. I raided my linen drawer for one-off large cloth napkins and also found colorful bandanas that work perfectly as the wrapper/mat. I have organized this chapter around a variety of situations where you find it necessary to pack a portable meal. You will find recipes for some of the ingredients in other chapters in this book. Not all the food is Japanese, but that is also true in Japan, and as I have explained, it is all about getting into an bento state of mind.

Bento Equipment

Bento gear and lunchbox culture, long established in Japan, have now gone global. Websites in multiple languages are devoted to this perfect portable meal, and to its preparation and paraphernalia. Bento boxes are compact, compartmentalized, and utilitarian. Of course, they can also be cute, cool, and chic.

You can find a limited variety of bento boxes at Asian markets and an unlimited variety online. But you can also find suitable stand-ins for both the boxes and the eating utensils in the plastic ware section in supermarkets and department stores, or and in the camping gear sections in sporting good stores. Many of these containers now have built-in (or removable) ice packs to keep food fresh.

Use colorful bandanas to wrap and carry these boxes Japanese-style, and then lay them out to do double duty as placemats. Check out the Resource Guide (p. 173) to find blogs and sources to get you started. I have focused only on cold lunches in this chapter, but there are many options for hot meals as well.

Helpful Bento Tips

Give the brown paper bag the sack and get into a bento state of mind! My friend, Patricia Hiramatsu, introduced me to Junko Ogawa when I told her I wanted to include a chapter on bento in this book. The three of us spent an afternoon together in the kitchen and house wares section of a Tokyo department store filled with bento paraphernalia. A few weeks later we made bento for her college age daughter in Junko's chic and compact kitchen. Junko's refrigerator was filled with transparent containers of cooked foods, home-made sauces, and ready-to-use garnishes. "Having these on hand makes my life easy," she explained. Junko is all about speed and efficiency and apologized for not making cute bento. But, they were colorful, nutritious, delicious, and attractive—who needs cute? Here are Junko's guidelines—I call them her "High Five." They were formed by years of practice and by a wonderful Japanese book: *Obento no Hiketsu* (*The Secret of Obento*), by Atsuko Matsumoto (Bunka Shuppan Kyoku, 2005.)

When choosing foods think about:
1 Five colors: white, black, green, red, and yellow
2 Five flavors: hot, sour, bitter, sweet, and salty
3 Five cooking methods: stir-fry, simmer, deep fry, steam, and roast (grill)
4 The food has to taste good cold.
5 Prepare in advance

When constructing the bento:
1 Drain liquids from the food.
2 Avoid mixing flavors by keeping foods separated in aluminum cups, lettuce dividers, etc.
3 Pack the food in tightly so there is no empty space for it to move around.
4 Cool food down before adding it to the bento.
5 If there is an element missing from the box include it in a drink: e.g., fruit or vegetable juices.

Junko's bento components:
1 Main dish
2 Cooked vegetable
3 Fresh Vegetable
4 Rice or Bread
5 Fruit or Sweet

Junko's top 5 bento recipes:
1 Chicken, pork, or meatballs boiled in water with ginger and leek. Store in cooking liquid in fridge or freezer.
2 Stir-fry vegetables and finish with a combination of bonito powder (without salt if available) and soy sauce, or use

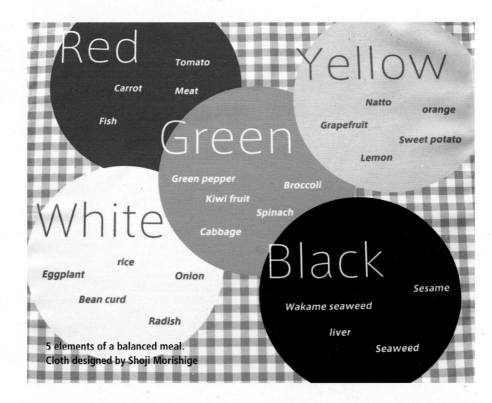

5 elements of a balanced meal.
Cloth designed by Shoji Morishige

curry powder and salt.
3 Make Seasoned Omelet Wedges (p. 34) with a variety of fillings: fried leeks, ground beef, or tuna.
4 Nori Rice: Dip small sheets of roasted seaweed in soy sauce. Alternate layers of them with layers of rice. Make sure a layer of nori ends up on top. The nori helps keep the rice moist.

Five flavorful sauces:
1 Ketchup: mixed with soy sauce, **or** Worcestershire sauce, **or** mayonnaise.

2 Miso paste mixed with yogurt—good for marinating fish or for marinating vegetables for a quick overnight pickle.
3 Thinly slice aromatics and herbs like leek, ginger, *shiso*, and parsley; soak them in cold water for 5 minutes. Wrap in a paper towel and keep in plastic ware in the refrigerator for garnishes and for a flavor punch.
4 Sweet and Sour Dressing: rice vinegar, sugar, salt, and dashi powder.
5 Sweet Soy Sauce: soy sauce, sake, mirin, and Dashi (Fish Stock).

Elementary School Sampler Bento

This VW beetle lunchbox was my son Brad's bento vehicle when he was a first grader in a Japanese elementary school. But he got it only after I sent him to school with a peanut butter and jelly sandwich, carrot sticks and a whole apple in a brown paper bag and he came home in tears. "I want a cute lunch like the other kids," he sobbed. Next day I put the same thing in a McDonald's kid's meal box, thinking that's pretty cute. "Not cute enough," he moaned when he returned the next day. Being the only foreigner, he wanted to fit in with his classmates, so I had no choice but to learn about bento. We picked out a book, *100 Obento Ideas*, and I worked my way through it for the rest of the school year. And what was the first lunch he picked out? A bologna sandwich! But it was the face of a little boy, bologna bangs and all. It didn't have to be Japanese food, but he needed a sampler that was delicious and, of course, cute.

These pinwheel sandwiches are stuffed with slices of cheese, vegetables and cold cuts. Brad used to call it "bread sushi." I also pack them for our grown ups' picnics, with slices of smoked salmon or roast beef. Cocktail franks are a standard side in Japanese kids' lunchboxes, but they are cut creatively into the shape of octopuses or flowers. Figuring they are cute enough on their own, I just score the little critters and stir-fry them in a little ketchup. Using an assortment of food is a must—green grapes alone would be fine, but try combining them with red ones. Tuck in a sweet treat like a cookie or chocolate covered raisins. Even if they start with that (you will never know) it's not enough to ruin an appetite. Don't underestimate the value of eye appeal—even for a five-year-old.

THE MENU
Pinwheel Sandwiches
Mini Cocktail Franks
Carrot Sticks
Red and Green Grapes

Pinwheel Sandwiches

Prepare these the night before and place in the refrigerator. All you have to do is slice in the morning.

Makes 4 servings
Prep Time: 30 minutes

12 slices of white or whole wheat bread, crusts removed
Plastic wrap
2 tablespoons butter or cream cheese, softened
4 leaves of soft leaf lettuce, rinsed and dried
4 slices of smoked salmon turkey, or ham
4 slices of cheddar, muenster, or American cheese

½ red, yellow, or green bell pepper, cut into 8 strips or
8 cucumber strips, watercress, or spicy sprouts

For the Spread:
2 tablespoons butter or cream cheese, softened or ¼ cup (65 ml) light mayonnaise mixed with 1 teaspoon mustard or tarragon

1 Set 3 slices of bread, in a vertical row, on top of a piece of plastic wrap. Set the wrap on a cutting board.
2 Take a rolling pin and flatten the bread. Spread lightly with softened butter or cream cheese or mayonnaise mixture.
3 Take the bread closest to you and overlap with the middle slice by ¼ inch (6 mm). Press the seam closed. Then take the middle slice and overlap it ¼ inch (6 mm) with the top slice. Press the seam together.
4 Place one lettuce leaf on the slice of bread closest to you. Overlap on the top of the lettuce the salmon, turkey, or ham on top of the second slice of bread.
5 Take the cheese, and overlapping with the meat slightly, set it on the third piece of bread.

6 Take the peppers (or sprouts) and set them, end-to-end, one third up from the bottom on the meat.
7 Lift the plastic wrap and the first slice of bread and roll the sandwich forward over the vegetables. Stop and press the bread together. Lift the plastic wrap and keep moving the bread forward until you have a complete roll. Wrap the plastic around the entire roll and twist the ends.
8 Repeat with the remaining ingredients. Chill for at least 2 hours or overnight.
9 Slice the roll in half, through the plastic wrap. Then cut into quarters and you will end up with 4 rounds.

Mini Cocktail Franks

These little links are a tasty addition to a kid's lunch. Score the tops with hatch marks and fry them in a non-stick pan over medium heat with a teaspoon of oil for one minute on each side. Add a teaspoon of ketchup and heat an additional minute until they get crisp and caramelize. Let them cool down before setting them into the lunch box.

Office Lunch Bento

If there is one thing that always tastes great the next day it is cold meatloaf. I usually make several small ones to keep in the freezer for quick lunches. Japanese-style meat loaf and hamburgers have a soft texture because they are made from a combination of beef, pork, bread, and eggs. The sauce can be anything from a ketchup and soy glaze to Teriyaki Sauce (p. 32) or a Sweet-and-Sour Sauce made from Sushi Dressing and ketchup. I also use ground turkey for a healthier and lower fat alternative to beef and pork.

Another "meat loaf" recipe came to me one day when I found myself with about a cup (250 g) of leftover filling for Japanese Pot Stickers (p. 64) and no more wrappers. I made a log out of the seasoned ground pork and chives, wrapped it in plastic to chill in the fridge. I am not keen on microwaving in plastic wrap so I cooked it in parchment paper in the microwave. For a sauce I used the classic dumpling dipping sauce—a blend of soy sauce, rice vinegar, and chili oil. Pretty clever of me I thought. But when flipping through a Japanese bento magazine there was a recipe for a microwave meat log! Sure enough (*yappari*)!

Make the mini-loaves and freeze them whole. Cut them when they are partially defrosted and set the slices on a soft lettuce leaf bed in your lunch container. This will keep your food cold until you are ready to eat. For easy eating, everything should be pre-cut. The Potato Salad, made with carrots and Japanese Kewpie brand mayonnaise, is creamy and delicious.

THE MENU
Mini meat loaf with Teriyaki Glaze
Japanese-style Potato Salad
Spicy Tuna Salad in Mini Tomato
Tricolor Cauliflower
Strawberries

Teriyaki Meat Loaf

Makes 3 loaves
Prep Time: 20 minutes
Cooking Time: 25-30 minutes

1 slice white bread or ½ cup (30 g)
  panko
¼ cup (65 ml) water or milk
¾ lb (375 g) ground beef (or use
  1 lb/500 g ground turkey entirely
  and do not add the pork)
¼ lb (125 g) ground pork
½ small onion, grated
1 large egg, beaten
½ teaspoon salt
¼ teaspoon pepper
½ cup (125 ml) Teriyaki Sauce (p. 32)
1 tablespoon ketchup

1 Combine the bread (or bread crumbs) with the milk or water in a mixing bowl, and let sit for 2 minutes until the liquid is absorbed.
2 Add the ground meat, onion, egg, salt, and pepper to the ground meat. Mix thoroughly.
3 Whisk together the Teriyaki Sauce and ketchup in a small bowl. Add 2 tablespoons to the meat blend and mix well. Set oven to 350°F (175°C).
4 Form 3 loaves (about 6 oz/175 g each) and set in a baking dish or on a foiled-line baking pan. Brush each loaf with the Teriyaki Sauce and baste with the Teriyaki Sauce every 10 minutes for a total of 30 minutes. Insert a knife into the center of one loaf, if the meat is no longer pink, the loaf is done; if not, continue cooking for another 5 minutes or until the meat is done.
5 Pour the remaining sauce in a small saucepan and heat over medium until it begins to bubble.
6 To freeze: pre-cut the meat loaf into slices and set it on a piece of aluminum foil. Drizzle the sauce onto the meat loaf and close the foil packet. Place the loaves in plastic zip top bag and label with contents and date.
7 To defrost: Remove one loaf from the freezer and place it in the refrigerator overnight. Place in the lunch box, semi-frozen. Be sure to separate the slices a bit so they will defrost by the time you are ready to eat. Eat cold or heat just before eating.

Gyoza Pork Loaf

Makes 1 loaf
Prep Time: 10 minutes
Cooking Time: 5-8 minutes

8 oz (250 g) Japanese Pot Sticker
  Filling (p. 64)
Parchment paper
1 teaspoon canola oil
1 tablespoon *Japanese Pot Sticker
  Dipping Sauce (p. 64)*

1 Shape the filling into a log about 4 by 2 inches (10 x 5 cm). Place in plastic wrap and chill in the refrigerator for 1 hour.
2 Tear a piece of parchment paper large enough to fold around the *gyoza* log. Brush the paper with a little bit of canola oil.
3 Unwrap the log and place it in the center of the parchment paper and enclose the loaf by rolling the top down and twisting each end to enclose the log.
4 Microwave on high for 5 minutes. Remove from the oven and carefully open the packet from the top. Check to see if the meat is done in the center. There should be no pinkness to the meat. Continue cooking in 1-minute increments until done.
5 Carefully remove from the packet (there will be lots of hot steam) and set in a pan with its own juices to cool in the refrigerator before slicing. Serve with the dipping sauce.

Japanese-style Potato Salad

Yields 1½ cups (225 g)
Prep Time: 15 minutes
Cooking Time: 10 minutes

1 large egg
1 large potato (2 medium), peeled
  and cut into 2 in (5 cm) chunks
1 carrot, peeled and diced
2 teaspoons rice vinegar
1-2 tablespoons Kewpie mayonnaise (Japanese brand)
1 slice ham, diced into ¼ in (6 mm)
  cubes
Salt and pepper to taste
½ mini-cucumber, cut on the diagonal in ¼ in (6 mm) slices

1 Fill a medium pot halfway with water and bring to a boil. Add the egg and cook for 8 minutes. Remove the egg, peel, chop, and set aside.
2 Add the potatoes and carrot to the boiling water and cook until fork tender. Drain and pour into a medium mixing bowl.
3 Add 2 teaspoons of the rice vinegar to the hot potato and carrot mixture. Mash a small amount of the potato slightly with a fork and mix together. Add the chopped egg, ham, and mayonnaise and mix together. Season with salt and pepper. Divide the potato salad into small cups and garnish with the cucumber.

Tuna Tomato Cups

Slice the top from a mini tomato (not cherry tomatoes) and hollow out the center from the tomato and fill with Spicy Tuna Salad (p. 88).

Traveler's Bento

Eki-ben, short hand for "station (*eki*) bento," is standard fare (couldn't help myself) for Japan's rail travelers. These boxed meals, available in kiosks right on the platform, usually contain regional specialties and are packed with disposable wooden chopsticks (*waribashi*).

American travelers today juggle bulging bags of burritos, salads that spill out of plastic containers, and pizza that drips onto the passenger sitting in the next seat. What a mess! In comparison, *eki-ben* are easy to eat, tasty, and tastefully arranged. I have taken to traveling with my bento box—but I call it *hikoki* (airplane) *ben*. But it can be your bus-*ben*, car-*ben*, or boat-*ben* as well.

Take an assortment of foods, cut them into bite-size pieces and set them into your box. Wrap the box in a cloth napkin or bandana, and pack a fork or chopsticks. It fits right in your carry-on. Use mini bagels cut in half and a slice of dense German bread cut into two triangles. In this box, I mix it up with Seasoned Egg Omelet Wedges (p. 34) and Chicken Balls in Teriyaki Sauce (p. 56), nested alongside. Whole gherkin pickles and olives on a skewer are a salty side. For sweets, a cupcake set in its own cup tucks in nicely with a few cherries. With careful planning this all fits nicely into this two-layered box. It is nothing fancy, but looks like a million bucks. You don't need a lovely bento box—a sturdy plastic container with sections will do—but it is a great conversation starter. I have had seatmates ask me where to buy the box. You can even bring your own green tea bag—airlines still serve hot water don't they?

Yield 1 lunch box
Prep Time: 30 minutes
Cooking Time: 20 minutes

THE MENU
Smoked Salmon and Chive
  Cream Cheese on Mini
  Bagels and Health Bread
Chicken Balls in Teriyaki
  Sauce (p. 56)
Seasoned Egg Omelet
  Wedges (p. 34)
Gherkin pickles and Olive
  Skewers picks
Cherries
Matcha Mochi Cupcake (p.
  162)

NOTE Use silicon baking cups (for cupcakes) for fresh vegetables and fruit. Place dressing or dips in the bottom of the cup and set the vegetables on top of the dressing.

Picnic Bento

We New Englanders are fond of "leaf peeping" in the autumn, but it is nothing quite like *hanami* (cherry blossom viewing), a truly national pleasure. In Japan, weather stations start to track the blossoms from south to north in early March, helping picnic planners choose their destination. And what revelry is in store! Pink arches of blossoms line parks, river walks, and temple grounds. Whole cities become one vast picnic blanket—actually, plastic tarps in most cases. Friends, co-workers, and families eat, drink sake, and sing beneath the floral canopy deep into the night. This elegant stacking box set, called a *jubako*, looks like its traditional lacquered wood, but is actually high quality plastic. I have no problem taking it for a walk in the park. Make your own stacking picnic bento boxes by purchasing re-useable plastic containers with tight fitting lids. Remember you want to open the box and "ooh and eat."

Fried chicken is a picnic favorite everywhere. Here I use drumettes and fry them Japanese Fried Chicken (p. 107). For less of a mess, Japanese moms usually wrap the tip of the leg with a bit of aluminum foil. Edamame cooked in their pods and salted, are a ready appetizer. The sushi balls are perfect with a variety of toppings (Although I never include raw fish on picnics). Or, instead of sushi, I'll make mini-sandwiches with Spicy Tuna Salad (p. 88) or homemade egg salad and potato salad and pre-cut them. Or make a whole layer of Pinwheel Sandwiches (p. 144) with assorted turkey, roast beef, or ham.

Serves 8
Prep Time: 1½-2 hours
Cooking Time: 1 hour

THE MENU
Japanese Fried Chicken (p. 107)
Salted Edamame in the Pod (p. 57)
Hayashi Sensei's Mini Sushi Balls (p. 45)
Steamed Assorted Vegetables with Mozzarella, Mini Tomato and Olive Skewers
Hard Boiled Eggs with Japanese Red Pepper Powder and Homemade Rice Sprinkles (p. 31)
Strawberries, Watermelon Balls, and Cherries

Teen Bento

Moms in Japan still do the bulk of food preparation and make bento according to the age and caloric needs of each family member. Boys'and men's lunches are packed with more calories than girls'and women's, and it is not uncommon to find two carbohydrates, like a sandwich and rice, in one box for a teenage or adult son. The volume of the boxes is also different. In the photo on this page is my friend, "J.J." 's son Ken's bento box that he used throughout his middle and high school years. She gave this to me because she knows I am bonkers for bento boxes and we thought it would be instructive. When J.J. made lunch, one layer would usually hold rice or some kind of rice dish providing the bulk, and the other layer would be a combination of vegetables and a protein. Japanese bento magazines give precise calorie counts and nutritional breakdowns for each recipe and the lunch in total. In my opinion, this is a Japanese national pastime.

It is a challenge to feed older kids. Most don't want to have anything too different from their peers, unless it is really delicious. Fried Pork Cutlets (p. 104) always worked in my house—they are good cold and make a great sandwich. I usually fried up a few extra cutlets when I was preparing this dinner so I could pack them for lunch the next day. Have a package of mini sub rolls in the freezer and make the sandwich with the frozen bread. It's like an ice pack and should be defrosted by lunch time. Variety is key. It makes things easy to eat by pre-cutting—whole fruit often gets thrown out. Oh, and that sprig of mint—it's a breath freshener. What teen doesn't want fresh breath?

THE MENU
Fried Pork Cutlets (p. 104) Sandwich
Steamed Broccoli with Spicy Mayonnaise
    Dressing (p. 28)
Spicy Sweet Potato Fries
Matcha Chocolate Coffee Cake (p. 160)
Watermelon balls and orange wedges

Spicy Sweet Potato Fries

These cook in about 15 minutes in a toaster oven. Make them in the morning.

½ sweet potato, peeled and cut
    into 2 in (5 cm) wedges
1-2 teaspoons canola oil
¼ teaspoon salt
Dash of red pepper powder
    (*togarashi*) or cayenne pepper
Dash of cumin or curry powder

1 Set the oven to 425°F (220°C). Cover the baking tray with aluminum foil. Set the potatoes in a bowl and and drizzle on the oil.
2 Mix the salt, pepper powder, and cumin or curry powder in a small bowl. Sprinkle over the potatoes and toss until they are well coated.
3 Arrange the potatoes on the baking tray and bake for 10-15 minutes or until the potatoes are browned.

Tonkatsu Sandwiches

Makes 2 sandwiches

2 mini sub rolls
1 cooked Fried Pork Cutlet, cut
    into 6 slices
4 soft lettuce leaves (Boston or
    red leaf)
Bull-Dog Sauce or Quick
    Tonkatsu Sauce (p. 32) mixed
    with ketchup

1 Slice rolls horizontally three quarters of the way through. Do not cut completely in half.
2 Set lettuce onto the bread. Arrange 3 slices of pork cutlet on the lettuce.
3 Drizzle the sauce over the cutlet and set in bento box or wrap each individually.

Vegetarian Bento

This is my favorite bento box (below). I love the chrysanthemum pattern and the way the flowers line up when the box is stacked. I walked past this small family owned lacquer-ware shop in the Ueno area of Tokyo every day for the month of January, lingering by the sale table just outside the door, but eyeing this box in the window display. "*Suteki desu ne*" I sighed to the shop keep conveying my desire to own the set. On our final day in Tokyo, when I went on a guerilla buying mission it was my last purchase of the day. I had held out long enough!

Hideko Itoh, our Japanese "niece," groaned when I said I wanted to put tofu in the vegetarian bento. "Why does it always have to be tofu for vegetarians?" She was right, and we decided no tofu in this Vegetarian's Delight! To make it more filling, we designated one layer for Yoshie's Delicious Crab Fried Rice (p. 85) (leave out the crab!). The Pumpkin Rounds (p. 136) fits right in with no wrapping, and mini tomatoes make an edible cup for a filling of egg salad. Marinate the asparagus spears in Wasabi Soy Sauce, (p. 28) and remove them from the marinade before setting in the box. A few berries in a muffin cup add another colorful touch—who needs tofu? But just in case, try the Tofu and Vegetable Scramble (p. 132) and make the bottom layer half rice and half tofu.

THE MENU
Pumpkin Rounds (p. 136)
Mini Tomatoes S tuffed with
  Egg or Tuna Salad
Steamed Fresh Asparagus
  with Soy Mustard Dressing
  (p. 133)
Mixed Berry Salad
Yoshie's Delicious Crab Fried
  Rice (without the crab) (p. 85)

Chapter Nine
Desserts and Drinks

When we arrived at our first home stay in the village of Tsukumi on the southern island of Kyushu, we were delighted to find ourselves surrounded by a ring of orange. Terraced hills of tangerine-like fruit called *mikan* in Japan (known as satsuma here in the states). This citrus fruit was a central part the community's economy. At that time, across Japan, *mikan* and other fresh fruits were the desserts of choice. You might be served one perfect Japanese pear (*nashi*) cut into wedges and divided among four people, or several luscious grapes that were peeled and plated. This was the era when a Tokyo "fruit parlor" sat on the nation's most expensive piece of real estate and sold $200 melons! But you might also be presented a cup of green tea with a Japanese style confection, *wagashi*, usually made with some kind of *mochi* (sweet rice cake). Chestnut and red bean purées might be sandwiched between waffle-like confections made in cast iron molds at famous shops. Western style cakes and cookies were limited and a simple loaf style-cake called *kasutera*, with its centuries old Portuguese pedigree, was very popular. These special treats were often served to guests or brought as gifts by grateful guests.

During the sticky summers, my boys, Brad and Alex, could count on a treat of shaved ice with flavored syrups (*kakigori*), available on most any street corner under a colorful banner with the character for ice (they learned to read that sign pretty fast). My friends' homes were equipped with small ovens that sat atop refrigerators, which they used to make mini cakes. We didn't have an oven, but it was at about this time when I learned how to make Steamed Ginger Lemon Walnut Cake (p. 163). To this day I love the simple flavors and springy texture unique to these steamed cakes. Today, everything has changed. Japan has long since embraced European-style pastries, breads, tarts and ice cream. Home baking and baking classes are wildly popular and most Japanese kitchens now have an oven big enough to turn out all kinds creations.

Many of the desserts in this chapter, I learned from my dear friend, Junko Joho, who teaches baking and dessert-making from her tiny, contemporary Tokyo kitchen. Known as "J.J." to her friends, I call her "Junko 911," as she has become a source for all kinds of help, both culinary and cultural. She came to my home in Boston with Emi Ono to teach a few classes to my students. She introduced us to Black Sesame Chiffon Cake (p. 166) that contains black sesame seeds and sesame oil and marries Japanese ingredients with Western techniques. It is a revelation.

Although rice cakes (*mochi*) stuffed with sweet red bean paste is a classic Japanese dessert, the relatively new technique of adding a strawberry has become very popular in Japan. J.J. showed us how to make the Mochi Dumplings with Strawberry and Red Bean Paste (p. 156) using a sweet rice flour in the microwave! And Crepes Stuffed with Red Bean Jam (p. 164) were inspired by a dessert J.J. and I had after lunch at a deeply urban Tokyo eatery.

Matcha, the powdered green tea once the domain only of traditional tea ceremonies, has become a trendy ingredient both in Japan and abroad. It is now used in ice cream, lattes, and cakes. It comes in small tins and is rather expensive, so I will give you plenty of recipes for using it. Try the easy blender-made Matcha Ice Cream, (p 168) or froth up your own Hot Matcha Milk (p. 171) with a little battery-powered hot milk whisk. A Japanese-American invention, Matcha Mochi Cupcakes (p. 162) are made with a sweet rice flour batter that gives the cake a chewy mochi-like texture and is gluten-free. I sent this recipe back over the Pacific for J.J. to try!

By now you know that I love *shiso* and that it is very happy in my garden. I concocted Sweet Shiso Ice Dessert (p. 167) while trying to figure out what to do with my "*shiso*-gone-wild-plants." I based it on a recipe for parsley sorbet, so this can be a palate cleanser between courses or a finale to any meal. Accompany your treats with a proper cup of green tea.

Fruit Cup with Mochi and Sweet Bean Topping

My friend Junko "J.J." Joho is not only a master of presentation but she's quick as well. With no prior notice or planning she whipped up this colorful and refreshing dessert in a few minutes and it looked great. J.J. used up the few strawberries she had left in a bowl, a lone tangerine, and half a grapefruit to create this dessert. This is a great way to use up bits of fruit or if you keep a few cans of mandarin oranges and pineapple on your shelf; this can be made without any fresh fruit at all.

The *mochi* made from sweet rice (glutinous) flour granules (*shiratamako*) can be formed into little balls or disks, as we did for this version, and boiled like little dumplings. They are mixed in with the fruit providing textural contrast. J.J. topped hers with chunky sweet bean paste and *kuromitsu*, a black sugar syrup that is more like molasses than brown sugar. I skip this for a lighter and more refreshing taste.

Tuck in some crushed ice around the fruit for a very refreshing dish. Mochi Balls are not hard to make but if you don't want to make them you can just add the sweet *adzuki* beans. It will still be a unique fruit salad.

Mochi Balls

Serves 4
Prep Time: 15 minutes
Cooking Time: 10 minutes

½ cup (65 g) sweet rice granules (*shiratamako*) or ½ cup (80 g) sweet rice flour (*mochiko*)
¼ cup (65 ml) water, plus more if needed
5 cups (1.25 liters) water for boiling the *mochi*

1 Have on hand a mixing bowl filled with water and ice cubes, set next to the stove.
2 Bring 6 cups of water to a boil in a medium saucepan and lower the heat to a simmer until you are ready to cook the mochi.
3 Add the sweet rice flour granules or sweet rice flour, whichever you are using, to a mixing bowl. Add ¼ water, a little at a time and mix together with a spatula until a dough forms and pulls away from the bowl. Add more water if needed, 1 tablespoon at a time. Now with your hands, mix the dough again. It should feel like the tip of your earlobe or play dough!
4 You can either pull little pieces from the dough to make ½-inch (1.25 cm) balls; or form a 12 inch (30 cm) cylinder (just like making a snake with play dough) and cut it into 28 pieces. Either way, they look, and feel like mini marshmallows! Set the balls on a plate.
5 You are going to boil the Mochi Balls in 2 batches. Bring the water back to a boil. Press your thumb into each ball flattening them slightly. Drop them into the boiling water as you go. Swirl with a spoon. When the balls have risen to the top (about 1 minute) remove them with a slotted spoon and transfer to the bowl of ice water. Repeat with the remaining balls.
6 Bring the bowl of *mochi* to the sink and carefully drain the water. Run a stream of cold water into the bowl with the *mochi*, swirling the little disks with your hands, for about 30 seconds. This will firm up the balls. Drain into a wire mesh colander. The *mochi* is ready to use.

Fruit Cups

Serves 4
Prep Time: 15 minutes
Cooking Time: 10 minutes

Fruit Suggestions
1 orange, peeled and cut into sections
1 grapefruit, peeled and cut into sections
Strawberries, hulled and cut in half
Kiwi, peeled, sliced, and cut into quarters
Melon balls: watermelon, cantaloupe
Pineapple sections
4 mint sprigs
1 can (7 oz/215 g) sweet *adzuki* beans

To Assemble the Fruit Cups

1 Set out 4 glass bowls or parfait glasses. Add the fruit and *mochi* balls alternately to each dish until ¾ of the way filled.
2 Add about 1 tablespoon of sweet *adzuki* beans to the top. Garnish with fresh mint.

Mochi Dumplings with Strawberries and Red Bean Paste

Ichigo Daifuku

Junko "J.J." Joho, baking teacher extraordinaire and a dear friend from Tokyo, came to Boston to teach a few cooking classes in my home. Her specialty is western style cakes and pastry, but she also makes wonderful Japanese desserts. She delighted the students with this contemporary combination of strawberry, red bean paste, and *mochi* dough. This confection does take a little bit of time and technique, but if you want to try something new, and don't mind a little clean up, it is well worth it.

The granular rice flour (*shiratamako*) used to make the *mochi* is available in most well stocked Asian grocers or on line. (If you cannot find this ingredient, I've provided a recipe for making the dough with regular Japanese sweet rice flour from Koda Farms that comes in a box and is more readily available. I have also experimented with a Thai brand of sweet rice flour. It does work, but the rice flour has a slight scent of Thai rice and is softer (p. 158). The dough is quite sticky, but you'll soon get the hang of it. It feels a bit like play-dough. The dough is very pliable and is drawn up around the strawberry and pinch closed like a dumpling. Choose flavorful medium size strawberries that will be easy to handle. The strawberries are enrobed in sweet bean paste and then wrapped in the *mochi* dough. Use the smooth *adzuki* paste (*koshi-an*) that comes in a pouch. If not you can make the paste from a can of *adzuki* beans (p. 164).

The trick to easy handling of the dough is cornstarch (not white flour) on your hands and work surface. The excess cornstarch is brushed off the confection before eating. J.J. made these in the palm of her hand, but she's an expert! I found that using a mini cupcake tin, to hold the dough and strawberry, was helpful to pull up and pinch the edges of the *mochi* over the strawberry.

This is a make-and-eat-operation—serve it the same day because the dough toughens if it's kept in the refrigerator. The combination of strawberry, earthy sweet bean, and chewy *mochi* is a winner. Serve it with green tea. *Gambatte*! (Go for it!)

Makes approximately 16
Prep Time: 45 minutes
Cooking Time: 8 minutes

16 fresh medium size strawberries
½ lb (250 g) smooth sweet red-bean paste (*koshi-an*)
1 teaspoon canola oil
1½ cups (200g) sweet rice flour granules (*shiratamako*)
1 cup (250 ml) lukewarm water
¼ cup (50 g) sugar
Cornstarch, for dusting
Mini cupcake tin (optional)

> **NOTE** If you are unable to find smooth sweet red bean paste in the package you can make your own with a can of sweet *adzuki* beans. See page 164 for instructions

1 Remove the stems from the strawberry, rinse, pat dry with paper towels, and set on a cookie sheet to dry.

2 Place the bean paste on a plate and spread it into a thick layer. Put the plate in the microwave and heat for 30 seconds. Remove the plate. Mix the bean paste with the knife and microwave for another 30 seconds, this will evaporate some of the moisture and make the paste easier to handle. The paste should not feel too dry or too sticky.

3 Make 16 balls, (2 inches/5 cm wide) from the bean paste. Set them on a plate and cover with plastic wrap and refrigerate until they are ready to use.

4 Drizzle the oil into a medium size microwave safe bowl. With a paper towel, coat the entire bowl with the oil. Wipe out any excess.

5 Combine the rice flour granules (*shiratamako*) and water in the bowl. Mix with your fingertips. Add the sugar and mix together until smooth. Heat for 2

minutes in the microwave. Remove and mix with a rubber spatula.

6 Place the mixture back in the microwave and heat for another 2 minutes. Remove and mix well. The batter should be smooth. Heat the mixture 2 more times in 30-second increments, stirring between each heating. The batter will be very sticky.

7 Cover your work surface generously with cornstarch. Turn the *mochi* onto the surface and sprinkle it with more cornstarch. The dough will be hot and you will need to work quickly. Knead gently for about 30 seconds. The surface will be smooth and the dough should feel soft, like the tip of your earlobe. With your hands, gently roll the dough into a thick log (about 12 inches/30 cm). This will feel like play dough. Cut the log in half and then cut each half into 8 pieces for a total of 16 pieces. Cover lightly with plastic wrap.

8 Have on hand a cornstarch dusted

baking sheet. Set the bean paste and the strawberries on your work surface. Dust your hands with cornstarch. Pick up a piece of the *mochi* and flatten it into a disc and stretch it by pressing the edges with your thumb and forefinger.

9 Set a ball of bean paste on the circle and flatten it almost to the edges. Take a strawberry, tip side down, and set it onto the bean paste.

10 Now gently stretch and pinch the dough over the bottom of the strawberry enclosing the berry. Pinch the dough together until sealed. Turn the straw-

berry over and lightly roll in you hands to smooth the sealed edge (like making a ball). Dust lightly with cornstarch. Loosely cover with plastic wrap. Repeat with remaining ingredients.

Shaping the Dumplings Using a Mini-cupcake Tin

1 Flatten the ball of bean paste. Mold it around the strawberry from the bottom up, leaving the tip of the berry exposed. Repeat with remaining strawberries.

2 Sprinkle cornstarch into each mini-cupcake tin depression, and, with your

fingers, coat the sides with cornstarch. Take one *mochi* ball and flatten it into a disc about 2 inches in diameter. Set the *mochi* into one cavity. Place a strawberry, tip side down, onto the *mochi*. Pinch the dough up and over the bottom of the strawberry, stretching the dough as you go and sealing the dough on the bottom. Carefully lift it out of the tin and set on a cornstarch-dusted platter. Repeat with the remaining ingredients.

How to Wrap the Strawberries

1. In a microwave safe bowl or dish add the water to the *shiratamako*.

2. With your fingers, mix the rice flour and water until the granules are dissolved. Then, mix in the sugar until smooth.

3. After heating the dough in the microwave, pour onto the cornstarch dusted surface.

4. Form the dough into a log and cut into the dough with a spoon and divide into 16 pieces. Cover with cornstarch.

5. Flatten the dough into a disk and set a ball of red bean paste into the center flattening it as well.

6. Set the strawberry, tip side down, into the bean paste. Bring opposite edges of the *mochi* up and over the strawberry. Pinch closed.

7. Turn the strawberry over and lightly roll in your hands to smooth the sealed edge (like making a ball).

9. Make sure the dumplings have a light dusting of cornstarch on them until you are ready to serve.

Mochi Dough Made From Sweet Rice Flour

This is similar to *mochi* dough made with sweet rice flour (*mochiko*) also referred to as glutinous rice flour, instead of shiratamako. *Shiratamako* is widely used in Japan but can be hard to find outside of Japanese markets. Sweet rice flour is more readily available at most Asian markets and now at some supermarkets. This dough will require more time when heated in the microwave. It is soft and when mixed, resembles mashed potatoes in texture.

Makes about 10-12

1 cup (150 g) sweet rice flour
⅔ cup (150 ml) water
¼ cup (65g) sugar
Cornstarch, for dusting

1 Mix the rice flour, water, and sugar in a medium size microwave bowl.
2 Place the bowl in the microwave and heat for 90 seconds. Take out the bowl, mix with a spoon, then return to the microwave.
3 Microwave for another 90 seconds. Remove from the microwave and mix with a spoon. The dough will be very sticky but it will hold together. Heat for 30 seconds. Remove from the microwave.
4 Cover your work surface generously with cornstarch. Turn the *mochi* onto the surface and sprinkle it with more cornstarch. The dough will be hot and you will need to work quickly. Knead gently for about 30 seconds. The surface will be smooth and the dough should feel soft.. With your hands, gently roll the dough into a thick log. Cut the log in half and then cut each half into 4-5 pieces for a total of 8-10 pieces. Cover lightly with plastic wrap.
5 Follow the procedure to wrap the red bean paste, strawberry, and *mochi* as above.

Black Sesame Seed Pudding

On a recent visit to Eriko Itoh's (my home-stay sister from 1972!) home in Yokosuka, (where she and her husband, Yukio, are now living in a multigenerational household with their daughter Hazuki, son-in-law Satoru, and granddaughter Mana) we spent the afternoon cooking together.

We decided to make Black Sesame Seed Pudding, a recipe Eriko had learned from a young chef, Yasuaki Kato, who owned a vegetarian restaurant in the suburbs of Tokyo. Black sesame seeds are un-hulled sesame seeds that are rich in calcium and protein and have a stronger taste than the hulled white seeds. You can find them in plastic jars at Asian grocers or at health food stores. It was made all the more special because her energetic granddaughter, Mana, was helping. As Mana dipped her finger into the dark sesame paste, I was struck by the fact that I was cooking with the great-granddaughter of Oishi Sensei (Dr. Oishi), our host father, who is the reason that all paths have lead back to Japan for my husband and me.

This recipe uses both half and half, and milk, at Eriko's we used only whole milk

Makes four ½ cup (125 ml) servings
Prep time: 25 minutes
Cooking Time: 15 minutes

2 tablespoons black sesame seeds, ground
3 tablespoons sugar
2 tablespoons sour cream or plain yogurt
1 cup (250 ml) half and half
1 cup (250 ml) milk
½ cup (125 ml) heavy cream
3 tablespoons water
1 packet (¼ oz/7 g) unflavored gelatin

1 Add the black sesame seeds to the bowl of a food processor or blender and pulse several times until you have a rough paste. Mix together the black sesame seed paste, sugar, and sour cream in a medium bowl. Set aside.

2 Pour the water into a small bowl and sprinkle the gelatin over the surface. Set aside for 3 minutes until softened.

3 Pour the half and half and milk into a medium saucepan and heat over low heat until just warm. Transfer to a measuring pitcher.

4 Slowly pour the warm milk mixture, in a steady stream, into the sesame mixture, stirring the whole time. Return these combined mixtures to the saucepan and cook over low-medium heat until it reaches 145°F (63°C) or until you see steam rising from the surface. Stir occasionally.

5 While the mixture is heating, add the heavy cream to a mixing bowl and whip the cream until it forms soft peaks. Set aside.

6 Turn off the heat. Add the gelatin to the warm milk mixture and mix until the gelatin is completely dissolved.

7 Strain the warm milk mixture into a mixing bowl through a tightly woven mesh sieve. There will be whole sesame seeds that do not go through the strainer, which is fine. Discard the sesame seeds from the strainer.

8 Fill a shallow bowl with ice cubes. Set the bowl with the strained mixture on top of the ice cubes and stir slowly with a wire whisk until the mixture begins to set.

9 Fold in half of the whipped cream until completely incorporated. Reserve the other half for garnish.

10 Ladle the pudding into small dishes and refrigerate for at least 2 hours. Garnish each bowl with a raspberry, a mint leaf, and a dollop of whipped cream.

Matcha Chocolate Coffee Cake

This recipe took on a life of its own. It started with a conversation about Matcha Mochi Cupcakes (p. 162) with my publisher, Eric Oey, who suggested Americans might like a regular white flour based cake with *matcha* powder added. I liked the idea, and expanded it by coloring only half the batter with *matcha*. Green and white, I thought, would make a lovely marble cake. My friend, Leslie Goldenberg, who did a lot of recipe testing for this book, is a great baker, suggested using chocolate. Now we had a triple flavored marble cake of vanilla, *matcha* and chocolate. We decided to experiment with small loaf pans, and the mini tri-color cakes came out great. The three flavors complement each other, and the soft texture of the cake is comforting and familiar. I hope you enjoy them. They are great with a cup of coffee or a glass of tea. Got any ideas for other flavors?

Makes 3-4 mini loaves or one 1.5 qt (1.5 liter) loaf pan

½ cup (125 g) (1 stick) butter, softened
1 cup (150 g) sugar
2 large eggs
1 teaspoon vanilla
1½ cups (235 g) cake flour
1½ teaspoons baking powder
½ teaspoon baking soda
½ teaspoon salt
¼ (65 g) cup plain yogurt or sour cream
¼ (65 ml) cup milk
2 teaspoons *matcha* powder
1 tablespoon warm water
2 oz (50 g) baking chocolate
2 tablespoons butter

Variation on the theme
Make just two colors—*matcha* being one of them
1 tablespoon *matcha* + 1½ tablespoons water

1 Set the oven to 350°F (175°C). Grease and flour a loaf pan. Set aside.

2 Cream the butter and sugar together in a standing mixer or with a hand mixer for 2 minutes or until fluffy.

3 Add the eggs, one at a time, beating after each addition. Add the vanilla to the mixture and beat again for 30 seconds and set aside.

4 Combine the cake flour, baking powder, baking soda and salt in a medium bowl. Whisk the dry ingredients together until they are thoroughly mixed. Whisk together the yogurt and milk in another bowl and set aside.

5 Mix the *matcha* powder and water in a medium bowl until it is a thick smooth paste. Add more water if needed. Set aside.

6 Add the chocolate and butter to a medium microwave safe bowl. Heat for 1 minute in the microwave and stir. Heat another 30 seconds until the chocolate and butter are completely melted. Set aside.

7 Add half the flour and yogurt mixtures, alternately to the creamed mixture, thoroughly combining after each addition. Add the remaining flour and yogurt mixture and mix thoroughly. You should have a smooth batter with no lumps.

8 Add one third of the batter to each of the chocolate and green tea mixtures. Mix each batter until smooth.

9 Spoon alternating colors of the batter into the prepared pans. Grease a flat knife or off-set spatula with oil and carefully smooth the top of each area, wiping the blade before going to the next color. With the tip of the knife draw a straight line down the center of the batter. Insert a knife, toothpick, or wooden skewer, into the pan, lightly swirl the colors into each other.

10 Set the loaves on the middle rack of the preheated oven. Bake for 25-30 minutes. Insert a toothpick into the center of the loaf. The cake is done when a toothpick comes out clean and the sides of the cake pull away from the pan. Be careful not to over bake, the cake will become dry. If you are using a large loaf pan the baking time will be increased. Check the loaf at 25 minutes and add more time as necessary.

11 Let it cool on a wire rack. Slice and serve.

Colorful Matcha Mochi Cupcakes

Welcome to the "Matcha Mochi Cupcake Club," which started when my friend, Grace Kim Niwa, who is married to 3rd generation Japanese-American Paul Niwa, told me about her mother-in-law's special *mochi* cupcakes. Mrs. Niwa Sr. told me the recipe originated form a Japanese American community cookbook. I tracked it down through some internet sleuthing to *Humblebean*, a Japanese cuisine website and subsequently to a Los Angeles Buddhist Temple's community cookbook, *Otoki*. The Temple cookbook committee kindly gave me permission to use the recipe. I spread the recipe around to several of my friends here to try and each came back with a slightly unique idea. Marie Doezema added the green tea powder to the cupcake batter and Shoko Kashiyama suggested sprinkling cinnamon on the cupcake with yummy results.

This is your perfect gluten-free cupcake. The base is the sweet rice (glutinous) flour, *mochiko*. It combines Japanese ingredients with classic western cake ingredients, creating the chewy texture of *mochi* from the rice flour. Instead of a filling of custard or chocolate, sweet *adzuki* beans are tucked in the center and create a toothsome jam. The flavor and color of the batter come from using *matcha*, the powdered green tea often associated with the tea ceremony. The center around the *adzuki* beans may look like uncooked dough, but it actually is *mochi*. They are very good warm as the sweet beans are jammy. Consume them within 2 days, as they tend to dry out. They can be frozen, but have to then be heated briefly in the microwave and served warm.

Yield Approx 16
Prep Time: 30 minutes
Cooking Time: 25 minutes

3 cups (450 grams) (1 box) Koda Farms *Mochiko*, sweet rice flour
1 cup (200 g) sugar
2 teaspoons baking powder
¼ teaspoon salt
2 teaspoons *matcha* (green tea powder)
3 large eggs
1½ cups (375 ml) milk
¾ cup (185 ml) canola oil
One 15 oz (400 g) can of sweet *adzuki* beans (optional)

1 Set the oven to 375°F (190°C). Line a muffin tin with paper or foil cups.
2 Combine the sweet rice flour, baking powder, salt, and *matcha* in a bowl.
3 Whisk together the oil and sugar in a separate bowl, add the eggs and milk. Whisk vigorously until thoroughly combined.
4 Add the dry ingredients to the oil mixture and mix with a rubber spatula until completely combined.
5 Place cupcake papers in the cupcake tin. Fill halfway with the batter. Add a scant tablespoon of *adzuki* beans. Spoon more batter over the *adzuki* beans to come just below the top of the paper.
6 Set the muffin tin on the middle rack and bake for 25-30 minutes. The tops will begin to crack.

Variations

Omit the green tea and add 1 teaspoon of vanilla
Sprinkle cinnamon on top of the un-baked cupcake
Sweet kabocha pumpkin purée (p. 136)

NOTE I have tried using a Thai brand of glutinous rice flour with mixed results. I find that Koda Farms Mochiko or other Japanese or Korean sweet rice flour works best. It is widely available in Asian grocers and on line.

Steamed Ginger Lemon Walnut Cake

Makes 2 small cakes
Prep Time: 20 minutes
Cooking Time: 35 minutes

I was first introduced to steamed cakes at a Chinese bakery in Yokohama's Chinatown. The cake had an almond flavor and a wonderfully light spongy texture. Baking is not a traditional form of home cooking in Japan, but now almost everyone has an oven, even small ones that sit atop the counter or fridge. When I first learned this recipe by Sadako Kono, like most Japanese I didn't have an oven…and I didn't miss it. You will see why if you make this recipe with a steamer, even if you have to rig one up.

Ginger juice is the base for the flavoring in the cake and gives it a subtly bracing taste. Powdered ginger would not give you the same results. I have added chopped crystallized ginger for a little extra crunch and ginger zing.

NOTE This can be baked in the oven but the texture will be quite different. Set the cake in a shallow tin of hot water, then bake at 350°F (175°C) for 25 minutes.

1 teaspoon oil
1 cup (125 g) flour
1 teaspoon baking powder
½ teaspoon baking soda
1 large egg
¼ cup (65 ml) honey
¼ cup (65 ml) molasses
1 tablespoon fresh ginger juice (p. 28)
1 tablespoon lemon juice
4 tablespoons warm water
3 tablespoons walnuts, roughly chopped
2 tablespoons crystallized ginger, finely chopped
1 teaspoon white sesame seeds

1 Grease 5 x 2 inch (13.75 x 5 cm) in diameter round aluminum foil baking tins or 2 mini loaf pans with oil. (You can use anything that will fit inside your steamer set up).
2 Sift the flour and baking powder together in a bowl. Then beat the egg, honey, molasses, ginger and lemon juices in a separate bowl.
3 Fold the flour and egg mixture together. Add the water and mix until completely combined. Add the chopped ginger and walnuts. Then pour the batter into the prepared pans.
4 Set up a steamer in a wok or in a large saucepan with a lid. Add about 3 inches (7.5 cm) of water to the bottom of the pot over medium heat. When the water just begins to boil, carefully set one cake onto the rack in the steamer. Reduce the heat to medium low. Place a linen or cloth towel around the lid. Be careful to tie the ends up around the top of the lid and away from the heat source and set on the wok or saucepan. Make sure the lid is several inches away from the top of the cake.
5 Steam the cake for about 35 minutes or until a skewer set in the center comes out clean. Periodically check the water level in the pan. Add water as necessary. Toast the sesame seeds in a dry skillet over low heat. Sprinkle on top of the cake.
6 Remove and cool on a rack. Repeat with second loaf. Slice and serve with green tea.

Crepes Stuffed with Red Bean Jam Anko Maki

This recipe was inspired by a meal at a restaurant called Sometaro in Asakusa, a wonderfully unpretentious area in downtown Tokyo. I was taken there by Junko "J.J." Joho, a savvy *Edo-ko* (someone with deep Tokyo roots). It is famous for *monjya yaki*, a Tokyo-specific savory pancake. After eating several of them, and with no room left to breathe, J.J. insisted I try *anko maki* for dessert—a red bean paste-stuffed crepe. "No" wasn't an option. And am I ever glad I gave in. One taste and I knew it would have a place in this book.

I make a stack of traditional crepes, spread the red bean jam onto each one, roll them into logs, and fry them in a skillet with butter. My friends love it. J.J. suggests using buckwheat flour for a healthy and earthy alternative. If you have an Asian market near you it is likely to have prepared *adzuki* bean paste in plastic pouches in its refrigerator section. The *anko* comes in smooth (*koshian*) or chunky (*tsubuan*). If not, follow the recipe below to learn how to take a can of the sweetened *adzuki* beans and turn them into a thick jam.

Makes 10-12 crepes   Prep Time: 35 minutes
Cooking Time: 20 minutes

2 tablespoons canola oil
2 tablespoons butter for frying the crepes
1½ cups (430 g) red bean paste, smooth (*koshian*)
    or chunky (*tsubuan*)

Crepe Batter
2 large eggs
1 cup (250 ml) milk
1 cup (125g) flour
Pinch of salt
2 tablespoons butter, melted

1 Add the eggs, milk, flour, and salt to the pitcher of a blender. Blend until smooth. Add the melted butter and blend again. Let the batter rest for 30 minutes.
2 Heat a small 6-inch skillet or crepe pan over medium heat for one minute. Put the oil in a small dish and set next to the stove. Pour the oil into the skillet and heat for 45 seconds. Pour the oil back into the bowl. Lightly wipe the skillet with a paper towel. Set the paper towel next to the bowl. Have a large plate by the stove.
3 Scoop a scant ¼ cup (65 ml) of batter with a ladle and pour into the skillet. Hold the handle of the pan and swirl the batter over the surface, making a flat thin crepe. Use the bottom of the ladle to smooth the batter out to cover the surface of the pan.
4 Let the crepe cook for 1 minute until bubbles appear. Slip a spatula around the edges of the crepe. Carefully lift the crepe and flip. Cook for 30 seconds. Flip the crepe onto the nearby plate.
5 Dip the paper towel into the oil and rub the surface

of the skillet. Repeat with the remaining crepe batter. Stack the crepes on top of each other.
6 To fill the crepe, spread about 2-3 tablespoons of bean jam in a 1-inch (2.5 cm) line across the lower third of the crepe. Roll the crepe forward and set on a plate. Repeat with the remaining crepes.
7 Melt 1 tablespoon of the butter over medium heat in a large skillet. Set half of the bean filled crepes into the skillet. Fry on both sides for one minute or until the crepe is light brown. Repeat with the remaining crepes. Serve with a cup of black or green tea.

To Make Bean Paste

One 15 oz (430 g) sweet *adzuki* beans
Once the beans are mashed they need to be
    heated either on the stove or in the microwave
    to evaporate some of the liquid and thicken the
    paste

1 Pour the beans into a bowl. Crush the beans with a potato masher with small holes, like a ricer, until fairly smooth. Transfer the mashed beans to a microwave safe plate and spread the mixture out with a spatula.
2 Starting in 1-minute increments, heat the beans. Remove from the oven and stir the mixture. Return the beans to the microwave and do this 1 or 2 more times minutes. You want the consistency of a thick jam. If you need to heat it further, do so in 30-second increments, stirring after each time. If using for Strawberry Mochi Dumplings (page 156) chill the mixture for at least one hour.

Variation

Top the bean paste with bananas or strawberries.

Variation

Buckwheat Flour Crepes

J.J. says that crepes made with *sobako*, buckwheat flour, are a perfect match for the earthy beans. This is not a delicate crepe; it is assertive and a little chewy. But she's right; it complements the sweet beans perfectly. My friend Francoise Matte, expert crepe maker, shared her recipe for buckwheat crepe batter. In her native France, this is used for savory crepes, so she was intrigued when I told her I would be using them for dessert. She pronounced them "c'est bon" and even preferred them to the white flour crepe.

Makes 8-10

⅔ cup (250 g) buckwheat flour
⅓ cup (125 g) white flour
2 teaspoons brown sugar
2 large eggs
1¼ cups (315 ml) milk
2-3 tablespoons oil for cooking (1 tablespoon for the batter and the rest for cooking)
¼ teaspoon salt

1 Combine the buckwheat and white flours and sugar in a mixing bowl. Add the eggs, milk, 1 tablespoon of oil, and salt and mix well. Let the batter rest for 30 minutes.
2 The batter should be the consistency of heavy cream. Proceed in making the crepes as described on page 164.

TIP To freeze crepes, stack between sheets of wax paper, wrap in plastic wrap and place in a half-gallon zip top bag.

Black Sesame Chiffon Cake

How often have you used toasted sesame oil when baking a cake? The aroma is wonderful! Junko "J.J" Joho and Emi Ono made this cake for a cooking class in my home. When they sent me the recipe, all the measurements were in grams and designed for Japanese-size bake ware. I told them not to bother bringing a chiffon cake pan to Boston because I had one. Uh-oh. After a lot of high level arithmetic—and after brushing copious amounts of flour from the scale into cups—we finally had a recipe that could be replicated in an American kitchen!

This cake is feather light with a distinctively nutty flavor. J.J. and Emi frosted the cake with whipped cream, but I serve it on the side with berries.

Makes one 10 x 4-inch (25 x 10cm) cake in tube pan
Serves 16
Prep Time: 30 minutes
Cooking Time: 50 minutes plus an hour for cooling

1½ cups (235 g) cake flour
2 teaspoons baking powder
10 large eggs, separated in whites and yolks
1 cup (200 g) sugar, ½ cup (100 g) for the meringue;
   ½ cup (100 g) for the sesame seed mixture
½ cup (60 g) black sesame seeds, toasted
½ teaspoon salt
½ cup (125 ml) water
½ cup (125 ml) sesame oil
½ cup (125 ml) canola oil

1 Set oven to 325°F (160°C). Have on hand a 10 x 4-inch (25 x10 cm) tube pan with a removable bottom.
2 Sift the flour and baking powder together and set aside.
3 Beat the egg whites in large mixing bowl until soft peaks form. Gradually add ½ cup (100 g) of sugar and continue beating until you have stiff peaks. Set the meringue aside.
4 Toast the black sesame seeds in a dry skillet on medium-low heat for 3-4 minutes or until the seeds begin to pop. Pour the sesame seeds into the bowl of a food processor. Pulse until the seeds are crushed.
5 Add egg yolks and the black sesame seeds to a mixing bowl. Mix well. Then add ½ cup (100 g) sugar, salt, and water and mix well. Drizzle in the sesame oil and canola oils and mix with a wire whisk.
6 Add the flour mixture to the sesame seed mixture, one third at a time, folding in after each addition. Mix until the batter is smooth.
7 Fold the meringue into the sesame batter with a rubber spatula in three portions. Pour the batter into the pan and bake for 50 minutes or until the cake is done.
8 Remove from the oven and turn the cake upside down. Some pans have special feet for this or place the tube onto the neck of a wine or soda bottle. Leave the cake in the pan until completely cool, about an hour.

Whip Cream Topping
½ cup (100 g) powdered sugar
2 cups (500 ml) heavy cream
½ teaspoon of vanilla
Raspberries, strawberries, and blueberries

1 In a mixing bowl, add the sugar and heavy cream and beat until the whipped cream is of spreading consistency.
2 Serve the cake with a dollop of whip cream with fresh berries.

Sweet Shiso Ice Dessert

Shiso is my favorite Japanese herb. A member of the mint family, *shiso* grows like a weed, which is both a good and bad thing. About 10 years ago, my friend Kyoko Wada gave me a *shiso* seedling and ever since I have eagerly awaited the arrival of summer to see what part of my garden has been taken over by this herb! Being so lucky as to have fresh *shiso* right out my back door for sushi, salads, and garnishes is a dream come true, but there can be too much of a good thing. My *shiso* plant produces more leaves than I can use, or press on people. Since you cannot freeze the leaves because they blacken and turn to mush, I searched for a way to preserve them. Leafing (excuse the pun) through a cookbook, I found just the thing—a parsley sorbet recipe that gave birth to this *shiso* ices. I have used this recipe as a palate cleanser between courses, as an icy bed for scallop ceviche, and as a sorbet at the end of a meal. The taste of fresh *shiso* now shines through, all year long!

Makes about 2½ cups (625 ml)
Prep Time: 3 hours (including freezing time)

20 *shiso* leaves
Juice of 2 lemons or limes
1½ cups (375 ml) water
¼ cup (50 g) sugar

1 Place all the ingredients into a food processor or blender and process until the *shiso* leaves are finely chopped.
2 Line an 8-inch (20 cm) square metal baking pan with 2 pieces of plastic wrap that extends about 3 inches (7.5 cm) beyond the edges of the pan. Pour the *shiso* mixture into the pan and freeze until solid, about 3 hours.
3 Take the plastic wrap and lift out the frozen mixture. Cut it up and put back into the bowl of the food processor. Pulse until slushy. Spoon *shiso* slush into a 1-quart (1 liter) plastic container and freeze.
4 Take the sorbet out of the freezer about 10 minutes before serving. Serve in individual bowls.

Matcha Ice Cream

The bitter green powdered tea, *matcha*, once the exclusive domain of Japanese tea ceremonies, is now widely embraced as an ingredient for making all sorts of desserts and is popular in and outside of Japan. The *matcha* powder makes a beautiful mossy green color. This frozen delight is about the aroma as well as the flavor—adding more *matcha* will increase the intensity of both. I also make this ice cream in the blender. When Hideko, my Japanese "niece" and I were making this, she only stopped adding the *matcha* powder when she could smell that grassy aroma. The taste was full bodied and perfect. Your nose will know!

Refrigerate the mixture for several hours before pouring it into the ice cream maker in order to facilitate its formation. Make sure your blender and ice cream freezer have at least a 5-cup (1.25 liter) capacity. Top it with sweet *adzuki* beans—think of it as Japanese hot fudge!

Makes 1 quart (1 liter)
Prep Time: 15 minutes + 2 hour chilling time for mixture
Freezing Time: 2 hours

2 tablespoons *matcha* powder
4 tablespoons warm water
1 cup (250 ml) half and half
2 cups (500 ml) heavy cream
3 large eggs
½ cup (100 g) sugar
½ teaspoon vanilla
⅛ teaspoon salt

NOTE Top with sweet *adzuki* beans or sliced fresh strawberries.

1 Prepare your ice cream maker according to manufacturer's instructions.
2 Mix the *matcha* powder and warm water into a smooth paste in a medium size bowl. Add the half and half and whisk the mixture together until the green tea paste is completely dissolved.
3 Add the green tea and the half and half mixture, heavy cream, eggs, sugar, vanilla, and salt in the jar of a blender. Place the lid on the blender and with your hand holding down the lid, blend for about 1 minute.
4 Open the lid and with a rubber spatula, scrape down the sides, cover and blend for another minute.
5 Remove the jar from the blender base and place in the refrigerator for 1-2 hours to chill the mixture. Then pour the mixture into your ice cream maker and proceed according to manufacturer's instructions. (It took about 20 minutes in my Cuisinart Ice Cream Maker)
6 Scrape the ice cream out of the ice cream freezer and store in a plastic container and place in freezer for at least 2 hours before serving.

Matcha Ice Cream (Front),
Black Sesame Ice Cream (Back)

Black Sesame Ice Cream

I first had this ice cream at the end of a traditional Japanese multi-course (*kaiseki*) meal with my friend of 25 years, Airi Tamura, a university professor. Most Japanese meals end with fruit, but I should have suspected something unusual was in the offing when I was served champagne at the end this traditional meal. A dark, creamy, comma-shaped scoop of ice cream was set before us on an elegant porcelain dish with a perfect berry placed beside it, just so. As with much Japanese food, we experienced the scent before the taste.

In Japan, the use of black sesame seeds has become popular in the last 20 years, using them in everything from savory to sweet dishes. The seeds are high in iron and calcium, and are naturally sweet, more so than white sesame seeds. Determined to re-create this memorable experience, I pored over ice cream recipes and came across one for peanut butter ice cream, in *Ice Cream for All Seasons* by Deb Tomasi and Suzy Gardner (ReTreat Publishing 1999). It worked. The ice cream has a full sweet nutty flavor with very little sugar. It's not a perfect match for the ice cream I had in Tokyo, but it is perfectly delicious.

Makes approximately one-quart
Prep Time: 30 mins
Freezing Time: 4 hours

½ cup (60 g) black sesame
   seeds toasted
3 large eggs
½ cup (100 g) sugar
2 cups (500 ml) heavy cream
1 cup (250 ml) half and half
½ teaspoon vanilla
⅛ teaspoon salt

NOTE The amount of the mixture could be greater than the capacity of your ice cream maker, so you may need to do this in two batches.

1 Have the cold insert of an electric ice cream maker chilled according to manufacturer's instructions.
2 Pulse the sesame seeds on the grind button in the jar of a blender until the seeds are finely ground and release a nutty aroma.
3 Add the eggs, sugar, heavy cream, half and half, vanilla, and salt to the blender. With your hand on the cover, press the blend button. Mix for about one minute, until the ingredients are thoroughly incorporated.
4 Place the blender jar with the black sesame mixture into the refrigerator to chill for 2 hours.
5 Pour the mixture into your ice cream maker and process according to manufacturer's instructions. It should take about 20 minutes to solidify.
6 Pack in an appropriate container and freeze for at least one hour before serving. Garnish with a sprig of mint and raspberries if you like.

Kenichi Kano and his two colleagues, Ms. Yamanaka and Ms. Senda, from the famous Kyoto based Ippodo Tea Co. came to my home at the end of their month-long tour of the United States and Canada where they made their way cross country giving tea making workshops. I served them Thanksgiving dinner in October and after the meal they treated my other guests and me to a tea tasting. Alan Palmer, a licensed tea ceremony teacher from the Urasenke school; Yori Oda, my former Japanese teacher; and an old friend, artist Paul Nagano; and I spent the next hour sniffing and sipping a variety of qualities of tea. The Ippodo tea was fresh and had a light newly mowed-grass aroma. The teas that had been sitting in my cupboard for awhile (oops) were hard to detect any aroma at all.

For the sake of research I took out my digital thermometer to check the temperature of the water. And the drama began. With a nod from Kano-san, Yamanaka measured the tea into the pot, poured the water and Senda-san set her digital watch and counted down the steeping time. "Ping!" One minute! Kano-san took the teapot and poured the tea into the cups. With great flair, he dripped every last drop into the teacups. The last drops containing the most flavor. It was an enlightening exercise and hopefully you will take the little bit of extra time it takes to make a satisfying cup of Japanese tea. *Cha* means tea and the various prefixes indicate the kind of tea.

Sencha

The steamed and dried rolled tea leaves that produce this green tea with which we are most familiar, is referred to as *ocha*. It is Japan's daily drink. Tea should be stored at room temperature in an airtight container. Mind the "best used by" dates on the packages—something I learned the hard way. Tea doesn't go "bad" but it does lose its fresh taste and potency. Boiling water is never poured on tea leaves. The water temperature should be about 170°F (80°C) and steeps for about 1 minute. You can brew an additional 2-3 pots of tea using the same leaves; no steeping necessary. The tea is a bit weaker, but still satisfying.

Makes 3 small teacups cups

1 cup (250 ml) hot water about 170°F (80°C).
1 tablespoon *sencha*

1 Have on hand a small teapot and 3 cups. Place the *sencha* into the teapot.
2 Pour the hot water first into the teacups and then from the teacups pour the hot water over the *sencha* into the teapot.
3 Wait one minute before serving the tea. Gently pour the tea back into each cup.

Hot Matcha Milk

Matcha

Matcha is the powdered green tea of tea ceremony fame. People spend a lifetime studying this meditative art. Every movement, when making and drinking the tea, is governed by a particular etiquette. The powder is whisked into the hot water so you are ingesting the crushed leaves making this an intense experience. The tea has a rich green color, distinct aroma, thick texture, and a slightly bitter taste. The accoutrements used to make the tea: pottery bowl, bamboo measuring spoon and whisk are simple practical things of beauty. However, you needn't wait to be invited to a tea ceremony to try a cup. Many enjoy it daily. The quantity is small and potent, like espresso. But unlike espresso, which is served in tiny cups, special deep tea bowls are used. Find a small bowl in your cupboard or use a mug.

1 Serving

¼ cup (65 ml) hot water
    (about 170°F-80°C)
½ teaspoon *matcha* powder

1 To cool the water to the proper temperature, pour the boiled water into a separate teacup.
2 Place the powder into a small bowl or large mug.
3 Pour the water from the tea cup lightly over the *matcha* powder. If you have a bamboo whisk, with quick back and forth motions whisk the tea until smooth and foamy. You can also use an electric latte wand or try a mini wire egg whisk.

Hot Matcha Milk

Prep and Cooking Time: 5 minutes
Makes two 4 oz (125 ml) servings

1 cup (250 ml) 2% (or low fat) milk
1 teaspoon *matcha* powder
2 teaspoons sugar

1 Pour the milk in a 2 cup (500 ml) microwavable pitcher. Heat on high for 1 minute.
2 Put the *matcha* powder in a small mixing bowl and pour on some of the warm milk. Stir until well blended. Set aside.
3 Add the sugar to the milk, stir and return to the microwave. Heat for an additional minute and remove from the microwave. Pour a little more hot milk into the *matcha* mixture, stir and add to the milk.
4 To froth the Hot Matcha Milk you can place the milk into a blender and blend for 1 minute. Or if you have an electric latte wand, set it in the warm milk and switch it on. Froth for about 45 seconds until the milk and *matcha* are well blended. Serve in two mugs or glasses.

Roasted Green Tea

Hojicha

This rustic Roasted Green Tea is one of my favorite drinks, hot or cold. The coarse brown leaf tea has a slightly smoky flavor. Just-boiled water is used for making this tea. Green tea is served in low round cups. Roasted Green Tea is usually served in tall, narrow cups.

Makes about 2 cups (500 ml)

2 cups (500 ml) hot water
2 tablespoons *hojicha*

1 Have on hand a large teapot (3 cup capacity). Boil the water and take it off the heat.
2 Place the *hojicha* in the pot. Pour the water over the tea and let steep for about 30 seconds. Pour into 4 teacups.

Acknowledgments

I didn't grow up with a Japanese mother or sister, but it feels like over the years I have acquired dozens and dozens of them. Long-term friendships and chance encounters all have contributed to my body of knowledge and understanding of Japanese culture and cuisine.

In particular I would like to thank the extended Oishi family for embracing the Samuels Family. We came to them as a young married couple through a study abroad program in 1972 with Colgate University and stayed at the home of Dr. Chikanori Oishi.

Oishi Sensei, passed away a few years ago, but he and his children and their children had long since become family to us. Eriko, his daughter, became my sister. Both his sons, Shingo and Seiichiro, are now doctors, Shingo in suburban Tokyo, while Seiichiro has taken over the sensei's practice in Tsukumi a small city on the southern island of Kyushu. Their children and ours have enjoyed "second generation home stays." Dick and I return to Tsukumi, our Japanese "home town" (*furusato*), as often as we can. In the winter of 2010, I cooked with Eriko, her daughter Hazuki, and her granddaughter, Mana, the sensei's great granddaughter in preparation for this book. We are all aware of how the sensei brought our families together and enriched so many lives.

A special thank you to Hideko, my Japanese "niece," who came from her home in Paris to spend 5 days planning, shopping, and cooking for this project's photo shoot. Her patience, skills and warm personality were invaluable. My dear friend Elsa Tian, my all-time cooking buddy, was the team leader in the kitchen. She worked with Akiko Tsuchiya, Sybil Solomon, Carol Halewood, Janet Washington, Leslie Goldenberg, Kyoko Wada, Grace Kim Niwa and Holly Jennings to help produce the lovely dishes for the photo shoot. My friend, Professor Merry "Corky" White, is a sociologist of Japan, a gourmand, gourmet cook and is deeply knowledgeable about Japanese cuisine. We have been a teaching tag team on bento programs. She has been a source of information and guidance throughout this project.

Yori Oda, my first Japanese language teacher, and I have remained friends for four decades. I practically failed Spanish in high school, but somehow Oda sensei managed to lay the foundation for me to go to Japan, have a full life of shopping, raising children, and being able to converse with those that didn't speak a word of English. *Sensei, domo arigatoo gozaimashita!*"

I was fortunate to have been introduced to Michiko Odagiri, my Japanese cooking teacher, who accepted a foreigner in her class and gave me the technical foundation for learning about Japanese cuisine. My fellow students kindly took me into the fold and treated me just like anyone else.

I re-assembled the same talented team who produced the photographs for *The Korean Table*. Catrine Kelty, food stylist extraordinaire, Heath Robbins, the gifted photographer and Mike Pettingill. This was a steep learning curve for them and I think they will never forget (or question) the proper placement of chopsticks.

Many thanks also to Eric Oey, Tuttle's publisher, for his faith and support in the project. Thanks to Bud Sperry, my editor, the definition of cool, calm, collected and very funny guy. Thank you to Chan Sow Yun, designer and June Chong, editorial supervisor, both from Tuttle's Singapore office, for their kindness, patience and attention to detail.

Recipe testers: Leslie Goldenberg, Russell Goldenberg, Joanne Rizzi, Grace Niwa, Elsa Tian, Diane Litvak, Janet Washington for questioning directions, ingredients, and to help make this a better book.

Legions of friends have contributed recipes and have enhanced my family's life in Japan: Akiko Nakajima and family, Shunichi and Kimie Sato, Yoshie and Andy Gordon, The Kai Family, Atsuko Fish, Kyoko Wada, Junko Joho, Emi Ono, Masashi Ishida, Takako and Yoichi Suzuki, Keiko Hayashi, Rico Mochizuki, Shoko Kashiyama, Airi and Susumu Yamakage, Patricia Gercik, Eri Kunimatsu, Noriyasu and Setsuko Tsuchiya, Taekyung Chung, Patricia Hiramatsu, Marie Doezema, Junko Ogawa and the Takeuchi family.

Thanks to Grace Kataoka for her eagle eye and knowledge of Japanese cuisine which was invaluable.

My friend and editor, Sheryl Julian, at *The Boston Globe*, has offered sage advice and patience as I went AWOL, for periods of time during this project.

To my sons Brad and Alex, who shared our adventures, sense of adventure and have always been adventurous eaters. Tofu, *furikake,* and dried squid is their comfort food. What would I have done if you had been "suki-kirai"—picky eaters? They have grown into true menschen.

And finally I would like to thank my husband, Dick, with whom I have been sharing this magic carpet ride through life. He read endless drafts, cajoled and exhorted me on and ate his way through this book—several times; my plate would be empty without you.

Bibliography

Cwiertka, Katarzyna J. *Modern Japanese Cuisine*. London: Reaktion Books, Ltd., 2006

Hayashi, Keiko. *Simple and Delicious Japanese Cuisine: Trumbull*. Connecticut and Tokyo: Shufunotomo, 1999

Hosking, Richard. *A Dictionary of Japanese Food Ingredients and Culture*. North Clarendon, VT: Tuttle Publishing, 1996.

Ingram, Christine. *Cooking Ingredients*. London: Hermes House, 2002

Kariya, Tetsu and Akira Hanasaki. *Oishinbo A la Carte*. San Francisco: Viz Media, 2009. This is a manga series of over 100 volumes on the quest for the ultimate Japanese meal. It is an exciting contemporary look into Japanese culture, food obsession, recipes and relationships. Each volume is devoted to one or two categories or types of food (rice, sake, sushi, and sashimi, etc.) There are 12 volumes in English.

McGee, Harold. *On Food and Cooking*. New York: Simon and Schuster, 1984.

Richie, Donald. *A Taste of Japan*. Tokyo: Kodansha International, 1985.

Shimbo, Hiroko. *The Japanese Kitchen*. Boston: The Harvard Common Press, 2000.

Shimbo, Hiroko. *The Sushi Experience*. New York: Alfred A. Knopf, 2006

Solomon, Charmaine. *Encyclopedia of Asian Food*. Singapore: Periplus Editions, 1998

Tomasi, Deb and Gardner, Suzy. *Ice Cream for All Seasons*: Appleton, WI: ReTreat Publishing, 1999.

Tsuji, Shizuo. *Japanese Cooking: A Simple Art*. Tokyo, Japan: Kodansha International, 1980.

Urakami, Hiroko. *Japanese Family-Style Recipes*. Tokyo: Kodansha International, 1992.

White, Merry. *About Japan, A Teacher's Resource*. The Japan Society, January 2009.

Yoshida, Mitsukuni and Tsune Sesoko, eds. *Naorai: Communion of the Table*. Hiroshima: Mazda Motor Corporation, 1989.

Shopping Resources

The internet has become a part of the consumer environment. To the best of my knowledge online references were operating at the time of publication.

www.asianfoodgrocer.com
www.everydayjapanese.com
www.amazon.com

Penzeys Spices
www.penzeys.com
phone order: 1-800-741-7787
black and white sesame seeds, natural wasabi powder, yellow mustard,

For Sushi Making
http://www.mysushiset.com/sushi-making-kits.html

Bento Blogs
www.Lunchinabox.net
www.justbento.com

Online sources for bento
www.reuseablebags.com
www.amazon.com
www.casabento.com
www.to-goware.com

Ebisuya Japanese Market
65 Riverside Avenue
Medford, Massachusetts
781-391-0012

HMart Shops

This is a large Asian supermarket chain, (with stores all over the United States. Their specialty is in Korean foods, but they carry a full range of Japanese products. Please check their website for online shopping as well as store locations: www.hmart.com

Mitsuwa Marketplace
This is the largest Japanese market in the United States with online shopping as well as stores in California, New Jersey and Illinois
www.mitsuwa.com

New Jersey
595 River Rd
Edgewater, NJ 07020-1104
(201) 941-9113

Illinois
100 E. Algonquin Road,
Arlington Hts., IL 60005
(847) 956-6699

California
There are 6 stores in California

21515 Western Avenue, Torrance
(310) 782-0335

Index

Published by Tuttle Publishing, an imprint of Periplus
Editions (HK) Ltd.

www.tuttlepublishing.com

Library of Congress Cataloging-in-Publication Data

Samuels, Debra.
  My Japanese table : a lifetime of cooking with family
and friends / Debra Samuels. -- 1st ed.
     p. cm.
  Includes bibliographical references.
  ISBN 978-4-8053-1118-9 (hardcover)
  1. Cooking, Japanese. 2. Cookbooks. I. Title.
  TX724.5.J3 S2595
  641.5952--dc22
                                        2010054353
ISBN 9784805311189

Distributed by

North America, Latin America & Europe
Tuttle Publishing
364 Innovation Drive
North Clarendon, VT 05759-9436 U.S.A.
Tel: 1 (802) 773-8930; Fax: 1 (802) 773-6993
info@tuttlepublishing.com; www.tuttlepublishing.com

Japan
Tuttle Publishing
Yaekari Building, 3rd Floor, 5-4-12 Osaki
Shinagawa-ku, Tokyo 141-0032
Tel: (81) 3 5437-0171; Fax: (81) 3 5437-0755
sales@tuttle.co.jp; www.tuttle.co.jp

Asia Pacific
Berkeley Books Pte. Ltd
61 Tai Seng Avenue, #02-12, Singapore 534167
Tel: (65) 6280-1330, Fax: (65) 6280-6290
inquiries@periplus.com.sg; www.periplus.com

Printed in Singapore   1106CP
15 14 13 12 11   6 5 4 3 2 1

In March 2011, during the final editing of this cookbook, a devastating chain of disasters—earthquake, tsunami, and nuclear accidents—occurred in northeastern Japan. We are all heartbroken for the Japanese people. Their stoicism and capacity to endure, embodied in the spirit and the word *gaman*, has been illustrated daily as the crisis deepened. I hope we will remember those souls who lost their lives and admire the courage of those who survived.

—Debra Samuels

Nori Maki Rolls—Real Home-style Sushi.

Hideko Itoh, my Japanese niece helps cook for the p

Teaching a sushi class to MIT students duri